Transitional Justice from State to Civil Society

This book is the first to offer an in-depth analysis of transitional justice as an unfinished agenda in Indonesia's democracy.

Examining the implementation of transitional justice measures in post-authoritarian Indonesia, this book analyses the factors within the democratic transition that either facilitated or hindered the adoption and implementation of transitional justice measures. Furthermore, it contributes key insights from an extensive examination of 'bottom-up' approaches to transitional justice in Indonesia: through a range of case studies, civil society-led initiatives to truth-seeking and local reconciliation efforts. Based on extensive archival, legal and media research, as well as interviews with key actors in Indonesia's democracy and human rights' institutions, the book provides a significant contribution to current understandings of Indonesia's democracy. Its analysis of the failure of state-centred transitional justice measures, and the role of civil society, also makes an important addition to comparative transitional justice studies.

It will be of considerable interest to scholars and activists in the fields of Transitional Justice and Politics, as well as in Asian Studies.

Sri Lestari Wahyuningroem is based in the Political Science Department, Faculty of Social and Political Science, Universitas Pembangunan Nasional Veteran Jakarta, Indonesia.

Part of the Transitional Justice series

Series editor: Kieran McEvoy, Queen's University Belfast, UK

For information about the series and details of previous and forthcoming titles, see https://www.routledge.com/Transitional-Justice/book-series/TRANJ

Transitional Justice from State to Civil Society

Democratization in Indonesia

Sri Lestari Wahyuningroem

Routledge
Taylor & Francis Group
a GlassHouse Book

First published 2020
by Routledge
2 Park Square, Milton Park, Abingdon, Oxon OX14 4RN

and by Routledge
52 Vanderbilt Avenue, New York, NY 10017

Routledge is an imprint of the Taylor & Francis Group, an informa business

A GlassHouse book

First issued in paperback 2021

British Library Cataloguing-in-Publication Data
Names: Wahyuningroem, Sri Lestari, author.
Title: Transitional justice from state to civil society: democratization in Indonesia/Sri Lestari Wahyuningroem.
Description: Abingdon, Oxon; New York, NY: Routledge, 2020. |
Series: Transitional justice | Based on author's thesis (doctoral – Australian National University, 2018) under title: From state to society: democratisation and the failure of transitional justice in Indonesia. |
Includes bibliographical references and index.
Identifiers: LCCN 2019050135 (print) | LCCN 2019050136 (ebook) | ISBN 9780367230593 (hardback) | ISBN 9780429288609 (ebook)
Subjects: LCSH: Transitional justice—Indonesia. | Trials (Political crimes and offenses)—Indonesia. | Indonesia—Politics and government—1998–
Classification: LCC KNW470 .W34 2020 (print) |
LCC KNW470 (ebook) | DDC 340/.115—dc23
LC record available at https://lccn.loc.gov/2019050135
LC ebook record available at https://lccn.loc.gov/2019050136

Library of Congress Cataloging-in-Publication Data
A catalog record has been requested for this book

ISBN: 978-0-367-23059-3 (hbk)
ISBN: 978-1-03-208455-8 (pbk)
ISBN: 978-0-429-28860-9 (ebk)

Typeset in Galliard
by codeMantra

Contents

Tables and charts

Tables

Charts

Acknowledgements

This book started life as my PhD dissertation at the Australian National University. I would like to thank those who support me during my PhD journey and during writing of this book. First and foremost, I thank my supervisor, Prof. Edward Aspinall, for his continuous support both while I was in Canberra and in Jakarta. His careful reading and detailed comments on every draft of this thesis have been the signposts that directed me onto the right track of writing and helped develop my intellectual (thinking and writing) skills. I am also grateful to my supervisory panel members, Dr. Tyrell Haberkorn and Dr. Lia Kent, for energising discussions and inputs, especially in the critical time when I did not have a clear idea of how I would shape this research project.

I thank Dr. Greg Fealy, Head of Department, as well as other teaching staff and administrative staff of the Department of Political and Social Change who were very supportive and helpful during my study at ANU. I also thank Dr. Annie Pohlman who convinced me to publish my manuscript and read my drafts. I was lucky to have chances to meet prominent experts during my study who were willing to share with me their thoughts and links, and to facilitate my research journey and involve me in their projects and teachings in Australia and Europe. They were Prof. Harold Crouch, Prof. Robert Cribb, Dr. Kate McGregor, Dr. Jemma Purdey, Dr. Tiong Djin Siauw, Dr. Vannessa Hearmann, Dr Jess Melvin, Matthias Hammer, Prof. Gerry van Klinken, Prof. Saskia Wieringa, Dr. Nursyahbani Katjasungkana, Dr. Ratna Saptari, Prof. Ben White, Prof. John Braithwaite, Prof. Hillary Charlesworth, Dr. Susan Harris-Rimmer, Dr. Cecilia Jacob, Dr. Victoria Mason, Amrih Widodo, Prof. Ariel Heryanto, Dr. Renee Jeffrey, Dr. Marcus Mietzner, Prof. Stephen Permentier, Prof. Michael Humphrey, Prof. Richard Chauvel, Prof. Klaus Neumann, Dr. Jacqui Baker, Dr. Sue Ingram, Dr. Eben Kirksey. Galuh Wandita, Patrick Burgess, Kamala Chandrakirana, my colleagues at Political Science Department, University of Indonesia –Nuri Soeseno, Dr. Chusnul Mariyah, and Prof. Valina Singka Subekti, Barbara O'Dwyer of Women's International League for Peace and Freedom (WILPF) Australia, and the great team at Australia's UN Women National Committee. I thank them for their enthusiasm for me, my work, and my research.

A special thanks to the Ausaid ANU office for being very helpful in making sure my study and adaptation as an Australian Leadership Award awardee went smoothly. Also, thank you to the Australian-Netherlands Research Collaboration committee for selecting me and helping me with preparations for the research fellowship in Leiden. During my short fellowship, I had the chance to meet prominent people involved in Indonesia's struggle for change, including great people who were stranded, stateless, in various countries in Europe after the 1965–1966 political turmoil. I had excellent group discussions with these great people.

Generous supports were also given by colleagues at the Universitas Pembangunan Nasional 'Veteran' Jakarta, my new habitation for academic life, during the writing of this book. I would like to thank the Rector, Vice Rectors, Dean of Faculty of Social and Political Sciences, teaching colleagues as well as the staffs for their warm welcome and assistance in supporting my professional career.

I cannot imagine doing my research and completing this book without the support and cooperation of my fellow Indonesians at home. I first thank my interviewees, 78 of them, and dozens of others who took part in group discussions, many of whom I have known personally for a long time. My years of involvement in the field of human rights and transitional justice gave me knowledge of the context as well as of people relevant for my research. Victims and survivors of various cases of human rights abuses deserve my greatest gratitude. Our interactions have been based on mutual trust, and I have learned so much from their strength and perseverance. Second, I thank friends who supported my field work and writing during my time in Indonesia, also the Asia Justice and Rights (AJAR) team, a great team which I was also part of for years, for providing office space and involving me in activities related to my research in Bali and elsewhere; Ella Lamasitudju and her dynamic team at Solidaritas Korban Pelanggaran Hak Asasi Manusia (SKP HAM) for assisting in Palu; Ikatan Keluarga Orang Hilang (IKOHI) for assisting field work in Lampung; and members of Koalisi Keadilan dan Pengungkapan Kebenaran (KKPK), a network which I am also part of, for allowing me to actively participate in meetings and other activities during my field work; and dozens of experts and volunteers, both in Indonesia and other countries, I worked with in organising the International People's Tribunal for the Indonesian 1965 Crimes against Humanity (IPT '65), which was held in the Hague, 10–13 November 2015.

My family also deserves all the credit for my achievements. I dedicate this book for them, especially for my late parents, Soegoro Hardjoamidjojo and Sampoernaningroem, who always guide me to walk on my journeys in their absence. Lastly, my most heartfelt and loving gratitude goes to the individuals that make my life a whole: my husband Agam, and my children Indis and Ero. Having Indis and Ero made us stronger, as the kids have their unique ways to teach us about compassion and patience. Autism gave us reasons to be persistent and to have big dreams together, the four of us as a team. This book was never my struggle, it wasn't my dream. It was, and it has always been, ours.

Glossary

ABRI Angkatan Bersenjata Republik Indonesia (the Republic of Indonesia Armed Forces)
Agitprop Agitasi dan Propaganda (agitation and propaganda)
Ampera Amanat Penderitaan Rakyat (Message of the People's Sufferings)
APRODI Aliansi Pengacara untuk Demokrasi Indonesia (Lawyers Alliance for Indonesian Democracy)
API Asosiasi Pembela Islam (Islamic Defenders Association)
Babinsa Bintara Pembina Desa (Neighbourhood Security Officer)
Badan Rekonsiliasi Nasional: National Reconciliation Body
BLBI Bantuan Likuiditas Bank Indonesia (Bank Indonesia Liquidity Support)
Bakorstanas Badan Koordinasi Stabilitas Nasional (Coordinating Agency for National Stability)
Bamus Badan Musyawarah (the DPR's Discussion Body)
BIN Badan Intelijen Negara (the State Intelligence Agency)
BPS Badan Pusat Statistik (The Indonesian Bureau of Statistics)
Brimob Brigade Mobil (Police Mobile Brigade)
BTI Barisan Tani Indonesia (Indonesian Peasants' Front)
Bulog Badan Urusan Logistik (the State Logistic Body)
DDII Dewan Dakwah Islamiyah Indonesia (Council of Islamic Missionaries)
DEMOS Democracy Research Institute
DK Dengar Kesaksian (Testimonials Hearings)
DKM Dewan Kehormatan Militer (Military Honour Council)
DPR Dewan Perwakilan Rakyat (The People's Representative Council)
ELSAM Lembaga Studi dan Advokasi Masyarakat (the Institute for Policy Research and Advocacy)
FBB Fraksi Bulan Bintang (Crescent Star Fraction)
FGolkar Fraksi Golkar (the Functional Groups Faction)
FKB Fraksi Kebangkitan Bangsa (the National Awakening Faction)
FKKI Fraksi Kesatuan Kebangsaan Indonesia (Indonesian Nationhood Unity Faction)

Forkot 66 Forum Studi dan Komunikasi Angkatan 66 (Communication and Study Forum 1966 Generation)

FPBB Fraksi Partai Bulan Bintang (Crescent Star Party Faction)

FPDIP Fraksi Partai Demokrasi Indonesia Perjuangan (the Indonesian Democracy Party of Struggle Faction)

FPDKB Fraksi Partai Demokrasi Kasih Bangsa (the National Love Democracy Party Faction)

FPDU Fraksi Perserikatan Daulatul Ummah (People State Union Fraction)

FPG Fraksi Partai Golkar (Party of the Functional Groups Faction)

FPKB Fraksi Partai Kebangkitan Bangsa (National Awakening Party Faction)

FPP Fraksi Persatuan Pembangunan (United Development Fraction)

FReformasi Fraksi Reformasi (Reformation Faction)

Front Nasional National Front

F TNI/POLRI Faksi Tentara Nasional Indonesia/Polisi Republik Indonesia (Indonesian National Military/Indonesian Police Faction)

FURKON Forum Umat Islam Penegak Keadilan dan Konstitusi

GBHN Garis-garis Besar Haluan Negara (the State Policy Guidelines)

Golkar Golongan Karya (The Party of the Functional Groups)

ICMI Ikatan Cendekiawan Muslim se-Indonesia (the Association of Indonesian Islamic Intellectuals)

IKOHI Ikatan Keluarga Orang Hilang Indonesia (the Indonesian Association of Families of the Disappeared)

Inpres Instruksi Presiden (Presidential Instruction)

IPPI Ikatan Pemuda Pelajar Indonesia (Indonesian Youth Student Association)

Kejagung Kejaksaan Agung (the Attorney General's Office)

Keppres *Keputusan Presiden* (Presidential Decree)

KINKONAS Komisi Independen Pencari Kebenaran untuk Rekonsiliasi Nasional (Independent Truth Commission for National Reconciliation)

KKP HAM 65 Komite Aksi Korban Pelanggaran HAM 1965 (1965 Human Rights Victims Action Committee)

KKPK Koalisi Keadilan dan Pengungkapan Kebenaran (the Coalition for Truth and Justice)

KKPK Kelompok Kerja Pengungkapan Kebenaran (Working Group for Truth-seeking)

KOAMPA Komando Aksi Amanat Penderitaan Rakyat (Message of the People's Sufferings Action Command)

Koneksitas (court) a joint civilian-military court panel

KontraS Komisi Nasional untuk Orang Hilang dan Korban Kekerasan (the National Commission for Enforced Disappearance and Victims of Violence)

KPKP Koalisi Pembela Kasus Priok (Defender of the Priok Case Coalition)

KPKPN Komisi Pemeriksa Kekayaan Penyelenggara Negara (Commission for Monitoring of the Wealth of State Officials)

Kodam Komando Daerah Militer (Provincial Military Command)

Kodim Komando Distrik Militer (District Military Command)

KOMNAS Perempuan Komisi Nasional Perempuan (the National Commission against Discrimination against Women)

Komisi Nasional Rekonsiliasi National Reconciliation Commission

Komnas HAM Komisi Nasional Hak Asasi Manusia (the National Commission on Human Rights)

Kopassus Komando Pasukan Khusus (Indonesian Army Special Forces)

Koramil Komando Rayon Militer (Subdistrict Military Command)

KPK Koalisi Pengungkapan Kebenaran (Coalition for Truth-seeking)

KPP HAM Timtim Komisi Penyelidik Pelanggaran HAM di Timor Timur (Inquiry Team on Human Rights Abuses in East Timor)

KP3T Komisi Penyelidikan Pemeriksaan Pelanggaran Tanjung Priok (Commission for the Investigation and Examination of Human Rights Violations in Tanjung Priok)

LBH Lembaga Bantuan Hukum (the Legal Aid Institute)

LBH APIK Lembaga Bantuan Hukum Asosiasi Perempuan Indonesia untuk Keadilan (Women's Legal Aid)

Lemhanas Lembaga Pertahanan Nasional (National Security Agency)

LIPI Lembaga Ilmu Pengetahuan Indonesia (the Indonesian Institute of Sciences)

Litsus Penelitian Khusus (the Special Investigation Unit

LoGA Law on Governing Aceh

LPK 65 Lembaga Pembela Korban 65 (Institute for the Defenders of 1965 Victims)

LPKP 65 Lembaga Penelitian Korban Peristiwa 65 (Research Institute for Victims of the 1965 Tragedy)

LPRKROB Lembaga Perjuangan Rehabilitasi Korban Rezim Orde Baru (Organization for Rehabilitation Struggle for New Order Victims)

LPS-HAM Lembaga Pusat Studi Hak Asasi Manusia (Institute for Human Rights Study)

LPSK Lembaga Perlindungan Saksi dan Korban (The Witness and Victim Protection Agency)

Masyumi Majelis Syuro Muslimin Indonesia (Council of Indonesian Muslim Associations)

MRP Majelis Rakyat Papua (Papuan People's Council)

MPRS Majelis Permusyawaratn Rakyat Sementara (Provisional People's Consultative Assembly)

MPR Majelis Permusyawaratn Rakyat (People's Consultative Assembly)

NKRI Negara Kesatuan Republik Indonesuia (Unitary State of Indonesia)

NU Nahdlatul Ulama' (Revival of the Religious Scholars)

Pakorba Persatuan Korban Orde Baru (Association of Victims of the New Order)

Pamong Praja Government officials

PAN Partai Amanat Nasional (National Mandate Party)
Pansus Panitia Khusus (Special Committee)
Parkindo Partai Kristen Indonesia (Indonesian Christian Party)
PBB Partai Bulan Bintang (Crescent Star Party)
PD Partai Demokrat (the Democratic Party)
PDIP Partai Demokrasi Indonesia Perjuangan (the Indonesian Democratic Party of Struggle)
Peradin Persatuan Advokat Indonesia (the Association of Indonesian Advocates)
Pepera Penentuan Pendapat Rakyat (Act of Free Choice)
Perpres Peraturan Presiden (Presidential Regulation)
Perpu Peraturan Pengganti Undang-Undang (Government Regulation in Lieu of Law)
Persahi Perhimpunan Sarjana Hukum Indonesia (Association of Indonesian Law Graduates)
PKB Partai Kebangkitan Bangsa (National Awakening Party)
PKI Partai Komunis Indonesia (Indonesian Communist Party)
PKS Partai Keadilan Sejahtera (Prosperous Justice Party)
PNI Partai Nasional Indonesia (Indonesian National Party)
Pokja Kelompok Kerja (Working Group)
PP Pemuda Pancasila (Pancasila Youth)
PPP Partai Persatuan Pembangunan (United Development Party)
PRD Partai Rakyat Demokratik (People's Democratic Party)
PSII Partai Syarikat Islam Indonesia (Indonesian Islamic Union Party)
Puspom Pusat Polisi Militer (Central Military Police)
RPDU Rapat Dengar Pendapat Umum (General Hearings)
REMHI Recuperación de la Memoria Histórica (Historical Memory Project)
Ranham Rencana Aksi Nasional HAM (National Action Plan for Human Rights)
RUU KKR Rancangan Undang Undang Komisi Kebenaran dan Rekonsiliasi (Draft of Law of Truth and Reconciliation Commission)
Sekber 65 Sekretariat Bersama 65 (General Secretariat of Victims of 1965 Tragedy)
SI Sidang Istimewa (Special Session)
SKP HAM Palu Solidaritas Korban Pelanggaran Hak Asasi Manusia Palu (Solidarity for Victims of Human Rights Violation in Palu)
TRuK Tim Relawan untuk Kemanusiaan (Voluntary Team for Humanity)
TVRI Televisi Republik Indonsia (Indonesian Republic Televison)
TNI/POLRI Tentara Nasional Indonesia/Kepolisian Republik Indonesia (Indonesian National Armed Forces/Indonesian National Police)
UDHR Universal Declaration of Human Rights
UU KKR Undang-Undang Komisi Kebenaran dan Rekonsiliasi (Law on the Truth and Reconciliation Commission)

YAPHI Yayasan Pengabdian Hukum Indonesia [Yekti Angudi Piyadeging] (Institute of Indonesian Dedication for Law)
YLBHI Yayasan Lembaga Bantuan Hukum Indonesia (the Indonesian Legal Aid Foundation)
Yon Arhanudse Batalyon Artileri Pertahanan Udara Sedang (Middle Air Defence Artillery Batallion)
YPKP 65 Yayasan Penelitian Korban Pembunuhan 65 (Research Foundation for Victims of the 1965–1966 Killings)

Chapter 1

Introduction

Transitional justice in post-Soeharto Indonesia

> This afternoon, as has always been the tradition of Kamisan, victims of human rights abuses gathered around and sat quietly in front of the Presidential Palace for thirty minutes. It was silent, as justice has been silenced in the history of the country. After thirty minutes of silence, Sumarsih got up and was getting ready to approach the Presidential Palace across the road. She held in her hand a letter addressed to the President. The same letter was sent every week with the same hope that the President would read and respond to it. For a few seconds, she stood there and stared at the palace. Then, accompanied by some friends and victims, she crossed the road. Every time they approach the palace gate, the dozens of police who guard the palace always stop them before they reach it. The police asked them to hand over the letter and promised to give it to the President, the promise they give every week. And as it has always been, she did not resist. She gave the letter without saying a word; turned around, and with others crossed the road and returned to where the rest of the victims were gathered. It has become a routine action, a ritual. As she and the others walked away from the Palace, their hopes for justice receded from the State's attention (Field note entry, 17 May 2013).

The event described above took place in 2013, as part of one of the peace demonstrations held every Thursday (*Kamis*) since January 2006 until today in front of the Presidential Palace in Jakarta. These weekly demonstrations are organised by victims of human rights abuses and other elements of civil society. Sumarsih, the woman who handed over the letter, lost her son, Wawan, during a student demonstration against Soeharto in 1998. The military killed Wawan and several other students at the event. No trial has ever been held on the case even though the Komnas HAM (*Komisi Nasional Hak Asasi Manusia*, National Commission on Human Rights) set up a team of inquiry to investigate it and found that a violation of human rights was committed by the state apparatus. Sumarsih decided to take matters into her own hands and worked with other victims and families of victims of human rights violations from various other cases that mostly occurred during the Soeharto presidency (1966–1998). They decided to pursue other methods, including the peace demonstrations that take place in front of the Presidential Palace every Thursday. Their only demand, which is also written in their letters, is for the President as the chief representative of the State to resolve cases of past human rights abuses and to end impunity.

Sumarsih's trajectory reflects the wider story of transitional justice—of how past human rights abuses are dealt with in a democratising society—in post-Soeharto Indonesia. Sumarsih and her colleagues had great hopes for truth and justice when the 1998 reform movement ended the three-decade-long authoritarian regime and created a democracy. Transitional justice quickly became a central theme of public discussions, and post-Soeharto governments were eager to adopt transitional justice policies and mechanisms. However, Sumarsih's struggle indicates the many failings in Indonesia's attempts to deal with past abuses. Transitional justice is, to say the least, an unfinished agenda.

Wanting to understand this unfinished agenda is what motivated me to write this book. I address two questions in this research. First: What is the situation of transitional justice in Indonesia, and how do we judge its successes or failures, as well as its impact on Indonesia's democracy? Second: What features of democratisation in Indonesia produced these outcomes? What factors facilitated or hindered transitional justice?

My research finds that Indonesia's transitional justice has been partially successful in terms of *procedure*. In other words, various mechanisms and institutions were set up to deal with transitional justice issues. But substantively it has failed in achieving its objectives of bringing justice to victims and strengthening democracy. The failings of state-sponsored transitional justice are related to the nature of the transition from the Soeharto's "New Order" regime to a new democratic regime under the leadership of five successive presidents. Indonesia's democratic transition combined elements of replacement, involving a total break from the outgoing regime, and transplacement, involving ongoing negotiations between elements of the old regime and the new regime.

In this book, I explain how these aspects of the transition shaped the outcomes of the various transitional justice processes. Adopting a new discourse on human rights and promoting transitional justice was useful both for elements of the outgoing government and for actor from the new regime. It helped them distance themselves from the New Order and to gain political legitimacy in the new democratic landscape. Meanwhile, the negotiated nature of the transition also influenced the implementation and outcomes of the transitional justice mechanisms that were adopted. In particular, it ensured that transitional justice mechanisms protected the interests of the political elite rather than foregrounding those of the victims. When democracy became more consolidated and elections took place, the new regime that resulted from the negotiations and compromises between the political elite of the New Order and the incoming opposition forces was no longer dependent on transitional justice as a source of legitimacy. The failure of institutional mechanisms to bring about meaningful outcomes was the result.

However, I also show that although formal transitional justice mechanisms failed to achieve their objectives, these failures did not stop the growth of initiatives to correct past wrongs at the civil society and local levels. On the contrary, the failures contributed to such efforts, in these cases, rather than transitional justice producing impacts on democracy, I argue that democracy enabled civil society and local actors to initiate transitional justice efforts from the grassroots. The effect of these grassroots efforts has, however, so far been limited.

In explaining transitional justice, other scholars have pointed to the effects of the nature of the political transition (Linton, 2006; Suh, 2012), but these effects have not been closely studied or thoroughly understood. Within Indonesia, both non-government organisations and victims of human rights abuses often acknowledge that the shape of Indonesia's political transition has had an impact on transitional justice, but most fail to connect their analysis to their strategies for demanding justice and state accountability. Activists often pay lip service to political analysis rather than integrating it into their understanding of what must and can be achieved in transitional justice. In this book, I hope to help bridge this gap between analysis and strategy.

For the past 19 years, I have been working with both non-government organisations and victims of human rights abuses. However, as I have also been trained as a political science scholar, during this period of transition, I realised that the outcomes of human rights campaigns are highly dependent on power dynamics within the state and the governing elite, and their relationships with civil society. This factor is emphasised in the comparative literature. When explaining whether the countries experiencing the "third wave" of democratisation prosecuted elements of the old repressive regime, Huntington (1991: 215) argues,

> In actual practice what happened was little affected by moral and legal considerations. It was shaped almost exclusively by politics, by the nature of the democratisation process, and by the distribution of political power during and after the transition.

In Indonesia, lack of discussion among proponents of transitional justice of power dynamics during and after the post-1998 transition resulted in a lack of political analysis and effective strategies among activists for ensuring the success of the measures they proposed. This lack of analysis led me to the two questions that I seek to answer in this book.

Transitional justice: emergence, concepts, and trends around the globe

The field of transitional justice study has taken shape over the last 20 years. Different scholars date the emergence of transitional justice differently. Arthur (2009) argues that for most activists and practitioners, the emergence of the transitional justice field was a consequence of the development of the broader human rights movement, especially within the context of democratisation in Latin America and Southern European countries in the 1970s and 1980s. Democratic activists and their allies in government sought to find new and creative ways to address past injustices. They began to develop the nascent transitional justice framework to strengthen their new democracies and to comply with the moral and legal obligations that the human rights movement was articulating, both domestically and internationally.[1] Some scholars who focus on transitional justice mechanisms argue that the origins of this approach date much earlier. Elster (2004) suggests that some mechanisms of transitional justice such as purges and trials were employed as long as 2,000 years ago during political upheavals in Athens.[2] Meanwhile, Teitel (2003: 69–70) states that the Nuremburg Tribunal in 1945 marked the initial 'phase' of transitional justice.

In its simplest form, transitional justice, according to a 2004 report of the United Nation Secretary General, is defined as "The full range of processes and mechanisms associated with a society's attempts to come to terms with a legacy of large-scale past abuses, in order to ensure accountability, serve justice and achieve reconciliation".

Attempts to settle cases of past injustices can take place through various measures and mechanisms. The mechanisms most referred to in the literature are those that involve prosecution, truth-seeking, reparations, and institutional reform in the form of lustration or vetting. Prosecution can occur on the domestic level, in hybrid, internationalised courts, or in international courts. The goals of prosecution are to redress the suffering of victims and to provide opportunities to establish or strengthen the judicial system and the rule of law in transitional countries. Such efforts also aim at reflecting a new set of social norms based on respect for human rights and can be a starting point for a process of reforming and building trust in government institutions (Van Zyl, 2005: 211).

Truth mechanisms are efforts to establish the truth about past abuses. They include the creation of truth commissions—bodies that are tasked with uncovering what happened during human rights abuses—or other national and international efforts, such as major historical research or documentation of violence and victims of violence, and exhumations. State authorities often use truth-seeking in response to the limited effectiveness of international and domestic courts in dealing with past atrocities (Hayner, 2001: 27). In other words,

1 Bickford, Louis. *Macmillan Encyclopedia of Genocide and Crimes against Humanity*. www.ictj.org.

2 See Elster, Jon, *Closing the Book: Transitional Justice in Historical Perspective*. Cambridge: Cambridge University Press, 2004. According to Elster, the meanings of these practices are understood by historical actors involved and got swept into a universal, homogeneous conception of transitional justice. Transitional justice, according to him, "is made up of the processes of trials, purges and reparations that take place after the transition from one political regime to another" (1). It is the aim of his book to present these practices in historical approach and build an analytical framework that can explain the variations among the cases. See also Paige Arthur (2009: 328).

when authorities lack the political will or ability to prosecute perpetrators—or believe it is too risky to do so—they often pursue truth-seeking as an alternative approach. In many contexts, truth comes together with reconciliation, because most experts believe reconciliation can only be achieved if the past suffering of victims is acknowledged.

Reparation policies consider the physical requirements of, or moral obligations to, victims and survivors of abuse. Reparations can include economic compensation and non-material efforts including symbolic recognition such as state apologies to, and memorialisation of, victims. Unlike prosecutions, truth, and institutional reform, reparation mechanisms focus more on victims' experiences and needs.

Meanwhile, experts believe reforming institutions that have histories of abusive behaviour, including the security forces and related institutions, is necessary in order to prevent recurrence of patterns of abuses and to establish a state-society relationship based on functioning and fair institutions. One concrete measure is to apply vetting as part of security sector reform.[3] In a broad definition, the United Nations (UN) defines vetting as

> Assessing integrity to determine suitability for public employment. Integrity refers to an employee's adherence to international standards of human rights and professional conduct ... Vetting processes aim at excluding from public service persons with serious integrity deficit in order to (re-)establish civic trust and (re-) legitimize public institutions (Office of the United Nations High Commissioner for Human Rights, 2006: 4).

Other than these mechanisms, there have also been extensive studies and debates on amnesties and their role in transitional justice implementation. Olsen, Payne, and Reiter (2010: 36) define amnesties as "official state declarations that individuals or groups accused or convicted of committing human rights violations will not be prosecuted or will be pardoned for their crimes and released from prison". Arguments for and against amnesties have been intense. For some scholars and policymakers, amnesties are a key mechanism for ensuring that consolidation of democracy can take place smoothly because they can forestall resistance to democratisation from elites who were responsible for past human rights abuses. Others see amnesties as serving the interests of repressive actors.[4] There has been a paradigmatic shift in the last decade within international human rights law and

3 The term 'vetting' is often used interchangeably with other words such as 'lustration', 'screening', 'administrative justice, and 'purging'. One important distinction is that 'lustration' usually is the term used to refer to post-communist contexts, while purging is targeting people for their membership or affiliation with a group rather than their individual involvement in human rights violations. See Duthie, Roger. "Introduction." In A. Mayer-Rieckh & P. de Grieff (Eds.), *Justice as Prevention, Vetting Public Employees in Transitional Societies* (pp. 17–18). New York: Social Science Research Council, 2007.

4 See discussion on amnesties in Olsen, Payne, and Reiter (2010: 35–37).

international criminal law circles, with many now seeing amnesties as no longer unconditionally lawful. However, to be legitimate, amnesties have to conform to legal norms, or comply with the standard of "qualified amnesties": they cannot bar prosecution for war crimes, certain treaty crimes, and crimes against humanity (Laplante, 2009: 4).

Globally, an increasing number of countries have adopted and implemented transitional justice mechanisms. Sikkink and Payne (2014: 36–39) have created datasets on various mechanisms of transitional justice around the world. Their data show a positive worldwide trend in state efforts to enforce accountability for human rights crimes. Prosecution and amnesties are the two mechanisms where use has increased most. Human rights trials, in particular, have occurred at both domestic and international levels. Their dataset shows that domestic human rights prosecutions have been used widely in Latin America and Central and Eastern Europe. The third largest number of prosecutions have occurred in Asia, after Europe and the Americas. From 1970 to 2009, countries in Asia implemented 17 per cent of the total number of domestic human rights prosecutions. In terms of international tribunals, Asia, Africa, and Europe are the three regions that dominate, in contrast to domestic prosecutions where the Americas are more prominent. Countries in Asia implemented around 32 per cent of international prosecutions around the globe. These international prosecutions included the hybrid, international-national tribunals in Cambodia and East Timor (Sikkink and Payne, 2014: 40). In the Asia-Pacific, Jeffery and Kim (2014: 22–27) also show that increasing numbers of countries have adopted transitional justice mechanisms since 1980.

The dataset developed by Olsen, Payne, and Reiter (2010) shows that there is a growing trend for countries in the Asia-Pacific to institute more than one mechanism. Out of 19 countries that had adopted transitional justice by 2009 only six countries instituted just one mechanism. Others had implemented two or more mechanisms either simultaneously or sequentially. The most commonly used mechanisms in these countries have been trials, truth commissions, and amnesties.

Even though a wide variety of studies and theories have been built around transitional justice and its positive relationship with democratic transition, recent literature (Humphrey, 2008; Lundy and McGovern, 2008; McEvoy, 2007; Meister, 2002; Stover and Weinstein, 2004) criticises aspects of state-sponsored transitional justice measures, including many of the mechanisms mentioned above. My experiences in working on advocacy for victims of human rights abuses in Indonesia have also given me insights into the weaknesses of mainstream propositions on transitional justice, some of which have not worked well in the Indonesian context. My experiences resonate with criticisms arising from the recent literature.

Humphrey (2008) argues that transitional justice, despite its success in making crimes against humanity visible and in putting pressure on states to be accountable for human rights abuses, also often becomes "tactics used by the State, a ritual performance to enact new beginnings, rather than an actual closure of the evil past" (Humphrey, 2008: 8). Meister (2002, 2005, 2012) questions the demarcation between "evil" and "justice" in transitional justice discourse. Transitional justice, he argues, does not address the structural inequities and injustices of the victims, encouraging victims of unjust political, social, and economic systems to accept only a minimal definition of justice. He argues:

> We must note, however, that the survivor stories that appear in the great documents of transitional liberalism [...] are almost never *about* systemic injustice as such. Rather, they are about a narrow class of victims (those who suffered physical torment) and a narrow class of perpetrators (their active tormenters). Although one might argue that focusing on these particular atrocities puts a human face on structural injustice, much of the recent writing on human rights in political transitions explicitly rejects this interpretation as incompatible with reestablishing (or establishing) the "rule of law". The rule of law in the aftermath of evil is expressly meant to decollectivize both injury and responsibility and to redescribe systemic violence as a series of individual crimes (Meister, 2012: 27 28).

Similarly, Leebaw (2011) argues that transitional justice has failed in achieving its goal to respond to systematic violence because it relies on criminal justice strategies to investigate experiences of *individual* victims and perpetrators. The adoption of a criminal justice framework depoliticises the process of making judgement. In her view, such depoliticisation hides the particular political and social values that frame the investigation and removes the problems from the political and historical context. All forms of political judgement are destructive to efforts for reconciliation or to the integrity of judicial processes. Thus, transitional justice is, in her words, "in tension with the pursuit of political mobilization on behalf of ongoing change to advance democratic reform or address the legacy of the past" (Leebaw, 2011: 18).

McEvoy (2007) views transitional justice mechanisms as top-down policies, designed and implemented by the state. He suggests transitional justice is a standard approach by which states are supposed to manage a democratic transition, and that it has become a "one-size-fits-all" formula adopted in many post-conflict or post-authoritarian regime settings (McEvoy, 2007: 414). Other scholars address their criticisms at the effectiveness of this state-centred approach, especially with regard to reconciliation at the grassroots level (Stover and Weinstein, 2004), and to the insufficient attention formal mechanisms often pay to local participation (Lundy and McGovern, 2008: 100). Kent (2012), taking the case study of the newly independent country of Timor Leste, criticised 'official' transitional justice as a toolkit developed by international organisations and funding agencies to promote individual values and individual rights. In Timor Leste's context, such values often contradict local perceptions of justice by which justice is seen as a broader social good. Accordingly, justice takes a long time to be achieved and should be based on locally embedded 'conversations', involving various international, national as well as local actors. As she concludes:

> In the gaps between local expectations and the form of justice that has been officially delivered, a conversation is continuing about how best to 'deal with the past'. What can be observed is that official transitional justice discourse and practice have contributed to the emergence of new narratives (based around concepts of 'victims' rights), encouraged emerging norms of identification (based around victimhood) and contributed to a new form of victim's rights politics. [...] The boundaries of this politics are being shaped and contested by a range of different actors: the national government and opposition parties; national and international human rights organizations; the UN; victims' groups; widows groups; and other interest groups (Kent, 2012: 205).

In line with such criticisms, recent studies of transitional justice acknowledge other ways of 'doing justice', including bottom-up approaches which incorporate local practices and local initiatives by civil society groups or communities. Launched in 1995, REMHI (*Recuperación de la Memoria Histórica,* Historical Memory Project) is a well-known local bottom-up mechanism in Guatemala. It is a truth mechanism organised through a project led by the Catholic Church that aims to document the atrocities committed during Guatemala's 36-year civil war. Another example is a truth-telling initiative in Northern Ireland called the Ardoyne Commemoration Project (ACP). This initiative is described as grassroots 'single identity truth recovery' project set up in the Ardoyne area of North Belfast, an area that suffered one of the highest casualty rates during the conflict in Northern Ireland (Lundy and McGovern, 2008: 284).

The main point made by advocates of bottom-up approaches is that initiatives should emerge from and be implemented by the community itself, mostly by using traditional justice and dispute resolution methods. The 'local' approach to transitional justice refers to justice measures that take place in the local where human rights abuses occurred (Horne, 2014a: 18–19). This bottom-up approach positions communities and those on the receiving end of violent conflict at the very centre of transitional justice (Lundy and McGovern, 2008: 291). As McEvoy (2007: 311) suggests, "the view 'from below' is really a way of providing a different vantage point in order to 'see' more clearly connections, accommodations, and relationships with institutions and structures 'from above'". Yet despite the acknowledgement of the centrality of the local communities, the concepts used in transitional justice approaches, such as truth and justice, often remain vague and are frequently defined by those who occupy prominent positions within traditional or local power structures. Often, these local initiatives are more associated with aspirational rhetoric than concrete political reality.

As well as grassroots initiatives, another alternative approach to transitional justice involves mechanisms initiated and established by regional governments. Such an approach involves representatives of the state at a lower level, and at the same time can accommodate local participation and practices. Regional state officials or elites sometimes initiate such policies, but mostly it is elements of civil society, including non-governmental organisations (NGOs) and victims, who initiate and sometimes lead such processes in collaboration with local governments. One example of this approach is the Greensboro Truth and Reconciliation Commission (TRC) in North Carolina, in the United States. The Commission was set up in 2004 and was claimed to be the first of its kind in the United States. The Commission started in the 2000s when a group of Greensboro residents and other concerned individuals recognised that problems in their community—including racism, distrust between police and African American residents, and poor working conditions—were connected to a tragic event on November 3, 1979 when members of the Ku Klux Klan, a right wing extremist movement, and the American Nazi Party shot and killed five protesters at a rally opposing the formation of the Ku Klux Klan. The Commission's mandate was to examine "the context, causes, sequence and consequence of the events of November 3, 1979" for the purpose of healing and transformation for the community.[5] The former Greensboro Mayor established a local Truth and Reconciliation committee, hoping that by establishing an accurate collective memory of the event, the community would better understand how to move forward (Williams, 2009: 144–145).

In Indonesia, various forms of transitional justice measures have also been initiated at the grassroots (Brauchler, 2009) and regional levels. Such initiatives have emerged in part as a response to the failures of state-sponsored measures. These measures have included documentation, exhumation, memorialisation, commemoration, and reconciliation. NGOs and victims' groups have been actively involved in documenting testimonies of victims as well as historical archives (Farid and Simarmata, 2004). Since 2008, they have also engaged in initiatives with regional governments. This book includes not only national initiatives but also grassroots and regional level mechanisms. Overall, however, discussion of these local approaches to transitional justice in this book is framed by analysis of the political dynamics of Indonesia's democratic transition and the outcomes of state-sponsored mechanisms at the centre.

Transitional justice in Indonesia

Indonesia's political transition started in 1998 with the fall, after 32 years, of the authoritarian regime led by General Soeharto, following an economic crisis that hit the country and massive demonstrations that took place in Jakarta and

5 See the website for more detailed information about the Commission, http://www.greensboro-trc.org/about_the_commission.php.

elsewhere in the same year (Aspinall, 2015; Robison, 2001; Robison and Hadiz, 2005). This change marked the beginning of a transition from an authoritarian regime to democracy, and made it possible for past human rights abuses committed during the authoritarian period to be acknowledged by the wider public.

After five successive presidents and four elections, there have been many attempts to bring about mechanisms for ensuring truth and justice with respect to past human rights abuses, and with regard to more recent abuses during or after the reform process. Indonesia is one of the many countries that has adopted more than one transitional justice mechanisms. In the beginning of the transition, truth-seeking was pursued for multiple cases, while legal reform also took place. Both processes later led to human rights trials. President Habibie (1998–1999) set up inquiry teams on conflict in Aceh and on the rioting and violence that accompanied regime change in Jakarta during May 1998. Komnas HAM as an autonomous state body also set up a number of fact-finding teams aimed at revealing the truth about human rights abuses, including those that had occurred in East Timor, the 1984 Tanjung Priok massacre, the 1989 Talangsari massacre, and some other cases of recent and past abuses. Trials began under Abdurrahman Wahid's (1999–2001) presidency, including trials on mass violence during East Timor's 1999 referendum for independence. In 2004, Indonesia finally passed a Law on Truth and Reconciliation. But a TRC had not yet been established when the Constitutional Court annulled the Law in 2006. From that time, the central government took no more significant efforts to deal with or resolve cases of past abuses. Chart 1.1 summarises the various kinds of transitional justice initiatives set up by the government in the early years of the transition.

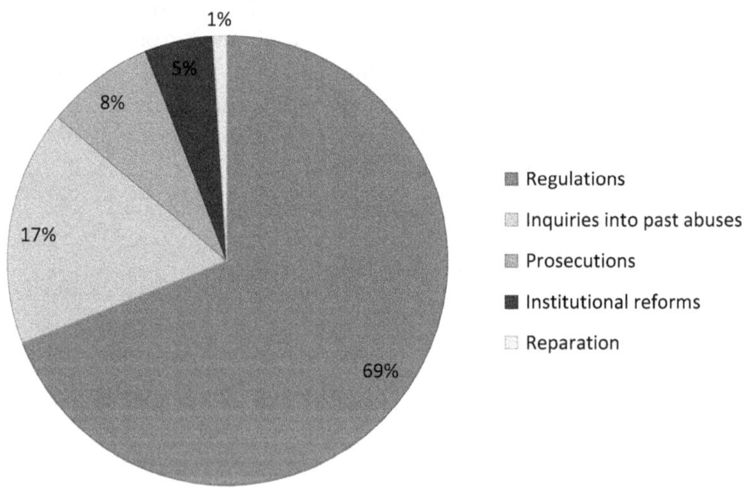

Chart 1.1 Transitional Justice Policies and Mechanisms in 1998–2004.
Source: ELSAM (2005).

The chart shows that law regulation that relates to the adoption of human rights norms into local policies were mostly chosen during the early period of reform (1998–2004). Within this period, Komnas HAM had a significant role in promoting and maintaining the momentum for human rights accountability through inquiries (truth-seeking initiatives) including for cases of past abuses under the Soeharto's rule (Pratikno et al., 2002; Setiawan, 2013).

Other than Komnas HAM and its truth-seeking initiatives, state institutions also pursued other options related to transitional justice. The MPR (*Majelis Permusyawaratan Rakyat,* People's Consultative Assembly)—Indonesia's supreme law-making body—passed Resolution No. V in 2000 which later served as the foundation for other measures for transitional justice. The DPR (*Dewan Perwakilan Rakyat*, People's Representative Council)—Indonesia's parliament—also responded to demands for human rights accountability and transitional justice by passing various laws and taking political decisions on some cases of human rights violations. For example, it passed Law No. 39 of 1999 on Human Rights and Law No. 26 of 2000 on Human Rights Courts. The judiciary was also active. The Supreme Court accommodated some demands that it deal with past abuse cases, especially the 1965–1966 violence—when hundreds of thousands of leftists were massacred by the army and its allies—by issuing a letter to the president and parliament recommending that they acknowledge and rehabilitate the rights of the victims in 2003 (Mahkamah Agung, 2003). Meanwhile, the security sector, including the military and the police, also took positive moves towards institutional reform and accountability. Chart 1.2 below shows initiatives

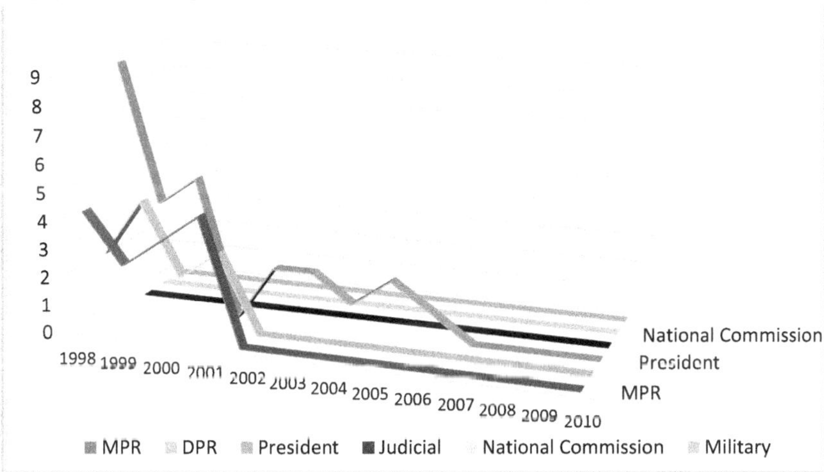

Chart 1.2 New Transitional Justice Policies Initiated by Different State Institution.
Source: Various documents and reports.

and policies related to transitional justice taken by these state institutions. It clearly shows that there was a flurry of law making and other initiatives in the early phase of the transition (1998–2001), but that the pace of transitional justice slowed dramatically after that.

In general, the adoption of transitional justice measures and human rights policies was positive in terms of the promotion of state accountability and human rights protection. However, some assessments suggest that the implementation of these measures was deeply unsatisfactory. Juwana (2003), in his assessment of human rights performance in Indonesia, outlines significant improvement in the human rights legal framework and a myriad of new human rights institutions, but he also acknowledges these things contributed little to improving the protection and fulfilment of human rights, resulting in a 'deficit in justice'. Likewise, the KontraS (Komisi Nasional untuk Orang Hilang dan Korban Kekerasan, National Commission for Enforced Disappearance and Victims of Violence), an NGO based in Jakarta, and the International Center for Transitional Justice (ICTJ) conducted an assessment in 2011 in which they acknowledged that during the 13 years of political transition to that point, especially in the early years of democratisation, Indonesia had taken positive steps to bring about legal reforms and create institutions for state accountability for past human rights abuses. However, they noted that there was a period after the annulment of the Law on Truth and Reconciliation in 2006, when all of these mechanisms stalled or stagnated (ICTJ and KontraS, 2011). Ehito (2015) relates the failure of transitional justice to the many ways by which the political elite contrived to obstruct efforts for justice by civil society groups. He explains that transitional justice in Indonesia "illustrates some of the larger and continued problems of governance in post-Suharto Indonesia where the rules of the game have changed, but many of the players remain the same" (Ehito, 2015: 88).

When relating transitional justice mechanisms to the aims of the rule of law, human rights, and peace, Indonesia is also failing. Various indices developed to measure performance in this area indicate Indonesia's failure. The World Justice Project in 2012 in its Rule of Law Index scores Indonesia at 0.52 on a scale of 0.00–1.00 and ranked it 55th out of 97 countries globally, 10th out of 14 countries in East Asia and the Pacific, and 7th out of 23 lower-middle-income countries.[6] In terms of human rights performance, Setara Institute, a Jakarta-based

6 The Index uses a definition of 'Rule of Law' based on four universal principles: "(1) The government and its officials and agents are accountable under the law, (2) The laws are clear, publicised, stable and fair, and protect fundamental rights, including the security of persons and property, (3) The process by which the laws are enacted, administered and enforced is accessible, fair and efficient, (4) justice is delivered by competent, ethical and independent representatives and neutrals who are of sufficient number, have adequate resources, and reflect the makeup of the communities they served". It categorises rule of law into eight factors, namely limited government power, absence of corruption, order and security, fundamental rights, open government,

research institute, scores Indonesia at 2.8 on a scale from 0 to 7. Its score for resolution of past human rights violations is 1.44, or the lowest among the indicators.[7]

Several scholarly writings assess Indonesia's transitional justice experience. Linton (2006) examines Indonesia's situation in accounting for atrocities, both authoritarian-era atrocities and those which occurred after *reformasi* began, by examining the law and legal processes. She not only looks at the normative/legal adoption of international norms into Indonesia's legal framework but also at the processes and outcomes of mechanisms set up to deal with cases of human rights abuse, including Komnas HAM, Human Rights Courts, *Koneksitas* Courts (a special court to prosecute perpetrators both from the military institution and civilians), TRC, and Commission for Truth and Friendship. She concludes that:

> The quality of accountability is so low that the flurry of 'transitional justice' has had little impact on changing society and taking Indonesia towards rule of law and democracy. Too often, the course of justice has been grossly perverted (Linton, 2006: 229).

Although there is a comprehensive legal regime in place (both law and mechanisms) and some improved statistical data, qualitatively, according to Linton, there is little actual improvement of the human rights situation in terms of accountability and justice. Furthermore, she argues that "accountability has too often been hijacked and skilfully used as platform to further aims that have nothing to do with the fundamental concepts that underpin the human rights paradigm, such as justice, fairness, non-discrimination and individual or state responsibilities" (Linton, 2006: 229).

Meanwhile, Suh (2012) looks at transitional justice from a slightly different point of view. She argues that Indonesia is a success story in adopting the transitional justice paradigm, but not in its implementation. The adoption of transitional justice was the result of international pressure, especially following the mass violence that took place around the East Timor referendum in 1999, and was also a consequence of the roles played by human rights NGOs as 'norm entrepreneurs'. She also argues that the fact that Indonesia is a latecomer democracy is an advantage because Indonesia had options to choose comprehensive

regulatory enforcement, civil justice, and criminal justice. Each of these factors also divided into sub factors. See the report Rule of Law Index 2012–2013, The World Justice Project, http://worldjusticeproject.org.

7 The indicators used in this index are (1) completion of past human rights violations, (2) freedom of expression, (3) freedom of religion/belief, (4) National Human Rights Action Plan and Human Rights institutions performance, (5) security and protection of citizens, (6) abolition of death penalty, (7) elimination of discrimination, and (8) right to economy, social, culture. See Human Rights Performance Index 2012, Setara Institute, in www.setara-institute.org/en/content/human-rights-performance-index-2012.

transitional justice mechanisms from various models and practices experienced in other countries. However, her findings suggest that transitional justice in Indonesia failed at the implementation level. She explains that:

> These comprehensive mechanisms, the ad-hoc human rights court system and the TRC, were adopted even though post-New Order Indonesia lacked the generally discussed preconditions for successful transitional justice [...] these comprehensive laws were adopted when other factors—nature of the transition, duration of the regime, quality of the judicial system, and the authoritarian regime type—were predicting the opposite, which gives us a good reason to pay attention to the impact of international influence (Suh, 2012: 13).

Without elaborating on these preconditions, she points to several factors contributing to the failure. First, international pressure on Indonesia to reform did not last long. Second, the new political elite chose not to alienate those who had formerly perpetrated or supported human rights abuses. Third, Indonesia lacked strong independent sources of pressure, or constituencies, that would support transitional justice policies based on a shared identity with victims of human rights abuses. On the last point, she argues that human rights NGOs failed to identify themselves or collaborate with political institutions or parties and were thus rather isolated politically.

I found these analyses helpful but ultimately unsatisfactory because they fail to explain *why* Indonesia produced poor outcomes in terms of substantive accountability and human rights promotion despite significant progress in the formal adoption of human rights policies and transitional justice mechanisms (Hadiprayitno, 2010a; Juwana, 2003; Linton, 2006; Suh, 2012). Most observers believe that the implementation of these policies has been flawed in many ways, resulting in a "deficit" of justice and accountability (Juwana, 2003; Hadiprayitno, 2010a) and even the "derailing" of transitional justice (ICTJ, 2010). The implication is that the situation of human rights protection has not improved (Juwana, 2003), producing no effect in terms of protecting rights-holders (Hadiprayitno, 2010a) or ending impunity (Linton, 2006). The transitional justice agenda, therefore, has been 'hijacked' by the new political elite in the Post-Soeharto period (Linton, 2006). Yet all of these analyses share the same argument in explaining these failures: lack of political will on the part of the state and ruling elite.

Explaining such poor outcomes of transitional justice and human rights as resulting from the lack of the state's political willingness is unsatisfactory because it assumes the state is monolithic, ignoring the fact that during the transition and in the period of what most scholars referred to as consolidation, state institutions and agents are willing to adopt transitional justice measures with different motivations and interests. These interests often collided with one another. In fact, some leaders were well informed and highly motivated to settle cases of past human rights abuses. Individual leaders are thus an important factor in determining whether or not transitional justice measures were introduced. Beyond the leadership aspect, state and political institutions chose to adopt transitional justice policies and mechanisms in an attempt to distance themselves from the Soeharto regime. Learning from the "tactical concessions" adopted during Soeharto's time (see Jetschke, 1999), especially the establishment of Komnas HAM which I explain in my next chapter, these leaders viewed transitional justice as a concession that could offer in order to gain political legitimacy in the new more democratic era, both from the international community and from the domestic public. I argue that the state and its leaders opted for and implemented transitional justice as a purely "tactical concession" without acknowledging the very reasons why violence had occurred. Tactical concession here refers to Risse and Sikkink (1999) understanding of governments' rhetoric response to pressure groups demanding adherence to particular norms, by underestimating the impacts of the changes or concessions they made (Risse and Sikkink, 1999: 66). Indonesia's transitional justice process was thus, from the start, politically superficial, as transitional justice was adopted only to respond domestic and international pressures for accountability of the repressive regime.

Assessing transitional justice and the implications for democracy

What is the situation of transitional justice in Indonesia? Has it been a success or failure, and how do we judge success or failure, including by taking into consideration the impact transitional justice has had on Indonesia's democracy? By success or failure, I refer partly to whether transitional justice mechanisms have completed their mandates and tasks as concrete "deliverables" or outcomes. But we also need to look at the broader impacts on Indonesia's democracy.

The use of various transitional justice mechanisms around the world has in the last decade been followed by various attempts to assess and evaluate their effectiveness and impacts. Such assessment is needed by governments, donor agencies, international organisations, civil society advocates, and scholars alike to help equip countries in transition with effective measures for settling past abuses.

Assessing the impact of transitional justice is not an easy task because transitional justice itself is a developing interdisciplinary field of inquiry. Duggan (2009), for example, acknowledges a number of challenges in assessing transitional justice methodologically, contextually, and politically. These include the complexity and unpredictability of the dynamics of democratic transitions, weak evidence of causality and problems of attribution, and dealing with traumatised victims and broken relationships within communities. All of these problems make it hard to assess the concrete results of transitional justice measures. However, various research efforts have been conducted and many of the findings suggest methods and criteria for assessment.

In general, there are three ways to assess transitional justice. First, it is possible to assess each mechanism individually, that is by looking at its formation, legal basis, implementation process, mandates, and results or deliverables. For some, the simple fact that a particular transitional justice mechanism is put in place can itself be considered a success. Establishing such a mechanism is not a small feat because transitional justice typically faces considerable resistance from those who are likely to be investigated or punished (Brahm, 2005: 6). The REMHI project, as mentioned earlier, is an example. The project was an initiative to support the work of any truth commission that might emerge in Guatemala from the Peace Accords in Oslo in 1994. Church leaders assumed that an official truth commission would be limited in mandate and time due to the resistance of the parties involved in the conflict, so they gathered data and information through documentation project to contribute to such a commission. Bishop Juan Gerardi, the leader of the project, was assassinated outside his home two days after its report. *Nunca Mas* (Never Again) was launched on April 24, 1998. A TRC (Comisión para el Esclarecimiento Histórico, CEH) was eventually established in 1997. Its establishment was considered a success for peace and reconciliation attempts in the country. It eventually used the information collected in the REMHI project. The point is that even though the initial REMHI project seemed to bear little fruit, its long-term impact was considerable; any early assessment may have missed this.

Second, it is possible to assess a transitional justice effort by looking at how successful it was at achieving its aims. If the former approach focuses on procedural analysis, the latter focuses on more substantive aspects of transitional justice. An example can be seen in the results and outcomes of the Timor Leste's CAVR (Commission of the Reception, Truth and Reconciliation). The Commission established the truth about the crimes against humanity which had been committed during the Indonesian occupation in 1975 until 1999 referendum through its reports *Chega* (Never Again) in 2006 (Hayner, 2011).

Third, it is possible to assess transitional justice mechanisms as an independent variable and to look at their impacts on other variables, especially democracy. Studies of the impacts of human rights trials on democracy have indicated a positive correlation. Single case studies such as the study conducted by Akhavan (2001) and Meernik's (2005) statistical analysis of the International Criminal Trial for Former Yugoslavia (ICTY) look at the effect of trials on democracy and peace building in former Yugoslav countries but provide slightly different findings.[8] Other scholars made comparative studies to test the effects of trials

8 Akhavan (2001) argues that ICTY's indictment was successful in marginalising ultra-nationalism and encouraging the emergence of moderate leaders. Moreover, it had positive effects on ethnic politics in Croatia and the integration of Serbia and Croatia into Europe. Meernik (2005), using statistical analysis to test the effects of international arrests and verdicts finds little impact on societal peace, however it had most effects to the strengthened roles of NATO and the US.

on democracy. Stromseth, Wippman, and Brooks's (2006) qualitative study of the former Yugoslavia, Rwanda, Timor Leste, and Sierra Leone argues that trials marginalised perpetrators but were less successful at promoting local judicial capacity and strengthening domestic support for accountability and justice. Comparing implementation of trials for human rights abuses in many countries around the world, especially Latin American countries, Sikkink and Booth Walling (2007: 427–445) found that holding human rights trials has not undermined democracy or led to an increase in human rights violations or conflict. They confirm that human rights trials correlate positively with democracy indicators as shown by the Freedom House database. A larger study of trials by Kim and Sikkink (2010) in 93 transitional countries between 1984 and 2004 confirms that countries with trials were less repressive and respected human rights better, even those civil war situations.

In terms of truth commissions, Hayner's (2001) often-quoted study finds that truth mechanisms contribute positively to the quality of democratic change. Wiebelhaus-Brahm makes a similar argument in his comparative study of truth commissions in 78 countries around the world (Wiebelhaus -Brahm, 2010). His database project with Dancy and Kim shows not only that truth commissions have become widespread around the world but also that they have positive effects on democracy (Dancy, Kim, and Wiebelhaus-Brahm, 2010). South Africa's TRC has become the model for many countries both because of its success and its limited nature. Boraine's (2001) book and Gibson's (2005) survey on the attitudes of South Africans towards their TRC find the TRC helped support the rule of law and reconciliation in that country. Other scholars conducting comparative studies on truth mechanisms also found positive effects on peace settlements (Long and Brecke, 2003) and levels of democracy (Kenney and Spears, 2005). Likewise, a quantitative study by Botha (1998), involving 56 countries in Eastern Europe, Africa, and Latin America, confirmed the positive correlation between truth commissions and certain measures of democracy.

An aspect of transitional justice mechanisms that is understudied is vetting or lustration. One study by David (2003) on Poland and former Czechoslovakia looked at the impacts of lustration policies in these countries on democracy and stability in their democratic transitions. Some other case studies have looked at this aspect, including an edited collection by Mayer-Rieckh and de Grieff (2007). The country cases show variation in how lustration or vetting impacts on democracy in countries in transition.

In evaluating the findings of such comparative studies of the effects of transitional justice processes on democracy, Sikkink and Payne (2014: 48–60) identify three positive impacts that transitional justice may theoretically have: deterrence, normative socialisation, and accountability-with-stability. The deterrence impact is adapted from both international relations and legal approaches and holds that enforcement or implementation of transitional justice will increase the likelihood of justice and democracy by subjecting would-be perpetrators of rights violations to fear of punishment. The normative socialisation impact sees transitional justice mechanisms as "high-profile symbolic and performative events that communicate and dramatize norms and socialize actors to accept those norms" (Sikkink and Payne, 2014: 49). Norm entrepreneurs, including local NGOs and intrastate organisations, promote these processes of communication and socialisation. Eventually, such processes lead state actors to behavioural change. Sikkink (2011) explored the impacts of both the deterrence and normative socialisation in explaining why human rights trials have positive impacts on human rights practices, an effect she termed "the justice cascade".

Meanwhile, Olsen, Payne, and Reiter (2010) develop the accountability-with-stability impact by looking at more comprehensive aspects of transitional justice mechanisms. By developing several measures and indicators of transitional justice and relying on data from Polity IV, they set up a database that aims at testing various hypotheses coming from the abundant literature on transitional justice.[9] Their findings lead to an approach they call "the justice in balance" approach. They suggest that any single transitional justice mechanism used in isolation will not lead to achievement of transitional justice goals but will worsen democratic outcomes. However, combinations of mechanisms, especially trials mixed with other mechanisms, are more effective. They thus recommend that transitioning countries should adopt a holistic approach to transitional justice involving sequential choices. Their analyses suggest two ideal sets of combinations: (1) trials and amnesties and (2) trials, truth commissions, and amnesties.[10] They say these combinations have had the most robust and positive effects on human rights and democratic outcomes. This finding resonates with an earlier study by Snyder and Vinjamuri (2003) on transitional justice in 32 post-conflict countries between 1989 and 2003. Snyder and Vinjamuri find that trials and truth commissions did not have much positive effect on democracy, human rights, and rule of law, but well-designed and thoroughly implemented amnesties did.

In this research, I look at both procedural and substantive aspects in order to assess transitional justice in Indonesia. Whether transitional justice mechanisms succeed or fail in procedural terms determines the outcomes with regard to larger objectives and helps shed light on how the different transitional justice mechanisms might interact to produce wider effects.

9 The database project attempts to fill the gap between knowledge and theory building on politics of transitional justice by testing how three political factors affect transitional justice achievements: characteristics of predecessor authoritarian regime, the type of transition, and the nature of new democratic governance. A large number of studies have found the authoritarian regime factor to be the most determining factor on transitional justice choices (Olsen, Payne, and Reiter, 2010).

10 Trials are certainly needed for ensuring state accountability for past crimes. However, trials alone are not a realistic option for many new regimes, as will typically not be possible to try everyone involved in past crimes nor to come up with the huge amount of resources needed for such efforts. The justice balance involves "the legal imperative for justice with protecting public safety by granting amnesty to perpetrator" (Olsen, Payne, and Reiter, 2010: 154).

In terms of procedural aspects, in assessing Indonesia's transitional justice experience, I look at the formation and implementation of each mechanism, including its legal basis, internal dynamics, and results or deliverables. Included in these aspects are also the access and involvement of victims and human rights groups, and other elements of civil society such as researchers and historians, based on the assumption that transitional justice processes should take place openly.

On the substantive aspects, I look at the outcomes of these mechanisms, relating each to the objectives and expectations that lay behind their implementation. These expectations, as Hazan (2006: 29) outlines, include the penal effectiveness of prosecutions and "show trials", the production and presentation of "truth", the therapeutic impact and effectiveness of public apologies, the effectiveness of reparations, and the process of building a common narrative. I found such expectations are also important for assessing transitional justice in Indonesia. In specific, I formulated questions to assess it during my meetings with various stakeholders, including victims of human rights abuses. First, has the particular transitional justice mechanism produced a democratised truth about past wrongs? The democratisation of truth can only occur when victims' narratives about their sufferings are brought to public attention and widely acknowledged, not only by the state but also by society at large. Second, have trials and prosecutions resulted in individual wrongdoers or state institutions being held formally accountable and sentenced? Such punitive justice is necessary to challenge the legacy of impunity of the New Order regime. Third, has victims' suffering been acknowledged as part of the initiatives of transitional justice? Acknowledgement of suffering can involve formal reparations to indicate state responsibility and to ensure the rights of each of its citizens. To be genuine, such acknowledgement should be institutionalised, programmed, and sustained. It can include memorialisation as a form of symbolic reparation and with the goal of educating younger generations about their nation's history. Lastly, has institutional and legal reform taken place to make sure truth and justice are accommodated formally as national policies and to ensure the non-recurrence of violations of rights? This would include, importantly, lustration policies to exclude from office individuals who committed human rights violations during their service.

In examining the procedural and substantive effects of transitional justice, I chose as my case studies two types of state-sponsored mechanisms that were adopted, or attempted in Indonesia in the years after 1998: prosecutions and the truth commission. To examine prosecutions, I choose the ad hoc human rights trials that were held in 2002 for the violence that occurred around the 1999 referendum in East Timor and in 2004 for the 1984 Tanjung Priok massacre. For the truth commission, I explore the state's attempt to establish a TRC between 2000 and 2004. These cases are examples of state-centred, or top-down, transitional justice.

The state-centred approach has been challenged by grassroots, or bottom-up, approaches which highlight an alternative transitional justice where the state has been ineffective in settling cases of past injustice. I therefore also look at initiatives from civil society groups, including NGOs and victims' groups, locally, nationally, and internationally. At the local level, I focus on grassroots reconciliation by Syarikat, an NGO based in Yogyakarta. The organisation has been attempting to reconcile local communities in Yogyakarta and some areas of Central Java affected by the 1965–1966 massacres of leftists. At the national level, I focus on the "Year of Truth" (*Tahun Kebenaran*) project run by the KKPK (*Koalisi Keadilan dan Pengungkapan Kebenaran*, Coalition for Truth and Justice), an NGO coalition whose members come from various regions in Indonesia. The project is a civil society truth-telling initiative on cases of past abuses between 1965 and 2005. At the international level, I look at two people's tribunal called the International People's Tribunal of the Indonesian 1965 Serious Crimes and the International Citizens' Tribunal on West Papuan Biak Massacre. I also look at measures implemented at the local government level, specifically Palu City's programmes for the victims of the 1965–1966 mass violence. This was the first formal policy by a local government that specifically acknowledged the 1965–1966 violence and tried to deal with its legacies.

In contrast to findings from Sikkink and Payne (2014), who argued that transitional justice can have effects at the state level, this study has found no such impacts in the Indonesian case. Rather, Indonesia experienced more positive impacts at the local and societal levels. Indonesia has adopted and implemented multiple transitional justice mechanisms at the national level. However, despite such procedural success, my research finds that these mechanisms did not result in justice as measured by the indicators mentioned above. On the contrary, transitional justice implemented at the state level resulted in total impunity despite all the policies and mechanisms that were tried. At the grassroots and local levels, however, transitional justice initiatives seemed to have produced more promising results.

Explaining transitional justice: the nature of the democratic transition

How do we explain such successes and failures of transitional justice in Indonesia? How did the political transition influence the adoption and implementation of transitional justice measures, and what aspects of the transition facilitated or hindered transitional justice?

With the flourishing of the 'third-wave' of democratisation since the 1980s, studies on transitions to democracy have acknowledged that nations undergoing transition faced dilemmas about whether to adopt a backward-looking focus on past injustice, by acknowledging the former authoritarian regime's role in past human rights abuses and trying to address these issues, or remain forward-looking and concentrate on rebuilding democratic institutions. Though most scholars of democratisation place emphasis on understanding the dynamics of the transitions themselves and the subsequent political consolidation, some also look at the problem of "settling the past account", in O'Donnell and Schmitter's words (1986: 30), or "the torturer problem" as Huntington (1991: 209) puts it.

This torturer problem confronts democrats with a choice between burying the past in order to avoid political instability initiated by spoilers from the old regime, and the moral and ethical demands to confront the crimes of the repressive period. O'Donnell and Schmitter acknowledge that how leaders respond will significantly influence the emergence of the new political system. Failing to analyse the past, in their view, might prevent a society from reaching a consensus on what was wrong in its history and therefore might damage attempts to form new societal bonds:

> It is difficult to imagine how a society can return to some degree of functioning which would provide social and ideological support for political democracy without somehow coming to terms with the most painful elements of its own past. By refusing to confront and to purge itself of its worst fears and resentments, such a society would be burying not just its past but the very ethical values it needs to make its future liveable (O'Donnell and Schmitter, 1986: 30).

In dealing with these past abuses, they argue, the "worst of bad solutions would be to ignore the issue", and that the least worst strategy, based on ethical and political considerations, is to hold trials for the wrongdoers (O'Donnell and Schmitter, 1986: 59).

Scholars often refer to two aspects of democratic transition that determine whether transitional justice measures are adopted and implemented. The first relates to the high degree of uncertainty in any political transition. Most of scholars emphasise the relative power of the actors who make the relevant policy choices, especially the political elite, both outgoing and in the new regime (Huntington, 1991: 208–280), the influence of the institutions complicit in past abuse (O'Donnell and Schmitter, 1986; Rosenberg, 1995), institutions in the new democracy (Elster,1998, 2004, 2006; Kritz, 1995; McAdams, 1997; Nalepa, 2008, 2010; Teitel, 2000), and the role of non-elite and public attitudes (Barahona De Brito, González Enriquez, and Aguilar, 2001; Finnemore and Sikkink, 1998; Skaar, 1999; Zalaquett, 1995). Clearly a tremendous number of factors contribute to how a democratic transition proceeds, giving rise to equally high uncertainty regarding the possibilities of transitional justice.

A second factor that has great influence on the adoption of transitional justice measures is the *nature* of the transition. Barahona De Brito, González Enriquez, and Aguilar (2001: 11 12) argue that transitional justice choices are strongly related to the types of political transitions undertaken. The more a transition entails defeat or total break with the old authoritarian elite and those responsible for human rights violations, the more possible it is for an incoming elite to choose thoroughgoing transitional justice policies. Accordingly, they argue that variations in policies and outcomes of transitional justice depend on where a country is located on a democratic transition spectrum. At one end are transitions by rupture that occur after a foreign intervention, revolution, or civil war that leads to the military defeat or sudden overthrow of dictatorial forces. In this type of transition, the old forces lose their capacity to manoeuvre. Their political, police, or military vehicles have been totally or almost completely destroyed. At the other end of the spectrum are negotiated, 'pacted', reform-oriented types of transition. In this type of transition, outgoing regime authorities retain some power and influence, and thus the incoming elite hoping to form a new democratic regime has to negotiate change with the old guard. Prosecutions, in particular, are more difficult in this type of transition, while reconciliation policies are more likely.

There is an abundant literature in political science that tries to capture the types of democratic transitions. Huntington (1991), for example, in his widely referred to book on third-wave democratisation categorises transitions into three types, based on his analysis of 35 third-wave democratisations. These types are transformation, replacement, and transplacement (Huntington, 1991: 124–125). Transformation is a type of transition where elements of the authoritarian regime spearhead reforms that lead to a democratic system. Such a decision typically requires the government to be stronger than the opposition. As shown by Huntington's case studies, this type of transition mostly occurred in strong and well-established military regimes where the government controlled all means of coercion against the opposition. Transformations are gradual, top-down processes of regime change.

The replacement type of transition, in contrast, does not happen by the willingness and decision of the authoritarian government. In the lead up to such a change, most of the standpatters—or the hardliner elements that support the regime—deny any need for change, while reformers in the government are either weak or non-existent. Democratisation occurs as the result of a strengthened opposition that overthrows the regime. In most cases, after the opposition groups come to power, conflict is transformed into competition among members of the former opposition about the nature of the regime they should establish. This form of regime change is sudden and initiated from below.

The third transition type is transplacement. This is a combination of the previous two transitions where, in the lead up to regime change, there is a balance between standpatters and reformers within the authoritarian government that makes the government willing to negotiate on regime change with the opposition. The opposition is strong enough to prevail over anti-democratic radicals but not strong enough to overthrow the government by themselves. As a result, democratisation happens as a result of processes of negotiation and compromise.

While Huntington's categories are useful for my research, Indonesia's transition does not match exactly any of these types; instead, it is a mixture of replacement and transplacement. This mixed transition relates to the nature of Soeharto's regime that, as proposed by Aspinall (2005), combined sultanistic with strongly authoritarian features. Such a combination resulted in democratic transition that occurred though considerable street disorder and the sudden resignation of Soeharto in May 1998, and at the same time showed "a high degree of continuity between the new democratic politics and those of the authoritarian past" (Aspinall, 2005: 269). The economic crisis during the last year of the New Order regime instigated mass protest and social unrest. Both the standpatters and weak reformers in the government lost their ability to manoeuvre. Violence was used to repress opposition groups, especially with the enforced disappearance of a number of anti-Soeharto activists (Collins, 2007).

Meanwhile, opposition groups strengthened in 1998 and mobilised popular protests demanding Soeharto step down and the government to undertake reforms. In May 1998, government leaders, most notably Soeharto himself, invited elements from the opposition to negotiate the direction of regime change. Most of these opposition leaders refused to deal with him, however, and his regime collapsed. After Soeharto stepped down on 21 May 1998, a series of compromises took place through several stages. The first stage involved recruitment of a new elite who were critical of the New Order into old political institutions. The Golkar (*Golongan Karya*, Party of the Functional Groups), the political party of the New Order regime, for example, made a drastic and sudden change in its membership in MPR (and DPR) to satisfy public demands for total reform (*reformasi total*). The second stage was the establishment of new political institutions, including various new political parties before the first post-Soeharto election in 1999. The third stage took place after the 1999 election, when most of the key political forces and leaders who were involved in the 1998 reform movement participated in the new power structure, including by taking senior governmental posts. At the same time, however, old forces—such as those representing the Golkar and the military—were never entirely excluded from the power structures of the new "Reformasi Order". The new regime was fundamentally a product of political compromise.

I will explore in more detail the nature of the post-1998 reforms in the next chapter. At this point, suffice it to say that the mixed nature of the transition affected the transitional justice measures adopted in the period of democratisation. The elements of regime change that resembled replacement pushed successive governments to adopt transitional justice in order for them to gain legitimacy and create distance between themselves and the New Order regime. However, the transplacement features, involving accommodation of elements of the New Order in formal politics, led to the failure of transitional justice outcomes at the implementation level. When the political elite started to consolidate and gain legitimacy through elections, transitional justice passed from the political agenda, and past injustices were regarded as being irrelevant. The era of progress in transitional justice was over.

Huntington's typology stresses the roles of 'government' and 'opposition' in each type of transition, which are central to my own analysis. In a replacement setting, the outgoing government is replaced by the opposition. In a transformation, the government is still dominated by the incumbent elite albeit with some structural changes. In a transplacement setting, the new government consists of elements of the old regime *and* its opposition. In the case of Indonesia's transition, where both replacement and transplacement elements took place together, it is important to look more closely at the opposition because, first, that opposition was not monolithic and second, and most importantly, it was the opposition that generated the transitional justice agenda. However, since the opposition was not monolithic, there was never a consensus on transitional justice among the opposition groups.

For the purpose of this research, I expand on Huntington's analysis by using Aspinall's (2005) explanation of opposition in Indonesia. In his book, Aspinall outlines the types of opposition that operated during Soeharto's last years of government. He categorises them into mobilisational opposition, semi-opposition, alegal opposition, and proto-opposition. The mobilisational opposition were groups that explicitly expressed demands to replace the regime with another system (Aspinall, 2005: 6). In doing so, these groups—such as students—tried to organise and mobilise a mass support base. The *semi-opposition* were those who participated in formal structures of the regime and were associated with "work-from-within" strategies of political reform. This group was more likely to engage in "compromise, partial and often unclear goals, and the utilization of regime language and ideological formulas to argue for political change" (Aspinall, 2005: 6–7). This group involved supporters of the legal political parties, such as the PDI (*Partai Demokrasi Indonesia*, Indonesia Democracy Party) and the mass organisations, such as major Islamic organisations like Nahdlatul Ulama (NU) and Muhammadiyah, which continued to command the loyalties of millions of Indonesians throughout the New Order period. The third group, the *alegal* opposition, was more fundamentally critical than the *semi-opposition*. It was characterised by dissidence: early participants or supporters of the regime, who later made moral appeals or calls for the regime to initiate reform, without wanting society to take action or organise their supporters behind a reform platform. Lastly, the *proto-opposition* was civil society organisations. These groups had limited and partial aims but were independent from the state structures. Even though they pursued limited aims, civil society organisations were a refuge for oppositional impulses during repressive conditions, and thus could harbour individuals who wished to transform the authoritarian regime.

Transitional justice was, above all, an agenda promoted by *proto-opposition,* notably by NGOs and other civil society groups, but it was also adopted by *semi-opposition* actors such as those associated with political parties. When the *semi-opposition* eventually managed to get into the new state structures after the 1999 election, they supported transitional justice measures. Transitional justice became a central part of the new post-Soeharto political order, agreed to by everyone, including elements from the outgoing regime.

Later in the consolidation period, the dividing line between the forces of the old regime and new democrats began to break down. Successive governments accommodated and absorbed all major political forces, producing remarkable stability in the Indonesian transition (Aspinall, 2010b; Slater, 2004, 2006). Such stability was also successful in drawing in potential spoilers, as Aspinall mentions:

> Spoilers have been accommodated and absorbed into the system rather than excluded from it, producing a trade-off between democratic success and democratic quality (Aspinall, 2010a: 21).

Facing massive pressure for political change after the fall of Soeharto, both the new and old elites had to fulfil the demands for state accountability to gain public legitimacy and international support. They needed to break from the New Order. Transitional justice became a useful tool for convincing both the national and international public that change was real. Reconsolidation of the elites, however, meant that transitional justice was no longer needed.

Research methods and data collection

I gathered most of my data during the period of 2012–2018 through interviews, group discussions, and participatory observations mainly in some areas in Indonesia. I interview no less than 78 informants which include victims and family of victims, human rights advocates, researchers, politicians, government officials, journalists, military retired, and religious and cultural figures. Out of these numbers, around 40 per cent of them were female informants. During my fieldwork, I observed meetings and events organised by NGOs and victims' rights groups as well as government institutions. I also got the opportunity to conduct fieldwork in the Netherlands in September 2013 when I interviewed political exiles and survivors of the 1965 mass violence in the country and conducted focus groups.

The secondary data I used for this research were gathered from various documents, clippings from national and local print and online media, as well as visual footage and documentary films. The documents included reports and proceedings from NGOs, and government-related official documents such as meeting proceedings in parliament, and legal documents from trials and the Constitutional Court.

I understand that my previous engagement as a human rights advocate who often criticised the government was not an advantage for me when trying to contact politicians, government officials, and military officers. Many of these people declined my requests for interviews, or failed to turn up for scheduled meetings. I acknowledge this situation as a limitation of my research. As a consequence, much of the information I need from official sources was gained from secondary data such as transcripts, books, or media reports.

Book structure

The next chapter of this book discusses democratisation in Indonesia, and how past injustices have been addressed by various transitional justice mechanisms. The main focus of this chapter is elaborating the nature of democratic transition in Indonesia. It explains that Indonesia's transition combined elements of rupture, or replacement, and negotiated or transplacement types of transition. This chapter also looks at how transitional justice discourse has been understood by the key actors.

My assessment of the situation of transitional justice in Indonesia is then divided into two parts. The first part discusses two state-sponsored transitional justice attempts in separate chapters. The first, Chapter 3, is on the ad hoc human rights trials on East Timor and the 1984 Tanjung Priok massacre. The second case, Chapter 4, covers the attempted establishment of a TRC. These cases represent two different mechanisms within the broad transitional justice paradigm, prosecution, and truth, which, as previously mentioned, are standard to top-down transitional justice efforts in many post-authoritarian countries.

When the attempt to deliver truth and justice through these state-sponsored measures failed, the initiative for transitional justice passed to the grassroots level. Human rights and victims' groups led new initiatives. I discuss this in Chapter 5. These initiatives range from local, national, and international level. Chapter 6 looks at local government-sponsored transitional justice efforts. The case study chosen for this chapter is Palu City.

Concluding the book, Chapter 7 reflects on the situation of transitional justice in Indonesia and explains the outcomes by relating them to the political dynamics during Indonesia's democratisation.

Chapter 2

Human rights, transitional justice and political transition in Indonesia

Introduction

Before I start my assessment of transitional justice efforts in Indonesia in later chapters, in this chapter I discuss the context of the political transition that enabled those efforts to arise. The chapter analyses the ways in which the idea of transitional justice emerged within the context of democratisation in Indonesia, and how the political dynamics of democratisation provided opportunities to address abuses committed under Soeharto's leadership. As I explained in the first chapter, existing writings on transitional justice in Indonesia, and Indonesian human rights in general, often separate the development of transitional justice policies from the political context in which they were chosen and implemented. This lack of deep consideration of political context has given rise to a generalisation in the literature that explains the failure of implementation of transitional justice as resulting simply from the absence of political will on the part of state leaders. The 'political will' argument does not explain why political reformers in the early years of *reformasi* chose to adopt these measures and attempted to deal with cases of past abuse. The 'lack of political will' argument is thus only relevant when we attempt to explain the failure of implementation, but not the adoption of such measures in the first place.

In this chapter, my discussion focuses on the dynamics of democratisation in Indonesia, and how past injustices have been addressed through transitional justice mechanisms introduced after the transition started in 1998. Specifically, the chapter elaborates on the nature of democratic transition in Indonesia, arguing that it involved a unique combination of rupture, or replacement, and negotiated, or transplacement, types of transition. The nature of the transition determined the adoption and implementation of transitional justice measures, especially trials and reconciliation.

I structure my discussion of the link between transitional justice and the dynamics of democratic transition into three periods: the early reform years which was the period of momentous change (1998–2000), the 'compromise' years (2001–2009), and lastly the period when transitional justice stagnated (2009 onwards). The periodisation I use is adapted from the assessment of transitional justice in Indonesia made by two non-government organisations (NGOs), namely the KontraS (*Komisi Nasional untuk Orang Hilang dan Korban Kekerasan*, National Commission for Enforced Disappearance and Victims of Violence) and the ICTJ and KontraS (2011).

The first part of the chapter provides an overview of human rights issues under the Soeharto regime, which allows us to better understand the power structure and strategies used to address mass violence in the political transition. I subsequently look at the political dynamics in each of the three periods of transitional justice implementation and discuss some of the elements that contributed to promoting transitional justice ideas.

Human rights under the New Order

In order to explain the nature of transitional justice in post-New Order Indonesia, it is necessary to first provide an overview of the legacy of violence that Indonesia inherited at this time. This requires looking at the structure of power under the repressive regime and categorising the human rights abuses that occurred under the New Order. As Olsen, Payne, and Reiter (2010) stress, much of the literature on transitional justice acknowledges that the duration of the regime, type of predecessor authoritarian regime, and the nature of past abuses are key factors contributing to success or failure of adoption and implementation of transitional justice in post-repressive contexts. They also look at types of transitions in correlation with three factors: the background of new democratic leaders, the country's past experience with democratic rules, and societal-level factors. All of these hypotheses or factors are tested in the database, using Polity IV's *Regime Transition Variable* in 72 countries where 84 transitions from authoritarian rule to democracy occurred during 1970–2004—excluding new democracies which emerged from periods of complete "absence of governments", i.e., Bangladesh (1972), Cambodia (1993), Guinea-Bissau (2000), Lesotho (2002), Liberia (1997), Pakistan (1973), and Sierra Leone (2002).

In the context of Indonesia, there is an extensive scholarly literature on the state-sponsored violence under Soeharto's New Order. Some of the literature argue that state violence was not distinctive of the New Order because state violence was common even before Indonesia became an independent country (Coppel, 2006). Other literature suggests that state violence did not occur in a vacuum but was conditioned by various social and cultural elements that helped to legitimate it, and which were therefore complicit in producing violence (Meister, 2010; van Klinken, 2007). Based on these two standpoints, one could argue that violence was a long-standing feature of Indonesian history, and that any political force in control of the state would be liable to use and justify it.

Putting such potential objections to one side, in order to assess the origins of transitional justice in post-Soeharto democracy, we still need to understand the main features of state violence under the authoritarian regime, and to recognise the central role it played in perpetuating authoritarian rule. For 32 years, Soeharto's New Order regime brought political stability and economic growth to Indonesia, but it used violence to eliminate political dissent and to maintain social order. From the regime's perspective, human rights was a threat to unity and nation building and thus had no place in the political order (Lubis, 1993: 74).

The key state agency that had the job of controlling society through the use of violence, was the security forces, which included both the military and the police. Many scholars have noted that unlike the military in other countries that sought power relatively late in a country's political development, the Indonesian military was part of its core political elite from the beginning (Crouch, 1978; Honna, 2003; Mietzner, 2009). When Soeharto seized power in 1965–1966, his rise represented the final victory of the military and its long-standing efforts to achieve dominance. Under his leadership, the military embarked on a nationwide modernisation project, adopting what it called a development approach and a security approach, in which the latter was supposed to provide a conducive environment for the former.

Violence as a means of controlling society and ensuring economic development became 'mundane' under the New Order regime. The regime restricted rights of expression, including in the media, restricted association, used the anti-subversion law to control dissent, and arrested dissidents who criticised the regime. This kind of violence was justified by the legal and political system and woven into the fabric of that system (Lubis, 1993). The banning of some national media, such as *Tempo*, *Detik*, and *Editor*, in June 1994 was an example of the regime's restrictions on civil and political rights. Similarly, the 1963 anti-subversion law was used extensively by the regime to criminalise peaceful dissent and detained hundreds of thousands of alleged political opponents without trial (Amnesty International, 1997). In other words, repression was systematic under the New Order; it was woven deep into the fabric of the regime's apparatus of social and political control.

When the *reformasi* process started, however, people promoting the transitional justice agenda paid scant attention to these cases of mundane repression—not least because the Habibie government (1998–1999) rapidly moved to repeal many of the most obvious restrictions on political expression and association. Rather, proponents of transitional justice focused on the gross human rights abuses which had taken place under Soeharto's leadership and in which large numbers of people had been killed, injured, or otherwise physically harmed. During the period from 1965 to 1998, such gross abuses can be categorised into three types: mass violence stemming from ideological conflict, state violence that aimed to defend the territorial integrity of the state, and repressive violence against opposition groups.

The key instance of mass ideological violence, and the bloodiest episode of civil unrest in Indonesia's political history, was the 1965–1966 mass violence. This violence stemmed from a conflict of ideology pitting right against left.

Briefly, during the 1950s and 1960s, there was increasing polarisation between left-wing and right-wing groups in Indonesia, which culminated on the night of 30 September 1965, when six senior generals and a lieutenant were kidnapped and murdered by a group calling itself a 'revolutionary council' and claiming to aiming to forestall a coup against then president Sukarno. The people involved in this attempt were mostly middle- and low-ranking military officers; their move was quickly countered by other elements in the armed forces led by General Soeharto. The military and its right-wing allies, such as various Islamic groups, used the opportunity to launch a violent crackdown on the left, particularly the PKI (*Partai Komunis Indonesia*, Indonesian Communist Party), which had been growing rapidly in strength in the preceding years. Violent mobilisation against left-wing groups and individuals quickly developed into what Gerlach (2010) calls a 'coalition of violence', involving the participation of right-wing groups especially those affiliated with religious organisations and political parties. The number of people killed from 1965 to 1966 is estimated to be between 100,000 and one million (Cribb, 1990).

State violence in Aceh, Papua, and East Timor were cases where human rights abuses occurred with the goal of defending the territorial integrity of the state. In these three areas, the military extensively used counter-insurgency operations to eliminate secessionist groups. Aceh and Papua are two resource-rich territories that contributed significantly to the national budget but received few development resources in return. Meanwhile, East Timor was invaded by the Indonesian military regime in 1975 on the pretext of fighting against communism. Economic and political disparities, and prolonged histories of human rights abuses, led to resistance against Indonesian authorities in all three territories. Violence against civilians resulted in hundreds of thousands of deaths (Human Rights Watch, 2001a, 2001b; Robinson, 2009). East Timor, as I discuss in Chapter 3, was granted a referendum under Habibie's presidency and later gained its independence in 1999.

Soeharto's military regime also used violence to silence protest and opposition in other locations in Indonesia, though this was typically less intense in the big cities than in peripheral territories. One incident of gross human rights abuse which became part of the transitional justice agenda during the reform period was the 1984 Tanjung Priok massacre. The incident took place following a period of political and religious tension that resulted in mass protests against the government. The military deployed thousands of troops and opened fire on the protestors in the Tanjung Priok area of North Jakarta, killing dozens of victims and wounding hundreds more. In the next chapter on trials, I discuss the incident in greater detail and how it was addressed during the democratic transition.

The deplorable human rights record under Soeharto became one of the major sources of criticism of his leadership during its final decade or so in power (Aspinall, 2005). As domestic pressure mounted against Soeharto's leadership in the 1990s, his government (Glasius, 1999a) was forced to introduce a policy of *keterbukaan* or openness in 1989 (Pratikno et al., 2002; Setiawan, 2013: 35–36). *Keterbukaan* was partly the result of fragmentation and competition among the political elite, especially between Soeharto and his military allies. Soeharto became powerful politically, enabled him and his cronies to control the country's economic resources and reduced the military's access and influence in national politics and business (Hefner, 2002: 268). Some elements within the military promoted *keterbukaan* and reform in an attempt to undermine Soeharto (Crouch, 1994: 86).

Strong criticism of the government also came from the NGOs. Although popular mobilisation was repressed during the New Order period, some intellectuals and other critics still managed to form NGOs in the early 1970s. Many of these supported—or criticised—the development activities and programmes that were increasingly carried out by the Soeharto government, allowing the number of NGOs to increase significantly (Aspinall, 2005; Eldridge, 1995; Hadiwinata, 2005; Uhlin, 1997). I discuss the development of NGOs in more detail in the first part of Chapter 5. Among the NGOs, the most critical of the government was the LBH, (*Lembaga Bantuan Hukum*, Legal Aid Institute) which later became the YLBHI (*Yayasan Lembaga Bantuan Hukum Indonesia*, Indonesian Legal Aid Foundation). LBH was initiated in 1970 in Jakarta by lawyer Adnan Buyung Nasution, with the support of other prominent lawyers such as Yap Thiam Hien, Loekman Wiriadinata, and Suardi Tasrief under the Peradin (*Persatuan Advokat Indonesia*, Association of Indonesian Advocates) (Culla, 2006: 132). Initially, LBH presented itself as part of the New Order project (Aspinall, 2005: 100). Political and financial support came from the Jakarta government under Governor Ali Sadikin and Soeharto's personal assistant Ali Moertopo. Soeharto gave his blessing to the establishment of the organisation (Aspinall, 2005: 101; Culla, 2006: 132–133). Its work initially focused on advocacy for those coming from lower-class backgrounds, making it a pilot project for a larger movement to modernise the rule of law and to make law accessible to the disadvantaged (Aspinall, 2005: 104; Culla, 2006: 138). When the organisation started, it worked on purely legal matters; later on, during the *keterbukaan* period it expanded its focus to engage in advocacy for vulnerable groups in society, notably in four 'structural' areas involving conflict with the state: civil and political rights, labour, land, and the environment (Aspinall, 2005: 104–105). Because of its work, LBH was widely known as the "locomotive of democracy".

In the early 1990s, with a growing numbers of critical middle-class intellectuals involved in NGOs, and limited space for them in the formal political institutions, NGOs became more critical of the government and its policies (Antlöv, Ibrahim, and van Tuijl, 2005: 4; Aspinall, 2005: 88–89). This is when the widely used term for NGO in Indonesia, LSM or *Lembaga Swadaya Masyarakat* (translated by Eldridge (1995) as self-reliant community institution), became synonymous with criticism of the government (Aspinall, 2005: 89), and when people began to view LSMs as anti-government institutions (Antlöv, Ibrahim, and van Tuijl, 2005: 3).

The Soeharto regime faced fierce criticism when the Santa Cruz massacre, in which Indonesian soldiers shot and killed more than 200 protesters in Dili,

East Timor, was widely publicised and captured the attention of the international community in November 1991. American journalists managed to film the event and smuggle the tape to the US where it was subsequently broadcast worldwide. As international attention and pressure mounted against the military's role in the massacre (Jetschke, 1999), the Department of Foreign Affairs had to respond to international condemnation of state violence in Indonesia in United Nations meetings and other international fora. The Department held a conference on human rights, led by senior diplomat Hassan Wirayuda, and proposed that the government should initiate an institution that worked to promote human rights (Pratikno et al., 2002). In response to mounting political pressure from his domestic opponents and international critics, Soeharto thus eventually agreed to establish the Komnas HAM (*Komisi Nasional Hak Asasi Manusia*, National Commission on Human Rights) (Setiawan, 2013: 36).

Komnas HAM was formed in 1993 by President Soeharto. Initially, many elements in civil society were sceptical about the role of Komnas HAM. However, after its first high-profile investigation into the killing of labour activist Marsinah in 1993,[1] followed by several other investigations, many critics of the government praised Komnas HAM and its work. Komnas HAM also did not face any major hindrance from the government or military. Setiawan (2013) believes the government's need to boost its image nationally and internationally was an important factor producing this outcome. Another factor was the quality of its members, especially the first chairperson, Ali Said, who was able to ensure that the institution maintained a good relationship with the government.

On the eve of *reformasi*, there was thus a widespread understanding in the public that the regime's human rights record was poor and that something needed to be done about it. Opposition groups focused their criticisms on both gross and mundane human rights abuses committed by the regime. This set the scene for the adoption of transitional justice measures as part of the post-Soeharto *reformasi* agenda. A large body of civil society groups had also emerged, with many allies in the media, who were committed to promoting a human rights agenda and were poised to take advantage of any weakening of the regime to do so.

1 Marsinah was a 23-year-old worker activist in a textile company called PT Catur Surya Jaya in Surabaya, East Java. On 6 May 1993, she disappeared from her rented room after organising a strike for 500 workers to demand a pay rise. Her body was found a few days later with signs of sexual assault and torture. Ten people from the company's management were detained and tortured during the investigation in Brawijaya Military Region. A trial was held in 1994 against these people, but in 1995 they appealed and were acquitted. Several civil society organisations carried out investigations, including the Human Rights Watch, and found military involvement in the murder. See for example, Human Rights Watch reports, 1994, http://www.hrw.org/sites/default/files/reports/INDONESI941.PDF. Accessed 20 May 2015; Weix, Gretchen Garnett. "Resisting History: Indonesian Labour Activism in the 1990s and the 'Marsinah' Case." In Brenda S. A. Yeoh, Peggy Teo, & Shirlena Huang (Eds.), *Gender Politics in the Asia Pacific Region* (pp. 120–136). London: Routledge, 2000.

The politics and periods of transitional justice in post-Soeharto Indonesia

In their assessment of how Indonesia's democracy has dealt with past human rights abuses, the KontraS and the International Centre for Transitional Justice (ICTJ) identify three phases since the beginning of *reformasi* that track the rise and then decline of efforts to promote justice and state accountability for human rights abuses.[2] I find this categorisation useful for understanding the trends and development of transitional justice in Indonesia.

The first phase was the momentous period of *reformasi* between 1998 and 2000 when a number of high-level inquiries took place, and Komnas HAM conducted an investigation into crimes against humanity in East Timor. These inquiries produced unprecedented findings implicating senior members of the security forces. During this period, two important laws were passed: the 1999 Law on Human Rights and the 2000 Law on Human Rights Trials. This was a phase where new and old elements of the elite opted for transitional justice as a means to boost their political support and legitimacy. For the military, this period was characterised by submission to the adoption of transitional justice mechanisms without significant opposition. Officers opted for transitional justice as a tactical concession, to demonstrate that they had understood public demands that they needed to reform their institution (Aspinall and Zain, 2013; Mietzner, 2009). At the time, they were trying to build new political arrangements with the new elite to find ways to maintain a political role.

The second phase, between 2001 and 2006, was characterised by what KontraS and ICTJ call 'compromised mechanisms' and included significant legal changes and the establishment of new transitional justice mechanisms. This period was important because the drafting of a Law on TRC took place during these years. However, relevant laws were poorly implemented, if at all, and the new mechanisms became seriously compromised. Attempted prosecutions failed, the Constitutional Court struck down the TRC law, and official inquiries proved to be ineffective. However, even though the executive failed to implement transitional justice measures, the parliament made recommendations for further inquiries into two cases of gross human rights violations: the 1998 Trisakti and Semanggi shootings (in 2004) and the 1997/1998 enforced disappearances of activists (in 2009). Therefore, rather than entirely agreeing with KontraS and ICTJ's periodisation, I argue that the period of compromised mechanisms lasted until 2009. This period was also marked by the continuing political rehabilitation of the military; former military officers ran as candidates in various elections. Susilo Bambang Yudhoyono set up a new political party as a vehicle that took him to the presidency in the 2004 election. Two military

2 See the ICTJ Report *Derailed: Transitional Justice in Indonesia Since the Fall of Soeharto* (p. 8). New York: ICTJ, 2010.

officers who were suspected of committing human rights abuses in the past, Wiranto and Prabowo, both ran for Chair of Golkar party at the same time, hoping to campaign for the presidency. Wiranto won the party's election, but lost in the presidential election.

The third phase of 'stalled reform' in Jakarta began in 2009 and continues to the time of writing and has been characterised by official reluctance to seriously enforce any transitional justice mechanisms. For example, the Kejagung (*Kejaksaan Agung*, Attorney General's Office) has failed to bring a number of important cases to trial. Several pieces of important legislation—including those establishing national human rights courts, requiring military actors to be tried in civilian courts, and establishing regional TRCs in Aceh and Papua—have not been implemented. In this period, military officers have had their own parties to take them to elections: PD (*Partai Demokrat*, Democrat Party) of Yudhoyono, Hanura (Hati Nurani Rakyat, People's Conscience Party) of Wiranto, and Gerindra (Gerakan Indonesia Raya, Great Indonesian Movement Party) of Prabowo.

As we can see from Chart 2.1, many of the mechanisms and policies were adopted and implemented in the early years of the transition. Institutional and policy reforms took place mostly under the governments of Presidents Habibie (1998–1999) and Abdurrahman Wahid (1999–2001). Truth-seeking and prosecution were mostly initiated during Abdurrahman Wahid's presidency and implemented under President Megawati's leadership (2001–2004). Transitional justice mechanisms and policies were not such a priority during Susilo Bambang Yudhoyono's presidency between 2004 and 2014.

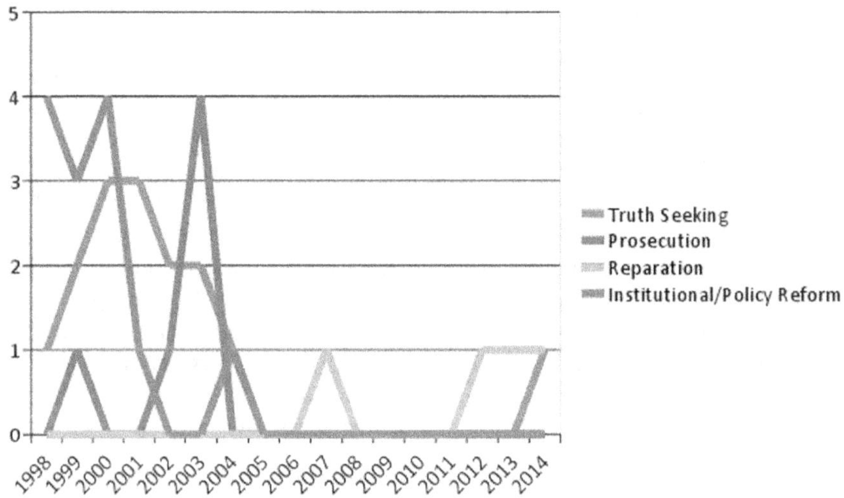

Chart 2.1 Transitional Justice Mechanisms and Policies Adopted 1998–2014.
Source: Various documents and reports.

I explore the dynamics of each of these periods in greater detail in later chapters when we examine particular cases. For example, in Chapter 4 I evaluate ad hoc human rights trials for two cases: the violence during and after the 1999 East Timor referendum, and the 1984 Tanjung Priok massacre. My evaluation includes consideration of the political dynamics within the periods mentioned here. At this point, however, it is useful to provide an overview of each period in order to review the major political changes and roles played by each major state institution with the goal of contextualising the adoption and implementation of transitional justice mechanisms. In particular, I investigate how the elements of rupture and transplacement in the political transitions impacted on how Indonesia's transitional justice agenda developed.

The period of momentous change, 1998–2000

In March 1998, in the midst of the worst economic crisis that Indonesia had seen for decades, the MPR (*Majelis Permusyawaratan Rakyat*, People's Consultative Assembly) approved Soeharto being reappointed as Indonesia's president for the fifth time. This decision outraged many elements in society, especially the pro-democracy groups and university students, leading to massive demonstrations in several big cities around the country between April and May 1998. The demonstrations grew larger after four University of Trisakti students were shot dead during a demonstration on 12 May in Jakarta. Over the next two days, massive riots took place in Jakarta and some other cities in Indonesia, resulting in thousands of casualties and the destruction of many commercial centres. Many rioters targeted the Chinese minority, including in the form of mass rapes of Chinese women; many non-Chinese were also killed. After this violence, in Jakarta, tens of thousands of students occupied the parliament building for days, demanding the parliament to convince the MPR to hold a SI (*Sidang Istimewa*, Special Session) to replace Soeharto.[3] Many national figures, including military retirees, joined the masses.

The economic crisis and social unrest diminished Soeharto and his New Order's capacity to make political manoeuvres. They used some violence to suppress the opposition, resulting in the enforced disappearance of several activists. However, violence did little to mitigate the crisis of trust. In the middle of this crisis, Soeharto invited some of the reformers from the opposition groups to discuss the situation. Most of the figures invited to the discussions represented Muslim groups, scholars, and political groups from the opposition. After negotiations with some prominent persons, Soeharto eventually stepped down on

3 In Indonesia's political history, only one MPR Special Meeting or SI MPR ever took place, and that was in 1966 when MPR asked Soekarno, the president, to present his report on the event of political chaos in 1965. MPR rejected Soekarno's report and dismissed him from office; it later appointed Soeharto to fill the position.

21 May 1998. Habibie was appointed to replace him, which was a disappointment for most pro-democracy activists. They saw Habibie as part of New Order, and viewed his appointment as going against the spirit of *reformasi* and the hope for a new democracy. Nevertheless, overall, the transition was relatively calm and smooth. Amien Rais, one of the opposition leaders who strongly called for Soeharto's resignation, said: "*Reformasi*, unlike revolution, required no radical and dramatic change. Revolution, if it failed, would only harm the nation" (interview with Amien Rais in Jakarta, 5 May 2012).

One important feature of this early period is that the ruling elite now needed new symbolic legitimacy to mark a clear break with Soeharto's regime and that human rights promotion played an important role to provide that legitimacy. This sudden break points to the rupture element of the transition. A particular feature of replacement, according to Huntington (1991: 142), is that such regime changes are marked by growing strength of the opposition and the weakening of the government's power until it collapses. A new regime then needs a new basis of legitimacy. The circumstances in which Soeharto took over from Soekarno's leadership in 1966 were similar. In both periods, supporters of the new regime used human rights to delegitimise the ousted leadership and at the same time became a tool for gaining legitimacy for the new regime (Lubis, 1993).

Many consider the period following the collapse of Soeharto's rule and the appointment of Habibie as marking the revival of human rights in Indonesia. The ideas of transitional justice became a promising tool for both predatory leaders of the old regime hoping to reinvent themselves, and to reformers seeking a new place in national politics. Both groups sought to convince the national and international public that a new era had truly begun. As a result, various important policies and legislation were introduced in this period. All of the state's key political institutions initiated and enacted various policies that promoted human rights and accountability. Two of these institutions, the MPR and the executive, were especially accommodating of demands for human rights promotion.

Only days after Soeharto stepped down, elements of civil society pressured Indonesia's supreme legislative body, the MPR, to conduct a special general meeting to revoke its support for Soeharto's presidency and plan for a new election. Some radical elements of the student movement were calling for the abolition of existing government institutions, so MPR members knew they needed to make major concessions. The SI, held in 10–13 November 1998, issued resolutions that set the stage for reform, including Resolution XVII on human rights. During the meeting, there was no debate or disagreement on the resolution.[4]

4 The only issue that was debated was an additional proposal from the FPP (*Fraksi Persatuan Pembangunan*, United Development Fraction) to include rights to access information. The article on this particular rights was then separated into a different article in the Resolution. See the discussion in Risalah Rapat Komisi E Sidang Istimewa MPR RI tahun 1998, Sekertariat Jenderal MPR RI, 1999.

This was surprising given the fact that the MPR had always rejected human rights in previous meetings during the New Order period, and the composition of the body had not changed. The Resolution mandated the government and state institutions to respect and promote human rights in society and to monitor the human rights situation. It also ordered the government to ratify international conventions and covenants related to Human Rights.[5]

After the 1999 election, the MPR passed more resolutions that gave wide space for policies related to human rights. This includes Resolution No. IV of 1999 which set out state policy for the next five years and explicitly acknowledged that policies under Soeharto's New Order regime had produced "various human rights violations, in forms that include violence, discrimination, and abuse of power". Further, the resolution called for a "just solution" to the protracted conflicts in Aceh, Irian Jaya (now Papua), and Maluku and committed the state to developing "a legal system that guarantees the supremacy of the rule of law and human rights based on justice and truth".

Later in 2000, the MPR issued TAP MPR No. V of 2000 on Strengthening National Unity and Integrity. The resolution acknowledged past crimes and called for a national commission for truth and reconciliation. The commission's mandate was to:

> Establish the truth by revealing abuses of power and human rights violations in the past, in accordance with the existing legal provisions and regulations, and implement reconciliation within the perspective of common interests as a nation. The steps after the revelation of the truth, are to acknowledge the past wrongs, deliver apologies, forgiveness, peace, enforcing the rule of law, give amnesty, rehabilitation, or other useful alternatives to uphold national unity taking fully into account the sense of justice in society.[6]

In the same year, the MPR issued another two resolutions related to security sector reform. One of the decrees separated the military from the police, with the former now to focus on defence and the latter on maintaining public security and order. Both decrees noted that the two institutions were responsible for respecting the rule of law and human rights. They also provided a scheme to phase the military and police out of politics and place them under greater civilian control.

The passing of these resolutions was a necessary condition that made further transitional justice policies possible. The MPR was the highest state institution (the Explanation, Chapter III Article 3, the Indonesian 1945 Constitution). Other institutions were subordinated to the MPR and thus implementation of its resolutions was obligatory. For example, when Indonesia's parliament, the

5 Tap MPR No. XXVII of 1998 on Human Rights, Articles 1–4.
6 Chapter 5, Article 3, TAP MPR No. V of 2000.

DPR, drafted the Law on TRC between 2000 and 2004, the main reason for doing so was because "it was mandated by the MPR"—according to the Chair of the Special Team responsible for the Drafting of the Law, Sidarto Danubroto (interview with Sidarto Danubroto in Jakarta, 10 October 2014).

Human rights NGOs and activists in these years believed they had the opportunity to get the state to adopt transitional justice measures by lobbying the MPR. Some of these activists, including then Komnas HAM commissioner Asmara Nababan, prominent activist Kamala Chandrakirana, and the ELSAM (*Lembaga Studi dan Advokasi Masyarakat*, Institute for Policy Research and Advocacy) director Ifdhal Kasim, held meetings with various MPR factions and commissions. Their lobbying efforts helped the MPR adopt points on truth-seeking and reconciliation in its resolutions (interview with Ifdhal Kasim in Jakarta, 22 September 2014). Their efforts were boosted by the fact that some of the MPR's members from the so-called group representatives (*utusan golongan*) were also reformists, including human rights activists such as Nursyahbani Katjasungkana, who were appointed to the body in November 1999 (interview with Nursyahbani Katjasungkana in Hague, 19 September 2013). The years from 1999 saw four amendments to the constitution that included changes in the MPR's role. When the MPR amended the Constitution for the second time in 2000, it recognised human rights and included specific provisions on human rights under one chapter that is Chapter X A.[7]

Successive executive governments also initiated and implemented various policies and institutional reforms that promoted human rights accountability. After Baharuddin Jusuf Habibie took over office from Soeharto in May 1998, public pressure mounted for accountability for recent cases of human rights violations, such as those which had occurred during Aceh military operations in the late New Order period and during the May 1998 riots in Jakarta. Habibie, in turn, promoted human rights policies. Immediately after taking office, he made human rights one of the official priorities of his administration. Many believed that he took this step because he wanted to distance himself from his image as Soeharto's favoured successor (Budiawan, 2004; Juwana, 2003: 647). Budiawan (2004: 5) argues that his decisions were partly driven by his personal motivation to be acknowledged publicly as a 'true reformer'.

Immediately after taking office, Habibie issued Presidential Decree No. 129 of 1998 on National Action Plan of Human Rights. The plan proposed four main

7 The chapter contains basic human rights that include the right to live; the right to establish a family and for a child to have the right to live, grow and develop; the right to prosper and improve, the right to be recognised and protected before the law and the right to work, equal opportunities in government and the right to citizenship status; the right to choose religion and the right of association and expression; the right to communicate and obtain information; the right to protection and the right to be free from inhuman treatment; the right to live in physical and spiritual prosperity; the right to receive facilitation and the right to social security and to own personal property; the right to life and the right to be free from discriminatory treatment.

pillars of human rights policy: first, preparation for ratification of international human rights instruments; second, dissemination of information and education about human rights; third, implementation of priority issues on human rights; and lastly, implementation of international human rights instruments ratified by Indonesia. His administration implemented some relevant activities, particularly ratification of international treaties: the Convention against Torture and Cruel, Inhuman or Degrading Treatment or Punishment was ratified in 1998, and the Convention on the Elimination of All Forms of Racial Discrimination in 1999. He also ratified three International Labor Organization (ILO) conventions.[8]

During his short term in office, Habibie also drafted and enacted the important Law No. 39 of 1999 on Human Rights. The law covers various basic human rights in 106 articles.[9] It also strengthens Komnas HAM which was established by Presidential Decree No. 50 of 1993. Habibie also established the National Commission against Discrimination against Women (Komnas Perempuan, *Komisi Nasional Perempuan*) under Presidential Decree No. 181 of 1998, following an investigation into the mass rapes of Chinese women in the 1998 May Riots.

In regard to groups that opposed the government, Habibie made surprising decisions. He released no less than 200 political prisoners, ranging from those who were imprisoned for their involvement in the Communist Party in the 1960s to those who were jailed for opposing Soeharto. In his memoir about his time in office, Habibie mentions his decision to release political prisoners as part of his '*reformasi*' agenda, along with the repeal of Law No. 11/PNPS year 1963 on Eradication of Subversive Activities (Habibie, 2006: 71, 113).

Habibie also initiated moves to deal with the separatism issue that was relevant in several outlying areas of Indonesia. Under his command, the Minister of Defence, General Wiranto announced the end of Military Operations in Aceh and proposed a special autonomy plan for the province. Controversially at that time, Habibie also endorsed a referendum or 'popular consultation' for the East Timorese to exercise the right of self-determination. After this vote—which was held in August 1999 and in which the East Timorese opted for independence—the Indonesian military orchestrated violence against locals, leading to international intervention on the ground and in support of investigations. Motivated by Habibie's decision to provide a referendum to the East Timorese, no less than 100 West Papuan leaders met with Habibie in Jakarta, 28 February 1999, and

8 These are the Convention on the Coalition of Forced Labor, Convention on Minimum Age for Admission of Employment, and Convention on Discrimination in Respect of Employment and Occupation.

9 The basic rights covered are right to life and the rights not to be abducted and/or killed, the rights to establish a family and bear children, the right to self-development, the right to justice, the right to freedom of the individual, the right to security, the right to welfare, the right to participate in government, women's rights, children's rights, and the right to religious freedom. See Law No. 39 of 1999 on Human Rights.

insisted on their right for self-determination as well. Instead of fulfilling this demand, Habibie offered special autonomy for Papua province similar to that planned for Aceh.

In terms of transitional justice mechanisms, Habibie set up two teams to investigate cases of past and recent violence. These were the 1998 Joint Fact-Finding Team looking into the Events of the May 1998 Riot and the 1999 independent commission to investigate violence in Aceh. The May 1998 Riot Team covered the violence that occurred in Jakarta, Solo, Palembang, Lampung, Surabaya, and Medan between 13 and 15 May 1998, a few days prior to Soeharto's resignation. In their report, the Team found that "the root cause of the May 13 to May 15 riots was the interaction of two key processes, namely the struggle on the part of the political elite in connection with the problem of maintaining the power of the national political leadership and the process of rapid economic and monetary deterioration".[10] Meanwhile, the 1999 Independent Commission on the Investigation of Violence in Aceh was established by President Habibie to investigate atrocities committed in the province since August 1996. The Commission found more than 5,000 cases of violence in its report, which was presented to President Abdurahman Wahid in November 1999.

Having set up these fact-finding teams, Habibie declined Komnas HAM's proposal to set up a truth and reconciliation mechanism for cases of past human rights abuses. Presumably, he did so as part of his negotiation with the military, the institution which was being scrutinised for its involvement in past abuses. Instead, he issued a Government Regulation in Lieu of Law (Perppu, *Peraturan Pengganti Undang-Undang*) on human rights in 1998 which later was rejected by the parliament.

On the 1965–1966 mass violence, one breakthrough under his leadership was the initiation of Law No. 3/1999 on General Elections, which included a provision to grant the right to vote to former political detainees, including those accused of being communists. Realising that this decision would invite controversy, Habibie also initiated an amendment to Criminal Code, which was subsequently passed by the parliament as Law No. 27 year 1999 on Changes to the Criminal Code related to Crimes against State Security. The Law explicitly stipulate that communist and Marxist teachings and ideologies are a threat to the nation, and thus serious criminal charges would apply to those who promote them.

In October 1999, Abdurrahman Wahid replaced Habibie, several months after the first post-Soeharto election was held on 7 June 1999. No less than 48 political parties, most of which were newly established, participated in these elections. Of the 462 national MPs elected, the Indonesian Democratic Party of Struggle (PDIP, Partai Demokrasi Indonesia Perjuangan) won 156 seats, making

10 Final Report of the Joint Fact-Finding Team Investigation of the 1998 May Incident, Jakarta, Solo, Palembang, Lampung, Surabaya dan Medan an Executive Summary, November 1998.

it the largest party in the DPR. Although the PDIP won most seats, Megawati Soekarnoputri, the chairperson of the party, did not automatically become the president, because the president was elected by the MPR. Political manoeuvres by a so-called *poros tengah*, or central axis, a coalition consisting of Islamic parties, and the Golkar, resulted in the MPR voting to make Abdurrahman Wahid president, with Megawati as his deputy.

Wahid had long been known as a human rights activist himself. Under his leadership, human rights became a priority policy area. His strong personal commitment to human rights was one factor that made transitional justice mechanisms an integral part of post-Soeharto political change. Wahid continued Habibie's move in releasing political prisoners, freeing at least 91 prisoners between October and December 1999, including persons imprisoned after the 1965 events. Wahid was the only president with a personal commitment to settle the legacy of the 1965–1966 mass violence. However, most of his initiatives in addressing the 1965 tragedy were based on this personal commitment, and were not institutionalised by his government or even in his leadership at NU, the large Muslim organisation which he had chaired between 1984 and 1999, some members of which were implicated in the 1965 killings. Thus, he appeared on national television on 14 March 2000 to apologise for the killing of alleged communists by elements of NU, and encouraged citizens to re-open the 1965 case as well as other cases of human rights abuse. He also urged the NU to carry out reconciliation. In addition, he issued two presidential decrees disbanding the security agencies the Bakorstanas (*Badan Koordinasi Stabilitas Nasional*, Coordinating Agency for National Stability) and the Litsus (*Penelitian Khusus*, Special Investigation Unit), a significant move for ex-political prisoners, detainees, and their families, because this unit had been in charge of ensuring the persons associated with the pre-New Order left were kept out of political posts, the civil service and other important positions. Wahid also called for a revocation of the ban on Marxist-Leninist ideology and teachings, known as the MPRS (*Majelis Permusyawaratn Rakyat Sementara*, Provisional People's Consultative Assembly) Resolution No. XXV of 1966, but the MPR was strongly against this proposal. He argued that the decree was unconstitutional because it restricted freedom of thought and expression and that Indonesia needed to liberate itself from 'fetishism' that led to the abuse of the state apparatus as a tool of political repression (Budiawan, 2004: 19). This proposal prompted huge controversies in society with some groups opposing it and lasting until the MPR rejected it on 29 May 2000.[11]

Wahid also invited all Indonesians living as political exiles to return home in a speech on International Human Rights Day 1999, and asked government

11 See the elaboration of this and the controversies following Gus Dur's proposal in Budiawan. *Mematahkan Pewarisan Ingatan, Wacana Anti-Komunis dan Politik Rekonsiliasi Pasca-Soeharto* (pp. 19–36). Jakarta: ELSAM, 2004. Budiawan also compares public reactions on Gus Dur's policies and proposal with Habibie's policies on the former political prisoners.

ministers to take step to restore the civil rights of former detainees and exiles. He passed an Inpres (*Instruksi Presiden*, Presidential Instruction) No. 1 year 2000 addressing the problems confronted by many Indonesians abroad who had not been able to return home after the 1965 coup, and he instructed the Minister of Law to take necessary measures to deal with this problem. Unfortunately, the Minister, Yusril Ihza Mahendra, then the Chair of the strongly anti-communist Crescent Star Party, did not carry out Wahid's instruction.

In terms of truth-seeking and national reconciliation efforts, Wahid's administration also drafted a Law on TRC to deal with crimes under the Soeharto regime. This law was eventually passed in 2004, after Wahid had ceased being president, but was then annulled by the Constitutional Court in 2006.

Although various policies on transitional justice were introduced during Wahid's administration, his subordinates in the cabinet did not always follow up on them. Moreover, politicians both in his administration and in the parliament considered some of his policies controversial and unworthy of their support. Wahid's actions and policies gave rise to some resistance during his term; there were many demonstrations, mostly organised by Islamic groups, against his proposal to revoke the Tap MPRS No. XXV of 1966, citing the dangers of atheism and warning of a potential rebirth of communism. His political rivals saw him as overreaching his powers and quickly moved to block any parliamentary debate over the proposed revocation. Anti-left vigilante and Muslim groups made their opposition known by descending on the presidential palace as well as threatening advocacy groups working on behalf of 1965 victims.

Eventually, Wahid had to step down after parliament accused him of corruption. His brief presidency, which lasted from October 1999 to July 2001, ended amidst scandals over the misuse of funds from the Bulog (*Badan Urusan Logistik*, State Logistic Body) and other abuses of power.

During this momentous period, parliament gained greater power after decades of being a rubber stamp for Soeharto. At the same time, the element of transplacement within the political transition was most obvious in parliament, which included representatives of different political parties which stood for various political interests, including some which had been supporters of the New Order. Transplacement which involves negotiation and compromise among the emerging elite, implies a low level of implementation of the transitional justice agenda.

The earliest form of compromise was the adaptation of the elements of the old regime to public demands for total reform (*reformasi total*). Golkar recruited members of a new elite who had been critical of the New Order. In 1999, for example, Golkar made a drastic and sudden change in its membership in the MPR and DPR to include such individuals. Another sign was the establishment of new parties by members of the old Golkar elite, including MKGR (*Musyawarah Kekeluargaan Gotong Royong*, Colloquy Familial and Mutual Cooperation) by former Minister of Women Empowerment Mien Sugandhi on May 1998, and PKPI (*Partai Keadilan dan Persatuan Indonesia*,

Indonesian Justice and Unity Party), by General Edi Sudrajat in December 1999. These new parties' main aim was to run in the 1999 elections. These new parties also recruited some individuals who were critical of Soeharto's leadership. Some other figures established new parties, including PAN (*Partai Amanat Nasional*, National Mandate Party) which was formed by pro-democracy activists led by Amien Rais, PKB (*Partai Kebangkitan Bangsa*, People's Awakening Party) led by Abdurrahman Wahid, and PK (*Partai Keadilan*, Justice Party) formed by university-based Islamic *tarbiyah* (religious education movement) activists.

After the 1999 election, most of the key political forces and leaders who were involved in and directed the 1998 reform movement were now able to participate directly in the power structure, either through the old parties or new parties including parties they established. As Aspinall (2010a) notes, most of the political figures who now dominated the succession of post-Soeharto governments had either been direct participants in the authoritarian regime or semi-oppositional players during Soeharto's New Order. As a result, in the following years, the dividing lines between the forces of the old regime and the new democrats became blurred as official politics accommodated and absorbed all major political forces and produced remarkable stability in the Indonesian transition. Such stability occurred in part because potential spoilers, who might otherwise have been tempted to undermine democracy, "have been accommodated and absorbed into the system rather than excluded from it, producing a trade-off between democratic success and democratic quality" (Aspinall, 2010a: 21).

The 1997 election, as with other elections under Soeharto's rule, had produced a Golkar majority in parliament. The PDI (*Partai Demokrasi Indonesia*, Indonesia Democracy Party) was at that time divided into those who sided with Soerjadi, a candidate backed by Soeharto, and the party's elected chair, Megawati Soekarnoputri. The majority of the party's members supported Megawati and decided to boycott the 1997 election. The composition of the DPR changed drastically after the 1999 election when the Golkar lost its majority, the largest bloc of seats was taken by Megawati's party, the PDIP, and a host of new parties also gained seats. The composition of both DPRs is shown in Chart 2.2.

This period of momentous change saw two different DPRs with very different compositions. Each passed an important piece of legislation on human rights. These were the 1999 Law on Human Rights passed by the 1997 DPR, and the 2000 Law on Human Rights Trials passed by the DPR elected in 1999. The 1999 Law on Human Rights was drafted to implement the 1998 Tap MPR No. XVII on Human Rights and was an initiative of the Habibie government. It was Muladi, the Minister of Justice, who drafted the law and submitted it to the DPR in April 1999 as part of a broader package of political reforms. Initially, the draft law was called the Law on Human Rights and National Commission on Human Rights. As discussed earlier, the Law enhanced and strengthened the

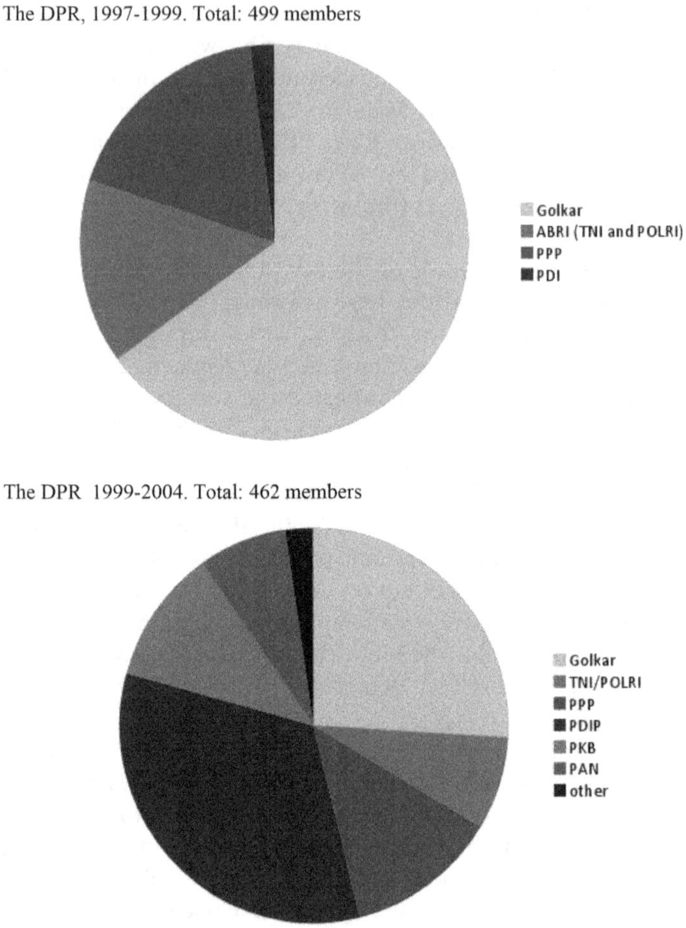

Chart 2.2 **The DPR, 1997–1999 and 1999–2004.**
Source: http://www.dpr.go.id.

role of Komnas HAM by providing the Commission with a legal basis more solid than a Presidential Decree. This was a response to the enormous public pressure for the government to investigate and resolve various cases of past violence and the resulting growing importance of Komnas HAM's investigations. All factions (*fraksi*—the Indonesian term for a party-based or other group within the parliament), except the ABRI (*Angkatan Bersenjata Republik Indonesia*, Republic of Indonesia Armed Forces) faction, agreed to the draft Law without proposing significant changes. The ABRI faction consistently opposed the law, especially its provisions for establishing a human rights court (Suh, 2012: 128–130). However, after the serious crimes that took place during and after the 1999 East

Timor referendum, followed by mounting pressure from the international community, ABRI and all other factions in the DPR had no option than to pass the Law (Suh, 2012: 130, see also Cohen, 2003).

Habibie responded to the international pressure by issuing a Perpu (*Peraturan Pengganti Undang-Undang*, Government Regulation in Lieu of Law) on human rights trials. The draft was proposed only three days before his accountability report to the MPR, which was rejected, leading to his replacement as President by Wahid. In March 2000, all factions of the newly elected 1999 DPR rejected the Perpu in a general session and requested the new government draft legislation on Human Rights Courts instead (*Kompas*, 13 March 2000). Wahid's Minister of Law, Yusril Ihza Mahendra, drafted a new Law on Human Rights Courts and submitted it to the DPR on 5 April 2000. On 14 June 2000, all factions of parliament agreed to work on the draft and passed it as a Law on 6 November 2000, or after only four months of the legislative process.[12] The Law says that cases of gross human rights violations that take place *after* the enactment of the law can be brought before a Human Rights Court. It also allows for trials of cases that occurred before the enactment of the law, but says that these must be tried through *ad hoc* human rights courts on the recommendation of the parliament. In other words, the law accommodated the retroactive principle, allowing past human rights abuses to be investigated and punished, albeit under special purposes. The use of the retroactivity principle in this way countered public suspicion that the Law was aimed at avoiding accountability for cases of past abuses.

In fact, the non-retroactivity principle was consistently debated in the drafting of both the 1999 Law on Human Rights and the 2000 Law on Human Rights Courts. This principle is stipulated in Article 1 of the Criminal Code, which was established in 1915 during the period of Dutch colonialism. It specifies that nobody can be held guilty for an act that was committed before a law against it came into effect. The ABRI faction at first consistently supported the non-retroactivity principle and opposed the government's proposal to apply the retroactivity principle both in the 1999 Law on Human Rights and in the 2000 Law on Human Rights Courts. However, they ultimately had to agree because the military was under massive pressure from both the domestic public and the international community to be accountable for its record of past human rights abuses. Seven other factions also questioned the government's proposal to include the retroactivity principle in the draft Law on Human Rights Courts.[13] The government

12 See the processes and statements from all parties, government representatives and all factions in the DPR, and the draft as well as the Law in "Proses Pembahasan Rancangan Undang-Undang tentang Pengadilan Hak Asasi Manusia", DPR Secretariat, 2000.

13 They were FGolkar (*Fraksi Golkar*, Party of the Functional Groups), FPBB (*Fraksi Partai Bulan Bintang*, Crescent Star Party Fanction), FReformasi (*Fraksi Reformasi*, Reformation Faction), FKKI (*Fraksi Kesatuan Kebangsaan Indonesia*, Indonesian Nationhood Unity Faction), FPDIP and FPKB (Fraksi *Partai Kebangkitan Bangsa*, National Awakening Party Faction). See Sekretariat DPR, Proses Pembahasan Rancangan UU Pengadilan HAM, 2000.

responded by emphasising that it wanted to establish ad hoc courts for special cases that took place before the Law was passed, and that it aimed to form a TRC which would also allow investigations of past crimes. NGOs and human rights activists intensively lobbied and convinced the factions to include the retroactivity principle. Eventually, all factions agreed to pass the law.

However, ironically, before the DPR completed the ratification of the Law on Human Rights Courts, the third amendment of the Constitution was passed by the MPR, stipulating non-retroactivity in its chapter on human rights (Article 28(I:1)). The amendment states that the right not to be charged retroactively is a basic human right that cannot be breached under any circumstances. For human rights activists, this particular article presented a dilemma. On the one hand, they believed it was important to protect human rights, but on the other hand the article would dramatically narrow the possibilities of investigating or prosecuting cases of past human rights abuses, most of which were not technically illegal when they were committed (Marzuki, 2012: 89). Amnesty International argued that this article would be used as "a backdoor for those responsible for the massive violations that have taken place over the years, including those who designed and directed policy" (Amnesty International, press release, 18 August 2000).

Marzuki (2012) argues that the article was included in the constitutional revision process as a result of intentional design by residual members of the New Order political elite who were still represented in the MPR and did not merely arise because of ignorance on the part of the politicians. The article turned the 1999 Law on Human Rights and 2000 Law on Human Rights Court into blunt tools. The fact that all of the perpetrators of human rights abuses were subsequently acquitted and that the 2004 Law on Truth and Reconciliation was later annulled, are some of the results of the article. According to Suparman, the article has effectively dug the grave (*menggali kubur*) of legal approaches for settling cases of past abuse. Problems that have arisen when investigators have tried to look into and punish past human rights crimes have occurred not only as a result of poor implementation of these laws; a fundamental legal problem has existed since their inception (Marzuki, 2012: 90–91).

The military in the period of momentous change

The period of momentous change was also marked by a positive attitude towards reform, at least in some aspects, on the part of the TNI (*Tentara Nasional Indonesia*, Indonesian National Armed Forces). Immediately after Soeharto's fall in 1998, media and public attention were focused on the exposure of New Order repression and human rights violations. Much attention was given to ABRI's primary role in these abuses as well as its *dwifungsi* or dual function—a doctrine adopted during the New Order regime that stipulated that ABRI played a role not just in defence but also in domestic politics. As one of their six core demands for *reformasi*, students wanted the military to be held accountable, and its dual function to be scrapped.[14] Pressure also came from the international community, especially following the referendum in East Timor.

Habibie's initiatives and policies to strengthen civilian groups and provide them with the opportunity to take leading political positions in the new democracy could potentially marginalise the military from political life for the first time since the 1950s (Mietzner, 2009: 197). The military had to make trade-offs in order to retain at least part of their political influence and positions. Elements within the military were therefore constantly negotiating with civilian politicians during the turbulent period of transition, under Presidents Habibie, Wahid, and Megawati. In the same years, internal struggle within the military was also intense. The situation was most obvious when Wahid took power. The TNI came under pressure due to Wahid's efforts to bring the armed forces under civilian control and his support for radical military reform. However, as Mietzner (2009) suggests, increasing military engagement in political affairs also depended on the quality of democratic rule. He concludes that, in the case of Indonesia's transition, "whenever the civilian polity was in crisis, the armed forces found entry points to increase their participation in politics" (Mietzner, 2009: 375). The political disorder that accompanied Wahid's rule thus provided many opportunities for the generals to strengthen their position and defend themselves against pressures for human rights accountability.

The TNI's earliest attempt to rebuild its image and demonstrate how it had broken with Soeharto's New Order came when it announced military reforms in 1999, or in the phrase used by Armed Forces Commander Wiranto', the 'New Paradigm', which consisted of four points (Mietzner, 2009: 201): the military was content not to be in the forefront of national affairs; the previous approach of occupying [political power] was changed into influencing; this influence was to be exerted indirectly rather than directly; and the armed forces acknowledged the necessity for role-sharing with other national forces.[15] Many elements in civil society saw this concept as half-hearted reform or *reformasi setengah hati.* In its research, the LIPI (*Lembaga Ilmu Pengetahuan Indonesia*, Indonesian Institute of Sciences) pointed out that the reform package indicated that the military preferred to share power rather than give it up to civilian leaders in the executive, legislature, and judicial branches. Moreover, the team noted that nothing had changed in the military's approach to handling security challenges, with it still using violence and repression against civilians (LIPI, 1999).

14 These six demands for reform, or *Enam Tuntutan Reformasi*, were: rule of law, eradication of corruption and nepotism, trials for Soeharto and his cronies, constitutional amendments, repeal of the military's dual function, and regional autonomy. See for example, Rais (2001: 1–2).

15 Honna (2003: 164–165) acknowledges that this New Paradigm concept was identical, both in wording and content, with the reform ideas formulated by moderate officers in 1996 and 1997 i.e., while Soeharto was still in power. Some progressive officers such as Agus Wirahadikusumah expressed their dissatisfaction with the use of these old formulae (Mietzner, 2009: 201–202).

In terms of human rights accountability, ABRI—whose name changed in 1999 back to TNI, the name it had used back in the early decades of Indonesian independence, as part of its attempt to distance itself from the Soeharto period—accommodated various aspects of the transitional justice agenda. The first relevant initiative was the ending of the Military Operation in Aceh followed in August 1998 by General Wiranto's issuing of a formal apology for abuses committed there. The TNI established a DKM (*Dewan Kehormatan Militer*, Military Honour Council) (similar to an earlier DKM set up in 1995 to look into the shooting of civilians in Timika, Papua), to investigate and try officers involved in the enforced disappearance of activists in 1997 and 1998. It also cooperated with Kejagung in establishing ad hoc civilian-military courts, referred to as *pengadilan koneksitas*, for several cases of past abuses including four trials on Aceh, and a trial for abuses committed in connection with riots that had occurred after a PDI congress in July 1996, often referred as *Kudatuli* (27th of July Riot, *Kerusuhan* 27 Juli).[16] With regard to the various laws and constitutional amendments related to human rights, military representatives in the DPR and MPR also expressed their disagreement but eventually cooperated with the end results.

Overall, the TNI complied and cooperated with the demands for human rights accountability, as long as they could be involved in the institutions and processes set up to respond to these demands. The *koneksitas* trials were conducted under the military's legal jurisdiction, even though civilians were also involved. When purely civilian human rights trials of senior officers seemed possible, the military would either arrange deals outside of formal institutions to protect their interests or completely disregard the judicial process. For example, the 1999 East Timor referendum resulted in investigations of military officers, but the military as an institution as well as its senior officers disregarded any attempts by Komnas HAM to get it to cooperate with the process. Thus, in the end Komnas HAM was able to bring indictments only against officers who were directly in charge in the field.

Some senior TNI officers also took their own personal, non-institutional, initiatives to come clean in the new transition period and so secure their positions in power. One example is A.M. Hendropriyono. In February 1989, Hendropriyono had ordered troops from the Lampung Regional Military Command, where he was the Commander, to attack the radical Islamic leader Warsidi and his followers in Lampung. The group was accused of being a deviant sect that wanted to rebel against the state and form its own Islamic state. No less than

16 The riot resulted from internal friction within the PDI where Megawati had been elected as party leader but the Soeharto government intervened by backing a rival faction headed by Suryadi. On the morning of 27 July 1996, Suryadi threatened to take over the Party's headquarters. His supporters, backed up by government troops, attacked the headquarters. A riot ensued and was followed by a government crackdown on opposition. The riot was blamed on activists of the PRD (*Partai Rakyat Demokratik*, People's Democratic Party).

229 people, including children and women, were shot dead and burned alive, according to a Komnas HAM's investigation (Komnas HAM, 2008).When Habibie appointed him as Minister of Transmigration in 1998, and later in the same year Minister of Labour, Hendropriyono immediately announced '*islah*', or an Islamic style of reconciliation with surviving victims of the massacre. In April 2000, he distributed 12 million rupiah each to a number of victims, and promised other material benefits as well as employment (group discussions with victims in Talangsari, Lampung, September 2014).

The military thus in formal terms at least adapted to transitional justice without significant resistance. The military, in particular the army, had to comply with the demands for state accountability to gain public legitimacy and international support. Its leading officers needed to break from any symbols and image that represented the New Order. Public pressure for accountability for past abuses made them see transitional justice mechanisms as a tactical concession, especially in the early years of *reformasi.* Openly resisting the transitional justice agenda would have damaged the military's role and bargaining in the new democracy, especially since several senior officers were running for political positions.

However, despite this formal adaptation, many of the reform policies, including transitional justice policies and mechanisms, eventually proved ineffective precisely because of the "entrenched network of political relationships cultivated by the armed forces" (Mietzner, 2009: 321). As we shall see, the military later undermined implementation of various transitional justice mechanisms which they had not openly opposed.

The period of compromised mechanisms, 2001–2009

The next period was characterised by transitional justice measures being used as tactical concessions by various leading political actors. The negotiation, or transplacement element of the political transition, was significantly stronger in this period, as the political tumult and mass protests of the early *reformasi* years faded, and as new political elites established their positions in power. During this period, political and military leaders often used transitional justice as a way to gain political support both domestically and abroad. This started when the draft Law on TRC was being legislated 2004 and when ad hoc trials for East Timor and the 1984 Tanjung Priok massacre were established in 2002 and 2005. I discuss these three mechanisms in more detail in the following chapters.

Even if a regime introduces transitional justice measures merely as tactical concessions, according to Risse, Ropp, and Sikkink (1999: 12), doing so can still "increase a regime's vulnerability to domestic mobilisation and provide additional leverage for external actors interested in ways to persuade a state to ultimately adopt rights-consistent behaviour". However, this was not the case with Indonesia. Not only did the policies adopted in this period not lead the state to adopt rights-consistent behaviour, it also created a pathway not to the settlement of cases of past injustice, but to a dead end. As I will later explain, the military was still a significant factor in this period. Even though various investigations and trials were implemented, most notably concerning military involvement in cases of human rights abuses, military elements had already consolidated themselves with conservative elites, especially after Wahid's impeachment, allowing them to retain influence in political life and to frustrate transitional justice efforts.

At the same time, Indonesia's democracy began to stabilise in this period, and the political elite was increasingly consolidated. The distribution of patronage through mechanisms such as elections and decentralisation, as Aspinall (2010) outlines, provided an 'absorptive capacity' that contributed to stability by neutralising three main potential spoilers: the military, ethnoregional elite, and militant Islamism. Stability was also the result of what Slater (2004) calls a style of cartel politics involving all or most of the major parties in power-sharing arrangements through cabinets and other important posts.

In contrast, transitional justice had little that was positive to offer potential spoilers or other elite elements which had benefited from the New Order regime. On the contrary, the adoption and implementation of transitional justice mechanisms would have implied ousting these elements from the political game, or at least damaging their reputations and circumscribing their authority. Unlike the first two years of the transition when transitional justice was adopted to gain public support and legitimacy for the new regime, the following years saw elite actors repeatedly making compromises or delaying transitional justice mechanisms to ensure that no elements from the old repressive regime would be disadvantaged or expelled from the power-sharing game.

Megawati Soekarnoputri replaced President Wahid in October 2001 after most parties abandoned Wahid and mobilised to oust him from office. As explained previously, many significant initiatives in the transitional justice area took place under Wahid, who also provided some of the foundation for future transitional justice mechanisms. Before him, though with an entirely different motivation, Habibie had also set up some of the basis for future human rights accountability and protection in Indonesia, even though his government did little about cases of past human rights abuses. Megawati's administration is also important in terms of transitional justice adoption and implementation with several important episodes of both prosecutions and truth-seeking occurring during her term in office. Ironically, however, these steps took place at the same time as an increase in political conservatism and a reconsolidation of the military's political role. Mietzner (2009: 225–235) describes the period under Megawati's leadership as one of "conservative revival". It was a period of a shifting in the civil-military relationship in favour of the armed forces. Because she did not trust the civilian alliance that had toppled Wahid and put her in power, Megawati gave concessions to the TNI in anticipation of potential challenges.

In terms of human rights, although Megawati responded positively to various demands for human rights accountability, most of her policies ended up allowing the military elite even more space to exercise their power and influence. Many of the important pieces of legislation passed during her presidency had already been drafted or proposed during Wahid's time. These included the Law on TRC passed by the DPR in 2004, and Regulations No. 2/2002 and No. 3/2002, both of which related to victims of gross human rights abuses (the former protects witnesses and victims; the latter outlines compensation and restitution mechanisms).

However, most of the important post-Soeharto human rights prosecutions took place during Megawati's presidency, including the two most important ad hoc human rights trials, both of which attracted attention from domestic and international actors. They were the human rights trials of military officers, militia leaders, and civilian officials involved in gross violations of human rights during and after the 1999 referendum in East Timor, and the trial of military officers responsible for the 1984 Tanjung Priok massacre. I discuss the trials of both cases in greater detail in the next chapter.

Several important investigations also occurred during Megawati's presidency. In 2002, Megawati set up a national investigation team on the violence in Maluku. Later, following up on Komnas HAM's investigation of the bloody Abepura incident in 2000 in which soldiers killed several dozen civilians,[17] she also supported the Human Rights Court to hear the case in Makassar in 2002. One military-civilian trial (a *koneksitas* case) was also initiated under her leadership in 2003 to try several military officers for their role in the 1996 PDI riot. Following the killing of Papuan leader Theys Eluay on 10 November 2001, she established a fact-finding team to investigate the assassination and in 2003 supported a military trial of the nine middle- and low-ranking military officers responsible.

Despite all this implementation of transitional justice measures under her presidency, the latter example shows the limits of her approach to human rights. For Megawati was, above all, a strong nationalist. Human rights, in her perspective, should be placed within the framework of nationalism and the NKRI (*Negara Kesatuan Republik Indonesia*, Unitary State of Indonesia). In her lengthy speech on Indonesian Independence Day on 17 August 2001, she made an apology

17 The Abepura case took place two months after a riot in Wamena in October 2000 and other violence between June 2000 and 2001. On 7 December 2000, two police officers and a security guard were killed in Abepura, a college town located around ten kilometres from capital city, Jayapura. Police believed the killings were carried out by pro-independence Papuan highlanders from Wamena who escaped into the hills. In response to the killings, police officers and Brimob troops retaliated under the Jayapura police chief's command. Police raided three student dormitories, rounded up people in other highlander settlements in the Jayapura area, beat and tortured them, and killed three students. See Human Rights Watch report. *Indonesia: Violence and Political Impasse in Papua* (2001).

towards both provinces Aceh and Papua for decades of human rights abuses. She promised to restore order, but with a condition that the two resource-rich regions would have to abandon hopes of independence. In her words:

> Apology is obviously not enough. It has to be followed by various efforts that guarantee the restoration in immediate future. Today we are making a fundamental correction in the two provinces, both by respecting the cultural identities of the people in both regions, and by giving autonomy for the local governments to manage their own domestic issues within the form of special autonomy. However, one thing needs to be clear. All of that shall take place within the maintenance of the integrity of the NKRI. Let me underline specifically on the integrity of the territory of our country. The territorial unity is not only an attribute of a country, it is also part of a stable global world order, where the changing of borders is no longer allowed. In this case, not only will we counter any movement that aims at separating a region from the NKRI, but the international community will never give their support.[18]

Furthermore, she introduced martial law in Aceh in 2003 after the breakdown of a Cessation of Hostilities Agreement (CoHA) there[19] and then divided Papua Province into Papua and West Papua provinces, which created confusion over the 2001 Law on Special Autonomy in that region and was seen as undermining anti-Jakarta sentiments in the territory.[20] Even though her father, President Soekarno, had been a target of the regime change of 1965–1966 and the crimes committed in that transfer of power had been covered up for decades by Soeharto's narrative about how he had saved the nation from communist subversion, Megawati chose to secure her position by avoiding the difficult subject of the 1965 tragedy. The only action she took was rewriting the history of what happened on 30 September and afterwards, by asking the then Minister of Education, Malik Fajar, to form a team of historians to publish a book on this subject for teaching and educational purposes. The team, led by Taufik Abdullah, started their project in 2004 and published a series of three books in 2012. However, the historical narrative presented in the books did not really change much from the state's version of the event, emphasising that the state engaged in an emergency response to the PKI's "betrayal". Megawati's administration also made a breakthrough by revising the secondary school curriculum

18 Official Speech of the President of the Republic of Indonesia Megawati Soekarnoputri, 16 August 2001. http://www.bappenas.go.id. Accessed 30 January 2016.

19 The deal broke off when the followed-up negotiation between the two parties failed in Tokyo. Quoted in Juwana, 654.

20 Presidential Instruction (Inpres) No. 1 year 2003 on the Acceleration of Proliferation of the Irian Jaya Province.

somewhat on the issue, including by removing the term 'PKI' from the name of the September 1965 coup—it had previously been referred to as the G30S/PKI (30th September Movement/PKI) in history books. In 2006, however, this new curriculum and the revised history text books used to teach it caused an uproar. The Attorney General was forced to investigate the then Head of the National Education Curriculum, Diah Harianti, and the previous head, Siskandar, for removing the term 'PKI' from the history books (*Koran Tempo News*, 15 March 2007). The Ministry of Education under Yudoyono put the term back in the history textbooks.

Human rights groups were aware of Megawati's sympathy for the military and her indifference to human rights. In an interview with Human Rights Watch, Hendardi, a prominent human rights activist explained:

> Megawati is very dependent on the military because she is aware that her own authority is weak. This is because although she is from the majority party, she only attained the presidency as a result of compromise with other parties. The TNI, however, is very strong, so she tries to accommodate their priorities (Human Rights Watch, 2003: 4).

The return of the military was underlined by the 2004 presidential election when many of the presidential and vice-presidential candidates were retired military generals. In response, activists became critical of the state's reluctance to end impunity and its willingness to allow the military to reenter politics. Munir, a prominent human rights lawyer, was among these activists. Just a month before the second round of the presidential election, Munir was murdered in a plot involving the BIN (*Badan Intelijen Negara*, State Intelligence Agency) on a plane taking him to Amsterdam to pursue his studies. Munir had long been known for his stubbornness in demanding justice for past human rights abuses and for his long-standing opposition to the military's extended roles in Indonesian politics and the economy. His murder was a massive shock for many civil society activists.

The 2004 presidential election was won by a retired general, Susilo Bambang Yudhoyono. Munir's murder was a big test for Yudhoyono's capacity and willingness to deal with human rights cases. He promised to bring the responsible parties to justice. A joint fact-finding team was established, which resulted in the prosecution of several people involved in intelligence work for the assassination. However, the master minds of the murder, senior officers in the BIN, such as the head of BIN AM Hendropriyono and Deputy Head As'ad who were named in the fact-finding team's investigation, were not indicted. Another senior officer, Muchdi PR, was put on trial but later acquitted.

Yudhoyono himself did not use his authority to push law enforcement offices, including Kejagung, to process the case. As far as human rights are concerned, he shared Megawati's reluctance to respond to victims' demands for justice and to implement initiatives proposed by both civil society and state institutions. These included any attempt to address the 1965–1966 mass violence.

His father-in-law, Sarwo Edhie, had been the head of the Army's Special Forces during the 1960s, and was widely believed to be one of the people in command of the slaughter of communists and their sympathisers at that time. It was widely believed that this personal connection mad him especially reluctant to deal with this case.

The pace at which transitional justice measures were implemented significantly decreased during Yudhoyono's presidency. Not only did prosecutions stop, the implementation of the Law on TRC, which was passed in Megawati's presidency in 2004, was also very slow. The passage of the Law took almost four years in total, with intensive meetings involving various elements nationally and internationally. I discuss this process in Chapter 4. The Law required the government to establish the TRC within six months of its issuance. Yudhoyono did not immediately implement the law, and for many months he left the process pending. In particular, he dragged his feet on the recruitment of commissioners. Meanwhile, civil society organisations, including victims' groups, requested a judicial review of the law due to three provisions they believed to violate victims' rights to remedy.[21] In December 2006, the Constitutional Court made a surprise decision by annulling the whole law rather than dismissing these specific provisions. The annulment of the law marked the end of the period of compromised mechanisms and the beginning of the next period—stalled reform, which I describe below.

Meanwhile, political dynamics in the parliament after Wahid's dismissal were surprisingly stable. As mentioned earlier in this chapter, this stability characterised Indonesia's transition overall. Despite the political tension under Wahid when he alienated most of his party allies, there was rarely real opposition to anyone who was in power (Aspinall, 2005, 2010) while the political elite consistently establishing collusive relations to keep major actors inside the political system and government (Slater, 2004, 2006). Even if competition occurred during elections, deals were usually made to share power shortly thereafter. Thus, although the PD's presidential candidate, Susilo Bambang Yudhoyono, won the first presidential election in 2004, the party did not win a majority of the seats in parliament. This situation caused Yudhoyono to offer political positions within his cabinet to other parties in order to secure his presidency.

Chart 2.3 shows that, as in the period between 1999 and 2004, the PDIP and the Golkar remained the two largest parties in the DPR. The composition remained similar to what it had been after 1999, except that the PD and the PKS (*Partai Keadilan Sejahtera*, Prosperous Justice Party) also won more seats. Another difference is that in this period there was no more TNI representation

21 These three provisions were: the TRC's power to recommend amnesties for perpetrators of serious crimes, a provision holding that cases that the TRC addressed could not be prosecuted in court, and a requirement that victims would only receive compensation if the relevant perpetrators were given amnesties. See ICTJ, Derailed, 29–30.

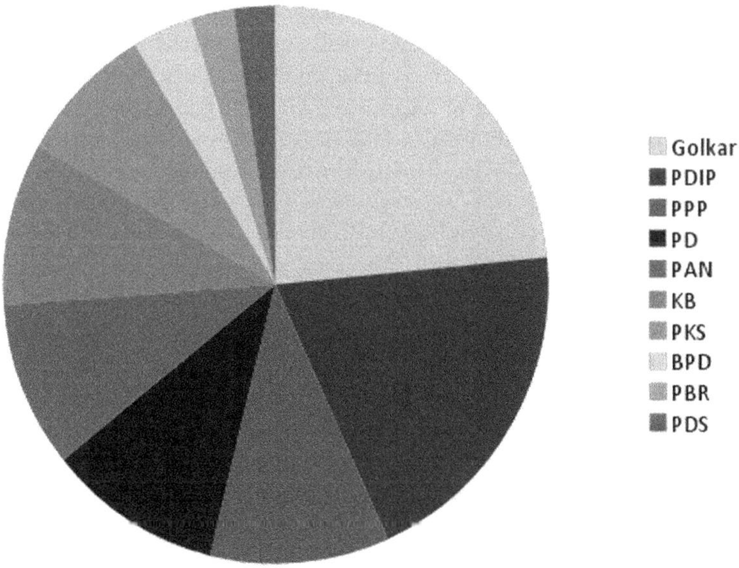

Chart 2.3 Composition of DPR 2004–2009.
Source: http://www.dpr.go.id.

in parliament. However, low levels of transparency continued to undermine decision-making processes in the DPR, with many decisions frequently taking place behind closed doors and involving informal compromises among small groups of party leaders and other members of the elite. For example, the DPR remained ambiguous on the case of the 1998 Trisakti and Semanggi shootings—these were cases of shootings by security forces of student and other protestors at large demonstrations during the period of regime change, in which several protestors were killed.

For these cases to be brought to court, the Law on Human Rights Courts required the DPR to recommend the establishment of an ad hoc human rights court. This was because, as explained above, the law required DPR approval for a court process for a crime that had occurred prior to the enactment of the law. After two years of lobbying by NGOs and students, the DPR set up a special committee to determine whether the case met the criteria of a gross human rights violation allowing an ad hoc human rights court to be established. In July 2001, based on the Committee's findings, the DPR had a plenary meeting to decide its support for a judicial investigation by Kejagung. Out of the ten factions, only three (the FKB, [*Fraksi Kebangkitan Bangsa*, National Awakening Faction], the FPDIP [*Fraksi Partai Demokrasi Indonesia Perjuangan*, Indonesian Democracy Party of Struggle Faction], and the FPDKB found the case to be a gross violation of human rights. Most factions (seven including the TNI) found no convincing evidence for such a violation. Komnas HAM nevertheless set up an inquiry team to investigate the cases. The team found new evidence and concluded that gross human rights violations had taken place against the demonstrators. The team also named 50 army officers who had used violence against the protestors, including Lieutenant General Sjafrie Samsoeddin who was in 1988 the Jakarta Military Commander and was later promoted in 2002 and again in 2010 as TNI's Head of Information and Deputy of Minister of Defense.

Komnas HAM and NGOs lobbied both the executive and the parliament to support this finding, revoke its 2001 decision, and establish an ad hoc human rights court to put the case on trial. In 2003, the DPR's Commission III on Law and Human Rights promised to review the decision and bring the case to a plenary meeting of the parliament. But it was not until after the new DPR was elected in 2004 that the decision was eventually reviewed. In June 2005, Commission III decided to recommend the cancellation of the 2001 decision to a plenary meeting, but this recommendation never got included in the agenda for a plenary meeting. In January 2006, the Meeting of DPR chairs (Rapim, *Rapat Pimpinan*) agreed to close any discussion on the case and decided that the 2001 decision could not be repealed.

However, in June of the same year the Bamus (*Badan Musyawarah*, DPR's Discussion Body) had a series of meetings and decided to ask Commission III to carry out a new inquiry into the case. Until the DPR elected in 2004 dissolved in 2009, it failed to make a clear decision on the cases. What is obvious in all those processes, however, is that there were frequently inconsistencies between the decisions made by individual parliamentarians and the interests of their parties as expressed by their leaders. According to Nursyahbani Katjasungkana, a PKB (*Partai Kebangkitan Bangsa*, National Awakening Party) member of parliament who was also a member of Commission III between 2004 and 2009:

> That has always been the case. One day these people (parliamentarians) support accountability. They said they would ensure that the cases (Trisakti-Semanggi shootings) would go to trial, but the next day, when it was time for decisions to be made, they suddenly changed their opinions. Apparently, the party's interests decide (interview with Nursyahbani Katjasungkana in Hague, 19 September 2013).

Despite its failure to support the recommendation for an ad hoc human rights court for the 1998 Trisakti-Semanggi shootings, the 2004–2009 DPR passed some legislation and made some recommendations. These included Law No. 11 of 2005 on Ratification of the International Covenant on Economic, Social, and Cultural Rights, Law No. 12 of 2005 on Ratification of the International Covenant on Civil and Political Rights, Law No. 13 of 2006 on Victims and Witness Protection, and a Recommendation for on the Enforced Disappearance of Activists in 1997–1998. They also established a Fact-Finding Team on the Death of Munir, and conducted Monitoring into the Civil Emergency in Aceh, under which the military pursued counter-insurgency operations. These decisions were in part facilitated by the inclusion of a number of individual politicians with personal experience in human rights issues and social activism in the DPR. These people, for example Eva Sundari of the PDIP, Nursyahbani Katjasungkana of the PKB and several others, maintained close relationships with human rights groups. They often lobbied other MPs, both from their own parties and from other parties, informally using 'personal approaches' (interview with Nursyahbani Katjasungkana, 19 September 2013). They considered such approaches necessary because, according to Eva Sundari, most MPs had very limited, or even no knowledge or understanding of human rights issues.[22] By using personal approaches, these DPR members from time to time succeeded in convincing other parliamentarians to produce legislation and recommendations that reflected a human rights perspective.

Such strong support for the adoption of a transitional justice agenda counters the commonly held view that parliament simply lacked the political will to seek justice for victims of human rights violations and abuses. Suh (2013: 235) argues that the DPR could not be condemned as a whole or considered a veto player against transitional justice. The fact that some parliamentarians showed support for human rights indicates that there was in fact sometimes political willingness, even if it was not strong.

This at best 'fragile will', as Suh refers to it, can be explained by the consensual nature of coalitional politics in Indonesia. This form of politics may have played a role in discouraging party politicians from supporting potentially divisive issues like transitional justice. As party leaders tried to reach political stability through making compromises on most contentious issues, they tended to be willing to make concessions to the interests of conservative military officers and party elites (Kim, Liddle, and Said, 2006; Mietzner, 2009). Moreover, none of the parties maintained a consistent stance on protecting and promoting human rights. As the Setara Institute's research findings show, party leaders tended to make the most important decisions, and they rarely considered human rights when doing so (Setara Institute, 2008).

The military

As discussed earlier, the conservative elements in the military reconsolidated their political position under Megawati's leadership. While various policies on transitional justice were implemented during Megawati's presidency, no senior

22 Sundari, Eva. "Parlemen dan HAM: Visi Tanpa Eksekusi". In Indriaswati Saptaningrum et al. (Eds.), *Hak Asasi Manusia dalam Pusaran Politik Transaksional. Penilaian terhadap Kebijakan HAM dalam Produk Legislasi dan Pengawasan DPR RI Periode 2004–2009* (p. XVII). Jakarta: ELSAM, 2011.

officers were punished for their involvement in past abuses. Military reform also stagnated, especially since pro-reform elements in the military, such as General Agus Wirahadikusumah, were sidelined. Conservative elements secured positions in power and even got promoted, as the example of Sjafrie Samsoeddin, mentioned above, shows.

Many senior officers simply ignored judicial processes that could lead to prosecution. For example, Wiranto was summoned by Komnas HAMs's investigation into mass violence in East Timor, but he never appeared before it. Komnas HAM, according to the 1999 Law on Human Rights, does not have *sub poena* powers, or the power to force witnesses or suspects to appear before its investigations. At the same time, some former military men continued to take individual initiatives to settle cases of past violence privately and outside of official processes. For example, Try Sutrisno, the former Armed Forces commander and Vice President tried to pursue private reconciliation with victims of the 1984 Tanjung Priok massacre even as the trial was taking place. This initiative was inspired by Hendroprioyono's '*islah*' for the 1989 Talangsari massacre.

The year 2004 also marked the repositioning of military individuals in political office. As Mietzner (2013b: 232) points out, conflict within civilian governments after the 1999 election and the internal consolidation of the armed forces increased the TNI's popularity in the eyes of the wider public. Such popularity improved the image of military officers and encouraged them to run in the 2004 presidential election and the local government elections that occurred thereafter. Significant numbers of military officers secured positions as heads or deputy heads of regional governments. The presidential election was won by Yudhoyono, who was known as a moderate officer in the TNI and had served as a minister under both Wahid and Megawati.

Stalled reform, 2009–2014

After 2009, transitional justice measures either failed to meet their objectives or were never implemented at all. Some trials took place under both military and civilian jurisdiction, but all such trials punished only lower-level officers or offenders and failed to bring the masterminds or higher members of the chain of command to justice. All of these offenders were eventually found not guilty in their appeals. Komnas HAM's investigations were blocked by Kejagung—which was required to approve prosecution after Komnas HAM sent it a recommendation—nor did they receive political support from the executive or the parliament. The Law on Truth and Reconciliation was also re-drafted by a team set up under the Ministry of Law and Human Rights, but the draft Law was never submitted to the parliament for enactment.

After Yudhoyono took over the presidency following his victory in the first ever direct presidential election in 2004—a position he regained for a second term in 2009—a period of stagnation set in, and there were even several reversals. Yudhoyono has, as Mietzner (2009: 316) argues, a "general disinclination to prosecute past abuses" or to settle cases of human rights abuses. In the end, however, his promises of human rights accountability proved little more than empty rhetoric. Yudhoyono was under little pressure to deliver on human rights; he did not find it necessary to adopt a transitional justice agenda to prove his reformist credentials. His victory in the direct election provided him with strong legitimacy and he also gained success with the Aceh peace process in 2005 (Suh, 2013: 245).

During Yudhoyono's period in office, Komnas HAM carried out several investigations, including an historic investigation into the killing of leftists and associated repression in and after 1965–1966. However, Kejagung refused to proceed with these investigations, and Yudhoyono never tried to push Kejagung to take action. As noted above, Yudhoyono also was very slow in implementing the Law on the TRC, before the Constitutional Court finally annulled it in 2006. Even though the Ministry of Law and Human Rights under his leadership started drafting a new law on the TRC, the process was painfully slow and the draft was withdrawn from the list of DPR legislative priorities in 2012.

The paralysis in the TRC Law shows that Yudhoyono was very reluctant to address the 1965–1966 violence in particular, given that this would have to be included in the proposed commission's investigations. Yudhoyono consistently demonstrated that he was reluctant to deal with this issue. Facilitated by his Advisor on Legal Affairs, Denny Indrayana, Yudhoyono held a meeting with the head of Komnas HAM and NGO representative Usman Hamid of KontraS in 2010, which was followed by a few other meetings with civil society groups, including victims, to discuss possible options for settling cases of past abuses. Yudhoyono seemed reluctant to include the 1965 tragedy in the issues to be addressed, most probably because it involved his late father-in-law Sarwo Edhie who, as noted above, bore significant responsibility for killings at that time (interview with Ifdhal Kasim in Jakarta, 22 September 2014).

The meetings never resulted in any concrete policy for settlement of cases of past human rights abuses. Instead, in 2011, Yudhoyono assigned one of the members of his President's Advisory Council, Albert Hasibuan, a former Komnas HAM commissioner, to establish a program for a national apology and resolution for victims of past abuses. There were also a series of meetings with scholars, legal experts, researchers, NGOs, and victims' groups to discuss this initiative (interview with Albert Hasibuan in Jakarta, 2 May 2012). However, it became a source of major public controversy when some elements, especially from religious groups, including NU, as well as members of the conservative political elite, vehemently rejected the idea of an 'apology' to victims of the 1965–1966 repression. According to these groups, the state should not apologise to communists, who they considered as being responsible for organising the coup and perpetrating past political violence (interview with Slamet Effendi

Yusuf in Canberra, 16 March 2013). But for Hasibuan, in a context where there were no other mechanisms to settle past wrongs:

> an apology to the victims could be an entry point for defining serious crimes and past injustice. This apology could be a legacy of Indonesian history ... and further we could then determine what kind of reparations were needed for the victims, not necessarily compensation (interview with Albert Hasibuan in Jakarta, 2 May 2012).

This initiative never bore fruit. Given the strong reactions against it from certain influential political leaders and mass organisations, Yudhoyono proved reluctant to finish what he started, and after two terms as president, he left no legacy on settling cases of past abuses or for improving human rights protection. Using seven variables to measure the handling of cases of past abuses, the Setara Institute scored Yudhoyono's performance in settling cases of human rights abuses on a 0–7 scale, giving him an average score of 1.14 in 2010 and 1.34 in 2012, highlighting his weaknesses in this area as seen below (Table 2.1).

The Institute concludes that Yudhoyono only used human rights as a rhetoric, hoping that past injustices would slowly fade from the public's memory. It also concludes that Yudhoyono used human rights issues to negotiate with his rivals in the military to win in his campaigns against the opposition from other parties (Setara Institute, 2012).

Yudhoyono largely controlled parliament through his own party and through his broader coalition. His party won the largest number of seats in the DPR in the 2009 election, though it fell far short of a majority. Both the Golkar and the PDIP numbers significantly decreased. Hanura and Gerindra, political parties led by former army generals suspected of involvement in various cases of human rights abuses, also won significant numbers of seats in parliament. The parliament elected in 2009 did not pass any legislation or issue any recommendations that supported the settlement of past human rights abuses. Overall, the legislative performance of this parliament was low, passing only 103 laws out

Table 2.1 Yudhoyono's Performance in Settling Cases of Human Rights

Variables	*2010*	*2011*
1.1. Enforced disappearance of activists	1.0	1.2
1.2. TRC	3.0	1.4
1.3. 1984 Tanjung Priok massacre	0	1.3
1.4. 1998 Trisakti, Semanggi I dan II shootings	0	1.3
1.5. Murder of Munir	2.0	1.2
1.6. Wamena-Wasior killings	1.0	1,4
1.7. Follow up recommendations of CTF	1.0	1.6
Total score	1.14	1.34

Source: Setara Institute Human Rights Index (2010, 2011).

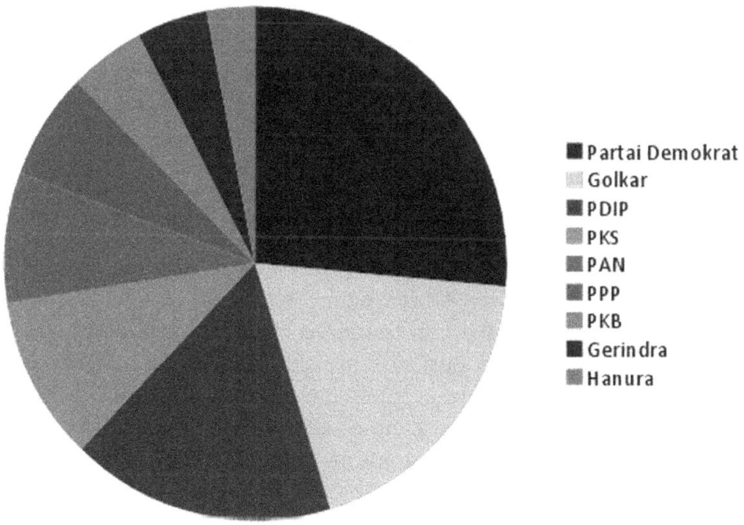

Chart 2.4 Composition of DPR, 2009–2014.
Source: http://www.dpr.go.id.

of 247 draft laws in its legislation program. Human rights groups also criticised the 2009–2014 parliament for failing to ensure that the executive implemented laws on human rights (*Suara Pembaruan*, 29 September 2014) (Chart 2.4).

Even so, the year 2009 marked a new peak for involvement of former pro-democracy and human rights activists, among them victims and relatives of victims of human rights abuse, in the political system either as parliamentarians or as government officials. Some victims of the 1997–1998 enforced disappearances of activists, such as Pius Lustrilanang and Aan Rusdianto joined Gerindra, the party led by the person who was said to be the mastermind of their kidnappings, Prabowo Subianto. Some others, such as Andi Arief, campaigned for Yudhoyono's candidacy and were rewarded with special positions in the executive government.[23]

Parties also nominally incorporated human rights in their political platforms. A survey by the Setara Institute (2008) found that of the 44 parties competing in the 2009 elections, 24 explicitly mentioned human rights in their platforms. These included major parties such as the PDIP, the Golkar, the PD, the PKS, and the PAN (Partai Amanat Nasional, National Mandate Party), but also parties identified with past abuses such as Gerindra and Hanura. Some also had special divisions on human rights, with the PDIP, the PD, and the Golkar enlisting

23 Andi Arief was appointed as one of the commissioners in PT Pos Indonesia, and later was appointed as one of the President's Special Staff on Disasters.

the help of former human rights activists to help them on the issue. However, in reality, these political parties did not demonstrate strong commitment to human rights protection, particularly in relation to cases of past abuses. By 2009, transitional justice had lost its significance to most mainstream politicians. In the words of a prominent human rights activist who was now in charge of the human rights division of the PD, "Transitional justice has lost its momentum".[24]

Conclusion

In this chapter, I have tried to contextualise the transitional justice agenda of settling cases of abuses by the New Order regime within the broader setting of the political transition that took place in Indonesia after the 1998 *reformasi*. I have explained how the elements of both rupture and transplacement in Indonesia's post-Soeharto democratic transition in some ways supported, and in other ways hindered, the adoption and implementation of transitional justice measures.

Such measures were adopted and implemented reasonably thoroughly in the early years of the transition, making these years a period of momentous change for human rights accountability in Indonesia. It was the rupture element of the regime transition that made this possible. The collapse of the New Order regime and of its legitimacy, meant that members of the old ruling elite needed to distance themselves from past abuses if they wanted to establish a political role in the new political order. This shift made the adoption of transitional justice measures a political necessity for many leading political actors.

However, as time passed and the tumult of the early transition faded, the element of transplacement became more prominent. Protests and disorder gave way to elite negotiations, gradual change, and the settling into place of a new political order. In this period, transitional justice lived on, but more in form than in substance.

24 A personal text message sent in response to my invitation for an interview, 2012.

Chapter 3

Prosecutions in cases of past human rights abuses

The East Timor and Tanjung Priok trials

> We demanded justice, and yes, we got the justice mechanisms through the ad hoc Court, but in the end, we didn't get the justice we wanted (interview with Wanma Yetti in Jakarta, 23 March 2012).

Introduction

This chapter discusses prosecutions of two sets of cases of gross human rights abuses through what were often called the 'double package' (*paket ganda*) trials: the trials of perpetrators of abuses in East Timor and Tanjung Priok. The first refers to a series of trials against those involved in mass violence following the 1999 referendum in East Timor. The latter refers to trials on a set of crimes that took place during Soeharto's New Order against residents of the Tanjung Priok area in Jakarta in 1984. Both trials took place through ad hoc courts that were established together in one policy package as a response to both national and domestic public pressure in the early years of the transition. Some of the perpetrators were found guilty; however, later all were acquitted in appeals. The prosecutors only tried persons who were directly involved in the violence and did not present officials in the chains of command to the courts.

In this chapter, I assess both the adoption of the trial strategy in these cases and the implementation of the trials within the framework of assessment that I explained in the first chapter. As argued elsewhere, and as I explain in greater detail in this chapter, the implementation of the trials was flawed in many ways (Cohen, 2003; Junge, 2008; Marzuki, 2012; Sulistiyanto, 2007). These flaws lead me to conclude that trials for cases of past abuses have been problematically successful, in the sense that they were implemented successfully but with highly complex and problematic designs and processes. Given the implementation problems, many activists and researchers from the start predicted the result would be complete failure in bringing justice. Their predictions were ultimately proven to be correct.

Later in this chapter, after analysing the implementation of the trials, I explain the flaws by looking at how aspects of Indonesia's political transition both facilitated the adoption of the trials as a policy, but hindered their implementation. I argue that the trials were a response to international and domestic pressures for accountability. However, for the new elite, the trials were more than a moral imperative: trials were held to provide them with legitimacy and to allow the old elite, especially the military, to remain at the centre of politics. Trials helped the new leaders of the government in the early years of the transition to gain support from both the public and from the international community. Similarly, the military had to accommodate to the process since the institution had gained much critical attention for its violence during the New Order. However, the military was able to influence the trial processes and results, both individually and institutionally, by intimidating the judges and victims and providing alternative settlement mechanisms to victims. For some individual military officers, these efforts were necessary tactical concessions that allowed them to remain active in the new political context. This argument is in line with my main argument for this book, that is, that adoption and implementation of transitional justice measures were highly dependent on the nature of Indonesia's political transition.

The first part of the chapter discusses the legacy of impunity in Indonesia. Despite policy and institutional reforms that have taken place since the 1998 *Reformasi*, impunity remains the country's greatest challenge in any implementation of transitional justice mechanisms. The discussion next turns to the first official attempts to hold human rights trials, and the formal legal base of these attempts, namely the 2000 Law on Human Rights Courts. The law was a product of creative legalism, combining the principles of justice and accountability with the political interests of the elite who were dominating the democratic transition. The next section discusses the background and implementation of ad hoc human rights trials for perpetrators of violence during the East Timor referendum in 1999 and the massacre at Tanjung Priok in 1984. The fourth section compares the two trials, looking at their processes and outcomes. This discussion is followed by an examination of the political conditions that help explain the processes and outcomes.

Impunity: the legacy of the past repressive regime

Impunity has been one of the main legacies of Soeharto's military regime. Those who committed past abuses have never been seriously punished; instead, they were often rewarded with better career opportunities in the military. For example, four of the 11 members of the Rose Team (Tim Mawar) who were involved in the enforced disappearance of activists in 1997 and 1998 were they were found guilty as charged in a military tribunal and subjected to minor administrative punishments, but were late promoted in their careers in the Special Forces (Kopassus) (KontraS, 2009).

In the amended Set of Principles for the Protection and Promotion of Human Rights through Action to Combat Impunity, submitted to UN Commission on Human Rights on 8 February 2005, UN defines impunity as:

> the impossibility, de jure or de facto, of bringing the perpetrators of violations to account—whether in criminal, civil, administrative or disciplinary

> proceedings—since they are not subject to any inquiry that might lead to their being accused, arrested, tried and, if found guilty, sentenced to appropriate penalties, and to making reparations to their victims.

Adding to that, the document states that

> impunity arises from the failure by States to meet their obligations to investigate violations; to take appropriate measures in respect of the perpetrators, particularly in the area of justice, by ensuring that those suspected of criminal responsibility are prosecuted, tried and duly punished, to provide victims with effective remedies and to ensure that they receive reparation for the injustice suffered, to ensure the inalienable right to know the truth about violations, and to take other necessary steps to prevent a recurrence of violations.

Impunity in Indonesia reflects the exact situation described in the above definition. The state, through its institutions, not only committed violence under the repressive regime but has not been able to bring about accountability and ensure the non-recurrence of such gross violations.

Accountability arises mostly as a direct result of trials within the legal system. Since *reformasi* started in 1998, Indonesia has made efforts in this regard. Several trials have been conducted of those who committed gross violations of human rights, mainly military and police officers.

There are three prosecution mechanisms for security officers who commit criminal and human rights offences. The first mechanism is through internal prosecution, which is commonly referred to as a military court or *pengadilan militer*. This type of trial is under the jurisdiction of the Supreme Court as regulated in Law No. 14 of 1970 on Basic Provisions of Judicial Authority, updated in Law No. 35 of 1999 the Amendment of Law No. 14 of 1970 and also Law No. 31 of 1997 on Military Tribunals. The KontraS (*Komisi Nasional untuk Orang Hilang dan Korban Kekerasan*, National Commission for Enforced Disappearance and Victims of Violence) analysed eight military trials on human rights cases that were held in the period leading to 2007.[1] It concluded that the law and its implementation contribute significantly to a climate of impunity in cases of human rights violence. The trials did not allow victims and witnesses to give evidence before the court, and the whole process lacked transparency. Moreover, senior officers could

1 These cases were the 1997–1998 enforced disappearances, the 1998 Trisakti shooting, the 1999 Semanggi II shooting, the 2001 enforced disappearance of members of Toyado village, Poso, the 2007 shooting of community members in Alas Tlogo, the 2001 Killing of Theys Hiyo Eluay and enforced disappearance of Aristoteles Masoka, the 1999 Beutung Ateuh Massacre in Aceh, and the 27 July 1996 incident: KontraS, *Menerobos Jalan Buntu, Kajian terhadap Sistem Peradilan Militer di Indonesia*, Jakarta, 2009.

intervene in the trials and intimidate witnesses. Moreover, according to KontraS, the Law on Military Trial contains many clauses that are contradictory to the Law on Human Rights and Human Rights Court (KontraS, 2009).

The second mechanism is commonly referred to as a *pengadilan koneksitas*, or a military-civilian court. These hold trials of either civilians or military personnel allegedly responsible for ordinary criminal offences. For cases related to human rights, there were two such courts established: one, in April 2000, for a trial on in relation to a massacre of Tengkyu Bantaqiah and his students[2] in Aceh, and one, in June 2004, the *Kudatuli* incident. The procedures and mechanisms for such trials are regulated in the Criminal Code (KUHP), Articles 89 to 94.

Third, are human rights courts which can try either security or civilian perpetrators of alleged gross human rights violations. Human rights trial can be ad hoc (for cases occurred before the establishment of Law on Human Rights Court) as well as human rights court (for cases after the establishment of Law on Human Rights Court) as explained in Law No. 39 of 1999 on Human Rights and Law No. 26 of 2000 on Human Rights Court. Until today, Indonesia had had two ad hoc Human Rights Courts for the 1984 Tanjung Priok massacre case and the Timor Leste'smass violence around the 1999 referendum. Meanwhile, there have only been one human rights court established, that is for the 2000 Abepura killings.

Komnas HAM named 137 perpetrators in its investigations for judicial processes in human rights trials. Out of this number, none was ultimately punished for the crimes committed, though some were punished on first instance, only to have their convictions overturned on appeal. The conviction rate is shown in Chart 3.1. None of these trials prosecuted high-ranking military officers for any cases of gross violations. The Komnas HAM (*Komisi Nasional Hak Asasi Manusia*, National Commission on Human Rights)'s investigations named some high-ranking military generals for their involvement within the chain of command, but none of these names were indicted by the Kejagung. Prosecutions only tried middle- to low-ranking military officials, and as shown in the graph, the eventual acquittal rate for human rights trials—after appeal—was 100 per cent.

In her assessment of human rights accountability in the period from 1998 until 2006, Meijer (2006) points to some factors that caused on-going impunity in Indonesia. These were power factors, legal factors, cultural factors, and international factors. The power factors referred to the role and influence of the military (and the police) in socio-political and economic life in post-reform Indonesia. These factors came as a result of the army's previous role based on its

2 Tengku Bantaqiah was a local Islamic leader who ran a pesantren (traditional Islamic school) in Beutong Ateuh, West Aceh. On July 1999, Indonesian military accused him of possessing firearms in the pesantren area, and on the 23rd of July military troops brutally fired on, and burned, the pesantren area. No less than 56 people died, including Tengku Bantaqiyah (Kusuma, 2007, in https://www.pantau.or.id/?/=d/426. Accessed 20 February 2018).

(major cases where a known number of suspects were named in Komnas HAM inquiries: Tanjung Priok, Abepura, East Timor, and Trisakti/Semanggi I and II)

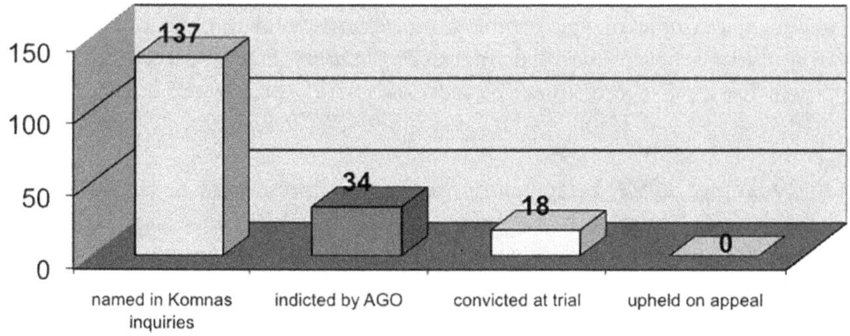

Chart 3.1 Convictions for Gross Human Rights Violations in Human Rights Courts.
Source: ICTJ and KontraS (2011).

dual function, the economic and political interests of the army, the complicity and rivalry between the police and the army, and paramilitary groups that fall outside the authorities' responsibility (Meijer, 2006: 75–92). Meanwhile, various legal provisions in Indonesia appear to support and legalise impunity. Meijer (2006) identified elements within Indonesian law that contribute to impunity, ranging from laws inherited from colonial rule, such as the KUHP and KUHAP (Criminal Procedure), to laws enacted during the earlier period of independence until the recent democratic period.

Establishing the human rights courts

A month after he came to office, President Habibie announced unexpectedly in a cabinet meeting on 9 June 1998 that he would give the East Timorese two options to resolve their tensions with the Indonesian government: extended autonomy within the Indonesian state, or becoming independent (Merdeka.com, 30 June 2016). Even though Ali Alatas, the then Minister of Foreign Affairs, had lobbied the UN and Portugal for an extended period of special autonomy before the referendum, Habibie insisted on holding it immediately with the two options.[3] The interpretations of this sudden proposal vary from those who argue

3 See the interview with Ali Alatas in *Tempo* (3 March 2003: 186). Alatas revealed that Habibie openly rejected the option to hold referendum with a 10–15 years transition period in East Timor. His rejection was in response especially to various criticism from pro-independence

that Habibie did it to gain support for his leadership from the West, to those who believe that Habibie was an impulsive individual who made the decision in a moment of 'emotion' with the belief that most East Timorese would opt to remain with Indonesia (Suryadinata, 2000: 344). His decision prompted strong criticisms from both military and civilian politicians. Megawati, whose party had won the largest number of seats in that year's election, accused Habibie of being an example of "government figureheads who tend to put their political ambitions before national interests" (*Jakarta Post*, 7 September 1999). Prabowo Subianto, the dismissed general who was then in self-imposed exile, said the decision was Habibie's "biggest blunder" (*Tempo*, No. 39/XXVIII, 29 November–5 December 1999).

On 29 August 1999, a day before the East Timorese went to the ballot box to vote for their future with Indonesia, President Habibie gave a speech urging the Timorese to reject independence and opt for special autonomy. The result of the referendum was a shock to many Indonesians, especially the political elite: almost 80 per cent of the East Timorese decided to separate from Indonesia and have their own independent state.

What followed after the referendum was even more shocking, not only to Indonesia's elite and public but especially to the international community. Groups of pro-integration militias who were trained by the Indonesian military engaged in massive violence in East Timor, resulting in numerous towns burnt and thousands of casualties. UN immediately called for a special session on 23–27 September 1999, and issued Resolution 1999/S-4/1 demanding the Indonesian government to bring those who committed wrongdoings to account and provide security for locals as well as international parties, including the UN. Furthermore, the resolution demanded the UN Secretary General form a special commission of inquiry consisting of international experts to investigate the violence that had taken place in East Timor since 27 January 1999. In the session, Indonesia's representative in Geneva explained that the government intended to establish a special inquiry team called the KPP HAM Timtim (*Komisi Penyelidik Pelanggaran HAM di Timor Timur*, Inquiry Team on Human Rights Abuses in East Timor). The team was later formalised by Komnas HAM under Komnas HAM Decree No. 770/TUA/IX/1999.

Habibie further responded by establishing a Perpu No. 1 year 1999 on Human Rights Courts, dated October 1999. The purpose was to establish a

groups as well as to a letter sent by Australia's Prime Minister John Howard that urged Habibie to choose the French solution to the New Caledonia issue by giving the East Timorese the option of independence after a period of ten years of transition. Initially the offer was to have extended special autonomy for East Timor, which was announced on 18 June 1998. Only on 27 January 1999, after Indonesia's Minister of Foreign Affairs lobbied the UN and Portugal, did the government under Habibie decide on two options: special autonomy or independence for East Timor. According to Alatas, in the meeting almost everyone was optimistic that the East Timorese would choose to stay with Indonesia, convinced by reports from the intelligence bodies.

new category of courts that could try cases of gross breaches of human rights. The parliament rejected the Perpu, and declared that it did not comprehensively list the types of crimes that could be categorised as 'gross human rights abuses'. It also did not regulate in detail the human rights court's processes, and the parliament stated that it should not have retroactive effect. As international pressure for prosecuting the Indonesian military was mounting, Habibie's replacement as president Abdurrahman Wahid, through his minister of Law and Human Rights Yusril Ihza Mahendra, prepared a draft Bill on Human Rights Court to replace the Perpu and submitted it to the parliament on April 2000.

The draft law was rapidly discussed then passed by Commission 3 (mandated for legislation related to law, human rights, and security) of the parliament on 23 November 2000 as Law No. 26/2000 on Human Rights Courts. The draft Law partially adopted the wording used to outline the mandate and powers of the International Criminal Court (ICC) under the 1998 Rome Statute, particularly Articles 5 to 8 of the Statute. Initially, the DPR (*Dewan Perwakilan Rakyat*, The People's Representative Council) avoided drawing on international precedents in the early discussions of the draft. Only when militia members in Atambua, West Timor, killed three UN humanitarian workers on 6 September 2000, and the UN insisted on the establishment of an international tribunal because international law was violated did both government representatives and committee members make reference to the Rome Statute of International Criminal Court (ICC) (interview with Albert Hasibuan in Jakarta, 2 May 2012 and Haryo Wibowo in Jakarta, 9 May 2016).

The fact that the law only partially adopted the Rome Statute affected how effective the human rights courts were going to be at holding trials on serious human rights abuses. The draft law empowered the Court to hear cases on gross violations of human rights but the law acknowledged only two forms of gross crimes: genocide and crimes against humanity. It did not include war crimes as understood in the Rome Statute. War crimes were likely to constitute a significant portion of cases that would otherwise be brought to court as many such crimes had allegedly occurred during the conflicts in Aceh, Timor Leste, and Papua (interview with Haryo Wibowo, 9 May 2016). Moreover, the law did not adopt important parts of procedural law mentioned in the Statute. These are the Rules of Procedure and Evidence and Elements of Crimes, two important instruments governing the functioning and operation of the Court (Abidin, 2007: 7; Santoso, 2003: 5). A fundamental difference exists between Komnas HAM, which is mandated to make initial inquiries into cases of serious crimes, and Kejagung which is in charge of the investigations, prosecutions, and examinations in these cases. While the former applies a human rights perspective and treats cases of serious crime as extraordinary crime, the latter treats these cases as regular crime as regulated in the KUHP. The KUHP and therefore Kejagung do not make room for treating human rights crimes as state crimes involving a chain of command, but rather see crime as an individual act driven by individual motives. So far, this difference has caused Komnas HAM's inquiries into prosecutions for cases of serious crimes to stagnate.

Many of the terms in the Rome Statute were also misinterpreted in the law, causing misunderstanding and distortion. For example, the phrase "directed against any civilian population" in the Statute was translated and understood as "*ditujukan langsung kepada penduduk sipil*" or "directly aimed at civilians". The translation of the article on command responsibility adopted from the Statute is also flawed. The exact words in the article of the Law (Article 42:1) are as follows: "*Komandan militer atau seseorang yang secara efektif bertindak sebagai komandan militer <u>dapat</u> dipertanggungjawabkan terhadap tindak pidana yang berada di dalam yurisdiksi Pengadilan HAM, yang dilakukan oleh pasukan yang berada di bawah komando dan pengendaliannya yang efektif*" (The military commander or someone who effectively acted as military commander can be held accountable for crimes under the Human Rights Court's jurisdiction, which were committed by the forces under his/her command and effective control). The word 'can be' or *dapat* in the article implies that there is no obligation on the courts to hold commanders responsible for the violence committed by their subordinates.

The partial adoption of articles from the Rome Statute within the Law was a political move, as we can see from the legislative processes in the parliament. As the law was from the start intended as a concession to respond to the public's demand for accountability for the East Timor and Tanjung Priok cases, tension developed among members of parliament on various issues discussed in the legislation. Four issues were hotly debate. First, was the definition of ordinary human rights and gross human rights violations or serious crimes, including its jurisdiction. Ordinary human rights violations are individual cases, which occur at certain times and locations, while gross human rights violations involve the elements of being systematic and widespread. This distinction was important because the human rights courts were empowered only to hear cases on gross abuses; ordinary crimes were supposed to be heard in the military tribunals. Second, was the procedure for the establishment of ad hoc human rights courts to try past cases, specifically whether this should happen by recommendation of the president and the parliament or either one. Third was the question of retroactivity, specifically whether the law could apply at all to cases that took place before it was passed. Fourth was the establishment of a TRC for cases of past abuses. Each faction's opinion on these matters is summarised in Table 3.1.

Table 3.1 shows the different opinions and political stances of the parliamentary factions in regard to the issues mentioned above. The TNI/POLRI (*Tentara Nasional Indonesia/Kepolisian Republik Indonesia*, Indonesian National Armed Forces/Indonesian National Police) faction objected to the definition and jurisdiction of gross human rights as defined in the Rome Statute and rejected the application of the retrospectivity principle. It believed that past human rights abuses could not be tried under any new law. Similarly, The Golkar faction

Table 3.1 Attitudes of Parliament Factions in Commission 3 on Four Issues Regarding the Law on Human Rights Courts

	Definition of Gross Human Rights Violation in the Draft Law	*Establishment of Ad hoc HR Court by Recommendation of Both President and Parliament*	*Retroactivity and Non-retroactivity*	*Truth and Reconciliation Commission*
F-TNI/ POLRI	Komnas HAM investigation potentially overlaps with jurisdiction under the Criminal Law (KUHP) and police investigation	No opinion	Against the principle of *nullum delictum noella poena sine praevia lege poenali* (one cannot be punished for doing something that is not prohibited by law)	No opinion
F-GOLKAR	Overlap with crimes definition under the Criminal Law (KUHP)	No opinion	Disagree, against *nullum delictum* in KUHP	Need more explanation of its role
F-PDIP	Needs clear definition	No opinion	Agree	No opinion
F-PKB	Crimes under human rights courts should include state violence by commission and omission	Prosecution for past abuses should be approved by Supreme Court	Agree	TRC is an alternative for settling cases of past abuses
F-KB	Needs a clear set of parameters of crimes under human rights court's jurisdiction	Potential for politicising cases of past abuses for revenge by political elite	Against non-retroactivity	Potential overlap with jurisdiction under ad hoc trials
F-KKI	Needs more definition	Could potentially be used as political revenge	Against non-retroactivity principle	Potential overlap with HR courts
F-PDKB	No opinion	Should be established by Supreme Court to avoid political intervention	No opinion	No opinion
F-PPF	No opinion	HR Courts under Higher Court	Cases of past abuses could potentially be used for political revenge	No opinion
F-Reformasi	No opinion	No opinion	Against non-retroactivity principle	No opinion
F-PBB	No opinion	No opinion	Agree	No opinion

Source: Summary of Processes of Legislation on Law on Human Rights Court, DPR Secretariat, 2000.

also criticised the definition of gross human rights violations used in the law, saying that it overlapped with the offences defined under the Criminal Code (KUHP). It also said that the retroactivity principle was against the KUHP. Most factions shared their uneasiness about retroactivity, believing that it could be used to exact 'revenge' for past abuses.

During the four months of the legislative process, civil society groups were also invited by the commission to give their input. The KontraS, the ELSAM, the London-based human rights NGO Tapol, and experts from the University of Indonesia gave inputs on the design of the law, including on the controversial articles mentioned above. For example, KontraS proposed to give the authority to establish ad-hoc courts to the Supreme Court instead of the President and the DPR—the commission ultimately rejected this proposal. Eventually, many of the inputs these groups gave were not reflected in the law, pointing to the fact that these civil society groups had limited influence on the legislative process.

Eventually, the Law was passed on March 2000 in a relatively short time, only six months after the 1999 Law on Human Rights was passed by the parliament. The Law said human rights courts should be established to punish cases of human rights abuses that occurred after the Law was passed, with the possibility for ad hoc prosecution of cases that had occurred earlier. This means that if the Komnas HAM made a recommendation to parliament for a trial of a case committed prior to 2000, the parliament could recommend the establishment of an ad hoc court to hear the case. It also opened up the possibility of settling cases of past human rights abuses through non-judicial mechanisms, notably through a TRC.

The passage of the Law provides a legal foundation for human rights trials mandated in the 1999 Law on Human Rights. Under international and domestic pressure, the Law accommodated cases of past human rights abuses and some provisions from the Rome Statute, including the acknowledgement of two serious crimes and their elements, and reparations for victims of violence. Overall, the law represented a high-water tide mark in post-Soeharto legislative action on transitional justice. It was a major concession to demands for greater state accountability, but one that was also marred by major compromises including the exclusion of war crimes and the requirement that human rights court can only take place by recommendation of the parliament. This latter provision means bringing the rule of law into politics. The adoption of the Rome Statute itself was political, and problematic. The Statute was established by the UN as world response to international serious crimes: genocide, crimes against humanity, war crimes, and, only recently adopted, political aggression (interview with Haryo Wibowo in Jakarta, 9 May 2016). It was not an international instrument for gross human rights abuses. The latter has been accommodated in various conventions, including the International Convention on Civil and Political Rights and International Covenant on Economic, Social and Cultural Rights (ICESCR), both were adopted by Indonesian government

2005. The lack of understanding, or worse, ignorance, of this nature of the statute, is another evidence that the state was basically making concessions to respond public pressure.

Trials on East Timor and Tanjung Priok

The ad hoc trial on abuses in East Timor took place in 2002, followed by the ad hoc Tanjung Priok trial in 2004. As with the passage of the Law on Human Rights Courts, the trials were a response to the outcry that followed the violence committed during the East Timor referendum. These were arguably the most significant trials in the post-Soeharto period of persons accused of being responsible for military atrocities. However, both trials suffered from fundamental flaws, including the fact that they indicted only direct perpetrators and ignored the chain of command so that the most senior commanders were not indicted.

Various reports and analyses have assessed the two trials in terms of their legal formal aspects and in connection to international (Cohen, 2003, ELSAM 2003, 2004a, 2004b; Junge, 2008; KontraS, 2009). I draw on these analyses in making my own assessment of the trials as one of the key mechanisms of transitional justice adopted in Indonesia, and in order to relate these trials to the surrounding political context of Indonesia's transition.

The context: the 1999 East Timor referendum and crimes against humanity

On the morning of Saturday 4 September 1999, it was announced that East Timor's people had voted to separate from Indonesia. From that point on, First Lieutenant Sugito of the Indonesian Army seemed to have no doubts about his duties as local military commander of the town of Suai. Nor did his colleagues in Suai's military, police, and civilian government. At 10:00 a.m., UN revealed the 78.5 per cent vote for independence. Just hours later, armed police and militias of the pro-Indonesian Laksaur group attacked the hamlet of Debos, shooting wildly and burning houses. One high school student was shot dead, and his body taken away in a police truck. Villagers fled into the grounds of Nossa Senhora de Fatima Church in the centre of Suai, joining hundreds of others camped there (McDonald, 2002: 13). This incident was typical of the wave of violence that enveloped East Timor immediately after its people voted for independence from Indonesia.

In fact, violence had already been widespread before the referendum took place on 30 August 1999. The result of referendum showed that 78.5 per cent of voters or 334,580 persons chose to reject autonomy and therefore opt for independence, against 21 per cent or 94,388 voters who chose autonomy and therefore desired East Timor to remain part of Indonesia (1.8 per cent of votes were invalid). After the announcement, violence broke out, resulting in mass killings, destruction and burning of property, and mass forced displacement. As the violence escalated, on September 1999, Komnas HAM made a statement on the situation in East Timor, referring to it as an "anarchical situation [involving] widespread terrorist acts perpetrated by both individuals and organized groups, witnessed and ignored by security personnel".[4] Thus, Komnas HAM recommended the establishment of an inquiry team to investigate the violence. The Indonesian government, as mentioned briefly in the previous discussion, in the same month had to agree to establish such a team after successfully lobbying the UN to block the establishment of an international tribunal.

Various accounts have been put forward to explain the violence. Robinson (2002: 243–244) outlines two different core explanations. One explanation came from the Indonesian officials and some external observers, who claimed that the violence happened spontaneously and was linked to the culture of 'amok', or spontaneous violence, among those who were frustrated with and angry about the results of the poll. The second explanation was advanced by most external journalists, human rights investigators, and The United Nations Mission in East Timor (UNAMET) officials. They insisted that the violence, both before and after the referendum, was designed by TNI officers at the highest level.

Robinson himself, based on his study of primary documents and field observations, argues that there is proof that the violence was to some degree planned and coordinated by the militia groups and the TNI. However, the evidence was not conclusive in pointing at any individuals or groups in the TNI as having masterminded the violence. Thus, he suggests it is necessary to consider two characteristics of the TNI to provide a comprehensive explanation of how the violence took place: the presence of a parallel chain of command within the institution, and the existence of a culture of violence within the TNI (Robinson, 2002). Cribb (2002) similarly suggests that to understand the violence in East Timor it is necessary to analyse the sub-culture of violence within the Indonesian military at that particular period of time. This sub-culture was rooted in two factors: military contempt for civilians since Indonesia's revolutionary period, and military triumphalism and impunity after the 1965–1966 killings (Cribb, 2002: 235).

All of these factors contributed to the violence. However, the trial was supposed to deal only with the systematic violence and to act upon the basis of evidence of gross violations of the human rights of civilians by the state.

The trials

There was wide consensus among credible investigators all that all the elements of crimes against humanity were present in the East Timor violence, and that perpetrators were militia groups with the involvement of the Indonesian military

4 See KPP HAM Timor Timur Report, Komnas HAM, 30 January 2000.

forces. Among the reports reaching these conclusions, as well as the findings of the Komnas HAM inquiry team, KPP HAMTimtim, there were also reports by Geoffrey Robinson (2003) as a UN mandated expert, an edited book by Richard Tanter, Desmond Ball, and Gerry van Klinken (2006), and a report by the UN's Serious Crimes Unit (SCU) (2006), as well as by the UN-initiated commission for truth and reconciliation, CAVR (Commission for Reception, Truth and Reconciliation in East Timor) (2005). Similarly, the CTF (Indonesia and Timor Leste's Commission for Truth and Reconciliation) report also mentioned the involvement of the Indonesian military as well as civilian government and defined their responsibilities as follows:

> In regard to crimes committed in support of the pro-autonomy movement, the Commission concluded that pro-autonomy militia groups, TNI, the Indonesian civilian government, and Polri must all bear institutional responsibility for gross human rights violations targeted against civilians perceived as supporting the pro-independence cause. These crimes included murder, rape and other forms of sexual violence, torture, illegal detention, and forcible transfer and deportation (KKP, *Per Memoriam ad Spem*, 2008: xiv).

Based on the KPP HAM report which was released January 2000 and its recommendation for prosecution, both the DPR and President Abdurrahman Wahid approved the establishment of an ad hoc human rights court for the mass violence cases associated with the referendum. However, when there was no debate around that decision, Kejagung followed up on KPP HAM's inquiry with an investigation. The Attorney General was Marzuki Darusman, previously the Chair of Komnas HAM. Its findings differed significantly from those of KPP HAM. Cohen (2003) summarises the differences in Table 3.2. As can be seen from the table, the basic difference was that Kejagung found much less evidence of human rights abuses, in terms of number and variety of cases, and of perpetrators and scope.

Such significant differences between the findings of the KPP HAM inquiry and the Kejagungs resulted in failure of the trials themselves in terms of implementation and outcomes. Only persons identified in the Kejagung investigation were indicted, and for the much narrower range of alleged crimes identified by the office. Cohen (2003) views the failure as symptomatic of the government approach from the beginning of the process and points to the absence of political will on the part of the Attorney General, Marzuki Darusman, and the highest levels of the Indonesian government. However, as I have argued in the first chapter of this book, explaining failures in the implementation of justice mechanisms as stemming from mere lack of political will on the part of government and state institutions is analytically unsatisfying. In the case of ad hoc human rights trial for East Timor, the fact that the government and politicians at large—including military representatives—agreed to trials being held indicates that some level of political will to resolve the cases judicially did exist. I return to this issue in the later part of this chapter.

Table 3.2 Differences between Findings of KPP HAM and Kejagung on East Timor Case

	Kejagung Case	*KPP HAM Report*
Patterns of crimes	Murder Persecution	Mass murder Torture and persecution Forced disappearance Sexual enslavement and rape Scorched-earth operation Forced displacement and deportation Destruction and loss of evidence
Occurrences	Four incidents: The Liquica massacre on 6 April 1999 The attack on Suai Church on 6 September 1999 The attack on Manuel Carrascalao's house on 17 April 1999 The attack on Bishop Belo's house on 6 September 1999	Sixteen primary cases, although not limited to them
Crime scenes	Three locations/regencies: Suai Dili Liquica	All 13 regencies of East Timor
Alleged perpetrators	Sixteen named individuals	More than 100 individuals, including those that allegedly executed the crimes directly, as well as Indonesian High Command
Time frame	April 1999 and September 1999	January to September 1999

Source: Cohen (2003: 11).

Based on the Kejagung's indictments, twelve trials were held from March 2002. Out of 18 defendants, only six were convicted and received sentences ranging from three to ten years. Later, all were acquitted on appeal. The trials did not establish clear command responsibility at the institutional level and strengthened the opinion promoted by many Indonesian officials that violence in East Timor was a classic case of *amok* or spontaneous clashes between unorganised groups in the society. The highest-ranking person held responsible was the commander (Pangdam Udayana) of the military region of which East Timor was a part, Major General Adam Damiri, who was convicted in August 2003 for violence in Licquisa Church in April 1999 and Covalima Church in September 1999. Like the rest, he was acquitted on appeal in the following year. We return to the reasons for these failures later in the chapter.

The 1984 Tanjung Priok killings

Tanjung Priok is a suburb in the northern part of Jakarta where the biggest port in Indonesia is located. In the late 1970s, after the New Order regime had successfully suppressed left wing groups, the government started to see Islamic groups as a potential source of opposition to its authority. In 1984, Soeharto's government announced a draft Law that stipulated that Pancasila, the state ideology, should be the only philosophical foundation of social organisations. Some Islamic leaders rejected this requirement, believing that Islam was the only appropriate philosophical foundation for religious groups, and expressed their objections while preaching in mosques.

On 7 September 1984, a Babinsa (*Bintara Pembina Desa* or a neighbourhood security officer) of a subdistrict military command (Koramil), Sergeant Hermanu, accompanied by a fellow security officer, Sukram, entered a small mosque (*mushalla*) in Tanjung Priok named As Sa'adah to search for posters and pamphlets he believed were expressing opposition to the government on the issue. He came back the next day with another officer, Samin, and insulted the locals by entering the mosque while wearing dirty shoes and throwing drain water on the wall in an attempt to make the posters illegible. The local Muslims were insulted because their place of worship had been dishonoured by the officers.

On 10 September, two locals from the neighbourhood citizens' association invited Hermanu to their office and asked him to apologise for the incident that had taken place two days earlier. Outside of the office, locals were outraged because Hermanu did not want to concede that his behaviour had been at fault. One local burnt the officer's motorbike. Four people were arrested that day by the KODIM with backup from the provincial military command (KODAM). Some of the locals came to Amir Biki, a local resident who had been active in the attempts to unseat the Sukarno government in 1966 and was now a businessman. He was known to have good connections with military officers, so the locals asked him to persuade the local KODIM office to release the four people who had been arrested. Amir Biki was not successful in approaching KODIM. He tried again the next day, just as local preachers were speaking in a rally to support a petition titled entitled *Ikrar Umat Islam Jakarta* (Jakarta Islamic Community Confession) drafted by local preacher Abdul Qadir Djailani. The petition urged the government to abandon legislative plans to oblige every formal association in Indonesia—including religious organisations—to adopt a uniform ideology (Burns, 1989: 63). Biki gave KODIM an ultimatum to free the detainees at no later than 11 o'clock that night. When the time expired, the mass meeting became a mass march to demand the release of the detainees.

KODIM officers, with backup from the higher-level Jakarta KODAM, sent hundreds of troops to confront the demonstrators who eventually opened fire on them. An unknown number were killed, and many injured. Some of the injured were evacuated to the Army Hospital. Others were detained and underwent torture in military and police posts, including at the North Jakarta KODIM and the Guntur Military police area office (Mapomdam) or RTM Cimanggis. Amir Biki was one of the victims killed in the incident.

The government accused those involved in the incident of being subversives. Starting in January 1985, more than a hundred persons were charged directly or indirectly for being involved in the Tanjung Priok incident and for committing 'political crimes' under the Criminal Code (Burns, 1989: 66). They underwent a court process and were sentenced to between ten months and 20 years in prison. The whereabouts of many others remain unknown. Reports from victims and relatives of victims suggest that as many as between 400 and 700 persons disappeared after the incident (ELSAM, 2004b: 2; Linton, 2006: 21).

When Soeharto resigned in 1998, victims and human rights groups demanded that those involved in the massacre should be punished. Compared to the East Timor case and other cases of past human rights abuses addressed early in the transition period, the way in which the Tanjung Priok trial eventually occurred was complex and involved various elements at the domestic level. A special feature of this case was that those advocating trials received support from influential national figures, organisations, and individual politicians from the post-Soeharto elite. In particular, Islamic groups and leaders which had themselves been targeted by Soeharto government policies at the time of the incident now found themselves in positions, if not of power, at least of political influence. For example, influential Muslim groups and organisations such as the Association of Indonesian Islamic Intellectuals (*Ikatan Cendekiawan Muslim se-Indonesia*, ICMI) and the Council of Islamic Missionaries (*Dewan Dakwah Islamiyah Indonesia*, DDII), both of which were strong supporters of President Habibie, supported a trial. These two particular groups helped in bringing the case to public attention.

After Habibie released political prisoners, including those associated with the Tanjung Priok case, in May 1998, several former political prisoners also joined the movement to redress the injustice. Support also came from influential individuals such as Ali Sadikin, Sri Bintang Pamungkas, and Buyung Nasution (Sulistiyanto, 2007, pp. 78). Individual politicians who supported the trial included A.M. Fatwa, a member of parliament who had been detained for his activities in the Petisi 50 dissident group and for his criticisms of the government for its role in the Tanjung Priok incident. Another supportive politician was Ahmad Sumargono, one of the leaders of the Crescent Star Party (*Partai Bulan Bintang*, PBB)—a party chaired by Yusril Ihza Mahendra who was the Minister of Law and Human Rights, and Ahmad himself.

In August 1998, victims and their families, led by Amir Biki's widow Dewi Wardah, made public detailed information on the killings and the victims

(Interview with Wanma Yetty in Jakarta, 2 September 2012). In October 1998, victims came to Komnas HAM and handed over the information which they proposed to be used to bring the case to court. Also in 1998, victims and various Islamic organisations held a mass prayer to commemorate the killings. Thousands of people attended the event, including prominent figures such as Amien Rais, leader of National Mandate Party (*Partai Amanat Nasional*, PAN), Yusril Ihza Mehendra, Said Agil Siradj of the Nahdlatul Ulama (NU), Islamic scholar Jalaluddin Rakhmat and human rights activist Munir (Sulistiyanto, 2007: 79).

During the early period of reform, the opportunity to re-open the case through formal judicial mechanisms seemed very limited. With the support of individual politicians from the United Development Party (Partai Persatuan Pembangunan, PPP) in the parliament, victims and human rights groups attempted to raise the case in the political arena. The PPP proposed to bring it up in the DPR, but both the military and Golkar factions in parliament opposed this step (Sulistiyanto, 2007: 78). Only when both the parliament and the executive enacted the Law on Human Rights Court in 2000, instigated by the mass violence during and after the East Timor referendum as explained earlier, was there an opportunity to re-open the case both in the judicial and political spheres.

As demands to re-open the case mounted, the military objected to trials or punishment of military officers involved in the incident. The former Commander of the Jakarta Military Command (Kodam) in 1984 when the killings took place, was Try Sutrisno—a man who later became Armed Forces commander and Vice President. He, not surprisingly, insisted that the case had already been closed and should not be re-opened (Sulistiyanto, 2007: 78). Later in 2001, just when the investigation by the Attorney General's Office was starting, he initiated an alternative method for settling the case by holding an *islah*, or Islamic style of reconciliation, with some of the victims. As noted in the preceding chapter, this was inspired by a similar initiative held with regard to the 1989 Talangsari masscare by Hendropriyono, who was the Minister of Transmigration in the Habibie government and later became the Head of Intelligence under President Megawati.

Sutrisno and six other military officers, including those who were named in the latter findings of the Komnas HAM inquiry into the case which was eventually released in June 2000, organised the first *islah* in Sunda Kelapa Mosque Jakarta on 7 March 2001. No less than 86 victims and families of victims signed the agreement, witnessed by Jakarta Military Commander General Bibit Waluyo and Nurcholish Madjid, a prominent Muslim scholar. The second *islah* took place on 18 September that year and involved the family members of Amir Biki. Under the *islah* it was agreed to establish a foundation called *Yayasan Penerus Bangsa* or the Heirs of the Nation Foundation in which Sutrisno would be an advisory board member. Sutrisno gave an amount of Rp. 300 million and six trucks to the foundation in addition to the Rp 2 million he paid to each victim (Akmaliyah, 2014: 168–190). Sutrisno also met President Wahid with some of the victims to convince him that the case was better settled through this mechanism (*Kompas*, 16 March 2001).

However, in March 2000, not long after Komnas HAM issued its report on the East Timor violence, the institution established a Commission for the Investigation and Examination of Human Rights Violations in Tanjung Priok (*Komisi Penyelidikan Pemeriksaan Pelanggaran Tanjung Priok*, KP3T). The victims and human rights groups had doubts regarding the independence of the team members and the quality of their work due to the involvement of Djoko Sugianto as the team leader. Sugianto was one of the judges who had sentenced some of the victims in subversion trials after the killings took place (Junge, 2008: 21). A month after the establishment of KP3T, President Wahid issued a Presidential Decree No. 53/2001 on the establishment of an ad hoc Human Rights Court for East Timor and Tanjung Priok.

KP3T worked over a fairly short time, just three months, and heard no less than 90 testimonies, including those from high-ranking military officers such as Rudolf Butar (former Commander of the North Jakarta District Command), Alif Pandoyo (former Operation Assistant in the Jakarta Military Command), Try Sutrisno, and Benny Moerdani (former Military Commander). In June 2000, KP3T issued its report. The report concluded that human rights violations were committed by both civilians and the military. For the civilians, trials had already been held and the wrongdoers had been punished. However, the violence committed by military personnel had gone unpunished and therefore the commission recommended trials. The commission also mentioned that there was no evidence of systematic mass killing of civilians as reported in the mass media and that some of the military had had to shoot demonstrators to defend themselves (*Kompas*, 16 June 2000; *Republika*, 17 June 2000).

That report did not satisfy victims and human rights groups because its findings and recommendations were too weak to proceed to a case of trials for gross human rights abuses. Some politicians, mostly from Islamic parties in parliament rejected the report and requested Komnas HAM to further investigate the case. Comparing the East Timor case with Tanjung Priok, Yusril Mahendra criticised Komnas HAM, "When investigating East Timor they were serious, but when investigating the Tanjung Priok case they were reluctant" (ICG, 2006: 9). This comment points to an important part of the politics behind the case, in which the Tanjung Priok case was mostly a priority of Muslim groups, in a context when they saw the state as intervening in response to violation of the rights of mostly non-Muslim Timorese. When trials for the Tanjung Priok case eventually occurred, they should thus be seen as partly an attempt to provide concessions to Muslim politicians and political movements.

In July 2000, President Wahid ordered the AGO to undertake further investigations. The AGO requested KP3T to supplement its report with more evidence including mass graves and the names of those involved in the chain of command. A KP3T follow-up team later added more details on the violence into its findings, including summaries of killings, unlawful arrests and detention, enforced disappearances, and torture. The report also named 23 people involved in the killings as needing investigation by the AGO, including Moerdani and Sutrisno. This second report was widely accepted.

On 21 March 2001, the parliament recommended the president establish an ad hoc Human Rights Courts for the 1984 Tanjung Priok case along with the East Timor referendum case. Together these two sets of trials were referred to as a *paket ganda* or double package. President Wahid then issued Decree No. 53/2001 on the establishment of Ad Hoc Human Rights Courts for East Timor and Tanjung Priok. Later, the decree was replaced by Presidential Decree No. 96/2001 issued by President Megawati.

The Tanjung Priok trials

Similar to the East Timor case, there were some differences between the Komnas HAM (or KP3T) report and Kejagung investigation that was later used as the basis for the indictments. Junge (2008) summarises the differences in Table 3.3.

As shown in Table 3.3, Kejagung was more specific in naming the offence as a crime against humanity. It also identified a wider pattern of crimes than had the KP3T report. This is slightly different from the East Timor experience where Kejagung identified lower offences and a narrower range of crimes than the Komnas HAM report. However, in both the East Timor and Tanjung Priok cases, Kejagung identified fewer perpetrators; in the case of Tanjung Priok it names only 14 soldiers, excluding high-ranking soldiers such as Try Sutrisno.

The trials were held and all 14 suspects were found guilty and sentenced to between two and ten years in prison. Most of those sentenced were low-ranking soldiers. However, only two officers were sentenced: Rudolf Butar Butar, the former Commander of North Jakarta Military District, and Sutrisno Mascung, the former Commander of Group III of VI Yon Arhanudse (*Batalyon*

Table 3.3 Tanjung Priok Trial, 2000

	Kejagung Case	*KP3T Report*
Offense	Crimes against humanity	Gross human rights violations
Patterns of crimes	Killings Persecution Attempted murder Torture Deprivation of physical liberty	Extrajudicial execution Arbitrary detention Torture Enforced disappearance
Alleged perpetrators	Fourteen low- and middle-ranking soldiers	Twenty-three low-level soldiers and High Command, including Try Sutrisno and Benny Murdani

Source: Junge (2008: 26), Komnas HAM (2000c: 20), ELSAM (2004: 7–15).

Artileri Pertahanan Udara Sedang, Middle Air Defence Artillery Battalion). Both of them appealed to a higher court and were acquitted, as were all the other defendants

Adoption and implementation of trials

Why did these trials take place, despite the significant obstacles in their way? Sulistiyanto (2007) argues that a coalition of actors within civil society demanding investigation of past abuses exercised such pressure that the new political elite had little choice but hold these trials. This proposition, in my assessment, is partly true. In both the East Timor and Tanjung Priok cases, a strong coalition of human rights groups, victims' rights groups, and international advocacy networks played a significant role in articulating and pressuring the Indonesian government to take accountability measures. In the East Timor case, the most powerful coalition united human rights NGOs in Indonesia and East Timor, international NGOs, and UN. In the Tanjung Priok case, the victims had already organised themselves sporadically before 1998. When Soeharto's regime collapsed, prominent human rights figures, such as the late Munir, started to approach and mobilise them to help them seek redress for the abuses they had experienced. Victims also allied themselves with other elements of civil society, especially those rooted in Islamic politics and social organisation. I explain more about this in Chapter 5.

Even though these civil society elements played a major role in pressuring the government to launch prosecutions, other significant factors also influenced the adoption of this mechanism. In line with my main argument about the conditions facilitating transitional justice in Indonesia's democratisation, these factors derived from the nature of Indonesia's transition.

As previously argued, one aspect of Indonesia's regime change was a sudden legitimacy crisis of the old ruling elite. This crisis potentially limited the opportunities for individuals connected with the New Order to attain positions of authority in the new political system. One way for such figures to survive politically was to improvise and adjust to public demands, including demands for human rights accountability. Try Sutrisno, Wiranto, and other high-ranking officers involved in the East Timor and Tanjung Priok incidents all joined the competition for political positions, both in the executive (positions in cabinet) and in parliament. Senior military generals such as Wiranto and Prabowo took part in leadership competition in the Golkar in 2004. Later, they formed their own political parties. Other senior generals took the same path by establishing and chairing new political parties, including Try Sutrisno and Susilo Bambang Yudhoyono, and ran for political positions in elections.

As part of this process of political adaptation, senior military officers adjusted to accountability mechanisms, even ostensibly far-reaching ones such as the trials on East Timor and Tanjung Priok. During the investigation and trials, even though there was plenty of evidence that the military was trying to influence and intervene in the trial processes, what many assessments did not discuss is the fact that high-ranking commanding officers were mostly accommodating to the processes. Albert Hasibuan, the team leader of KPP HAM on East Timor, explained that:

> There was resistance from the military ... [They] tried to stop it but later they became cooperative. All the soldiers responsible for the East Timor case came when we asked them, including Wiranto. Based on that we formulated the charges, which were legally and morally constructed. Wiranto was held responsible because he held command responsibility (interview with Albert Hasibuan in Jakarta, 2 May 2012).

Another factor influencing the trials was the confluence of interests, even a temporary coalition, between civil society actors such as human rights groups and other NGOs, and the new emerging political elite, many of whom had backgrounds in 'semi-opposition' during the late Soeharto period. This coalition also occurred in the context of the deep crisis of legitimacy of the Soeharto's regime. Many of the new elite—for example, leading members of political parties—were themselves engaged in the race to gain political legitimacy and public support and wanted to distance themselves from the New Order and its practices. This short-term goal explains the new elite's willingness to take a stand against impunity and to support then popular demands for human rights accountability—notably in the case of the Tanjung Priok case. Overwhelming support from various political forces to re-open the case and establish an ad hoc court points to cooperation between a wide-ranging coalitions, many of whose members were brought together by a shared Islamic identity.

A major factor in the success of the Tanjung Priok was the support the effort gained from members of the political elite. One of the reasons for that support is that several key activists and former political prisoners involved in cases had in fact been close to the New Order. Though they ended up being repressed, they were not politically distant from the regime. Amir Biki, for instance, was one of the activists in a group commonly known the Angkatan 1966, of the 1966 generation that had protested against Soekarno and the communist party in 1966. They subsequently formed the Forkot 66 (*Communication and Study Forum*, Forum Studi dan Komunikasi Angkatan 1966) in which Biki also played a prominent role. Biki and some Muslim activists eventually became involved in the PPP, though he maintained good connections with various official networks, including the military. However, he became critical of Soeharto's New Order from the early 1980s, at the same time that the regime itself was becoming increasingly suspicious of Islamic politics (interview with Beni Biki in Jakarta, 16 May 2012).

Meanwhile, the massacre in 1984, as mentioned above, led to the arrest of other well-known figures including AM Fatwa, Abdul Qadir Jaelani and Syarifien Maloko. At the time of his arrest and trial, Fatwa was the secretary of the

Petisi 50 dissident group headed by Ali Sadikin. The group released a statement on 17 September 1984, only five days after the incident in Tanjung Priok, criticising Soeharto's repression of Islamic groups. Jaelani was a Muslim preacher who was outspoken in his criticism of Soeharto and Pancasila ideology. Maloko gave a short speech on the day of the massacre but managed to escape and hide in Merak for more than a year before he was also arrested and jailed. The three of them, together with a few others, were sentenced to between ten and 16 years in jail.

After the New Order collapsed, and signifying the political transformation of opposition groups, all three joined new political parties established after 1998. Fatwa joined PAN while Jaelani and Maloko joined PBB. After the 1999 election, both Fatwa and Jaelani became members of parliament. Maloko was elected as an MP in the Jakarta provincial parliament.

The success of the movement for the Tanjung Priok trials was largely due to mobilisation of support within parliament by politicians such as Jaelani and Fatwa and others who were sympathetic to them. For example, Beni Biki explained that the Tanjung Priok case was initially not included in the agenda for the DPR general session in 1999. However, with the help of the PBB politician Hamdan Zoelva, Beni managed to fulfil the requirement of having at least 40 MPs provide their signatures to support the inclusion of the case in the agenda (interview with Beni Biki in Jakarta, 16 May 2012). The PBB and many of its prominent members, including Hamdan Zoelva and Yusril Ihza Mahendra, were involved in the early investigation of, and advocacy on, the case with victims and human rights groups. At the same time, many members of the PAN—which was linked to the modernist Islamic organisation Muhammadiyah which in turn had connections with many affected by the post-Priok repression—also sympathised. PAN's leader Amien Rais made public appearances and gave statements demanding the government take responsibility for the violence. Likewise, another prominent Islamic party, the PPP, also strongly supported the coalition since Amir Biki was its cadre and activist. Other Islamic organisations such as DDII and the newly established mass organisation FURKON (*Forum Umat Islam Penegak Keadilan dan Konstitusi*, Muslim Forum of Justice and Constitution Enforcement), led by another of Amir Biki's brothers, Faisal, also took part in the coalition.[5] All in all, there was strong political support for action on the Tanjung Priok case, including from many well-connected actors. It helped that the case became a major focus of various Islamic movements and organisations.

5 Faisal and his organisation, along with other militant organisations, received funding from the military, led by Wiranto as Habibie's Military Chief and Kivlan Zen as Army Strategic Reserve Command (Kostrad) chief of staff, to establish a civilian security guard or Pamswakarsa to 'secure' the Special General Session of MPR in 1998 against student protestors and others. See the *Jakarta Post*, June 28, 2004.

Unlike the Tanjung Priok case, there was relatively little organisation and mobilisation around the East Timor case. Partly for this reason, investigations into abuses in East Timor, failed to gain the support of most of the Indonesian political elite. As discussed earlier, the international community and Western states were instead the main actors demanding accountability from the Indonesian government for what it had done in East Timor. On the Indonesian side, there was some lobbying and campaigning for trials, but most of this was done by human rights groups such as ELSAM and KontraS, as well as by some individuals and organisations who were part of the more radical fringe of student and mass-movement politics (these included some individuals and organisations who had close connections with the PRD). Although the national media regularly reported on developments in the investigations and trials, the Indonesian public and politicians were not well informed about the gross human rights abuses that had occurred in East Timor. For the Indonesian public, the issue was more about the inability of Habibie's government to keep East Timor as part of the Indonesian state. There was also considerable hostility to foreign intervention in what was considered a domestic affair.

This hostility to international pressure continued even after the trials in Indonesia were over. On 24 February 2003, while the trials were taking place in Indonesia, SCU established under Kejagung in Timor Leste (the formal name of the new state) released an indictment to the Dili Court, requesting a warrant against eight Indonesian military officials for crimes against humanity committed at the time of the referendum. Some international and national organisations welcomed this indictment because previously the SCU had only indicted militia groups in Timor Leste. However, the fact that an institution under the political jurisdiction of the Timor Leste's government released the indictment made the indictment ineffective in pressuring the Indonesian government and its military officials to comply.[6] Kiki Syahnakri, the Commander of Martial Law during the referendum, opposed the indictment and said, "We will not consider the call, because the national courts dealing with the Timor Timur case has not yet completed" (*Direito*, 2003: 2; *Tempo.co*, 24 July 2003). Likewise, Wiranto refused to respond to the indictment and denied the charges against him. He claimed that it was an attempt at character assassination by the UN (*Liputan6*,

6 There was a controversy around the indictment by the Serious Crimes Unit. The controversy was around who actually developed the indictment. The UN spoke person Fred Eckhard in New York stated in 25 February 2002 that Timor Leste's Attorney General's Office (AGO) released the indictment, and the UN involved with advisory assistance. However, the indictment could be traced back to the time when the SCU was still placed under UNTAET. SCU was established by UN Resolution No. 1272 in October 1999. Its mandate was to investigate serious crimes that took place around the referendum. When UNTAET was finishing, UNMISET (UN Mission in East Timor) was established and SCU was placed under the new body. When the Republic of Democratic Timor Leste was formally established, SCU was placed under AGO, but still worked under UN supervision and resources.

8 February 2015). The Indonesian government, represented by the Minister of Foreign Affairs Hassan Wirayuda, also rejected the indictment on the basis that it violated Indonesia's national jurisdiction. The Indonesian Attorney General was reluctant to follow up. In fact, it was not only the Indonesian government which felt disinclined to hold such a tribunal, but Timor Leste's government also did not make it a priority, believing it could potentially damage bilateral relations between the two countries. In an interview with the Australian Broadcasting Corporation (ABC), Xanana Gusmao, former Fretilin leader who was imprisoned by the Indonesian government and subsequently became Timor Leste's president said:

> We went there (to Indonesia) last month to congratulate, to pay respect to President Megawati. We met the minister of co-ordination and he told us the same question as I feel in East Timor, please, we are in a very difficult situation economically, socially, culturally, ethnically, we have enormous challenges, we will not forget but it must not be our priority (*ABC* interview transcript, 10 October 2001).

As international pressure to establish a tribunal mounted following the failure of the Indonesian ad hoc courts to punish Indonesian military officials, the two governments came up with a proposal to set up a bilateral truth commission called the Commission for Truth and Friendship (CTF). Again, to the larger public in Indonesia, this was not a -priority issue and it therefore gained very little attention from politicians. The Indonesian Foreign Ministry was in charge of the process for establishment of the Commission (interview with Nursyahbani, September 2013).

Assessing processes and outcomes—comparing the two trials

As explained in the first chapter, the parameters used to assess the success of transitional justice mechanisms, including the prosecutions discussed in this chapter, are both procedural (processes and results) and substantive (outcomes), though of course procedural aspects tend to determine the substantive outcomes. Procedural aspects include elements such as transparency, participation of civil society groups and victims, security and protection for victims and judicial actors, as well as the independence of the procedure from political influence.

In both cases, there were some elements of success in these procedural aspects, including access for the public to both processes and findings. Civil society groups, including victims' rights groups, were involved and gained access to the processes. Two NGOs that were involved in monitoring and advocating for the victims were ELSAM and KontraS. For the East Timor trials, international engagement was very intense as the issue directly concerned the international community, especially UN. However, involvement of victims and human rights groups from East Timor was minimal because the trials took place in Jakarta. Kejagung turned down the option of having long distance communication with the victims through teleconference facilities to accommodate their testimonies. This was one of the major controversies in the process because it meant victims had very limited opportunity to testify.

Public support for the victims and the processes was also very different between the two cases. The East Timor trials were supported and closely monitored by several human rights groups in both Indonesia and East Timor and by international observers. But there was little interest from the broader public. Meanwhile, the Tanjung Priok trials received a great deal of attention from the public mainly because victims had been mobilised from early on after Soeharto's resignation, and also because prominent Muslim organisations, parties, scholars, and politicians were sympathetic. Many Muslims believed the Tanjung Priok massacre was an example of how Muslims had suffered injustice and repression under the New Order. When the international community pressured the Habibie administration to adopt punitive measure to enforce accountability for mass violence in East Timor, these organisations and individuals insisted the government should do the same for Tanjung Priok case.

In March 2001, the spokesperson of the DPR Sutarjo Suryoguritno argued that an immediate response to the two cases of human rights abuses was needed to "prevent intervention from outsiders" (*Jakarta Post*, 22 March 2001). However, most observers (e.g. Junge, 2008; Juwana, 2003; Suh, 2012; Sulistiyanto, 2007; Tapol Bulletin 68, 2002; Interview with Ifdhal Kasim in Jakarta, 22 September 2014 and Patrick Burgess in Jakarta, 22 March 2012) believed that the possibility of external intervention applied only to the East Timor trial, and not to the Tanjung Priok case. That the government chose to hold the Tanjung Priok trials, out of many other potential cases of past human rights abuses, points to an ideological reason, namely a desire to balance prosecutions on the East Timor case where the victims were 'Catholic', with a case which had a more 'Islamic' flavour.[7] Some even feared that the East Timor trial could indicate that the government might again suppress Muslim groups as had happened during Soeharto's time. As Masdar Mas'udi, a NU moderate scholar, said, "This [decision to have hold only the East Timor trial] could create sensitivity that is the religious sentiment, knowing that the government only takes the side of one particular religion" (*Kompas*, 5 February 2000).

In summary, even though the trials of both cases were open, the level of public involvement and engagement was different. The new political elite also responded differently to each case, giving more attention and support to the Tanjung Priok trials than to the East Timor trials, as the former resonated more with their domestic political interests and outlooks.

7 It should be noted that I could not find strong evidence to support this claim based on my interviews with some of the key politicians involved in this decision.

In terms of the processes, observers assessing the implementation of the trials found both legal and non-legal flaws. The legal flaws came from the weak indictments and evidence presented by the prosecutors as well as poor prosecutorial strategies (Cohen, 2003; Junge, 2008; Sulistiyanto, 2007). Prosecutors failed to bring strong and credible evidence and sometimes presented irrelevant testimonies and documents (Junge, 2008). Prosecutors also did not present coherent and credible accounts to justify convictions for crimes against humanity. All of the assessments point out that prosecutors did not act on the basis of the findings of the Komnas HAM inquiry teams, deciding not to include the most senior officers in their indictments. All of these factors point towards lack of professionalism and independence on the part of the Kejagung.

The lack of credibility and professionalism on the part of the prosecutors from the Attorney General Office can be explained by two factors: the individual quality of prosecutors, and the fact that the office was a part of the executive. Most prosecutors in Indonesia did not have any background in and understanding of human rights issues. The Attorney Generals themselves were mostly career prosecutors who lacked experience in human rights issues. The first non-career was Andi Ghalib who came from a military background and was appointed by Habibie in 1998. Under Wahid, two non-career Attorney Generals were appointed: Marzuki Darusman (1999–2001) and Marsillam Simanjuntak. Before his appointment, Darusman was one of the first commissioners of Komnas HAM and the Chair of KPP HAM East Timor. He was also a senior Golkar politician. When he became the Attorney General, Albert Hasibuan replaced him as the KPP chair. As the Attorney General, Darusman played an important role in convincing Wahid to remove Wiranto from his position as Coordinating Minister for Political, Legal, and Security Affairs for his alleged role in the East Timor violence (interview with Albert Hasibuan in Jakarta, 2 May 2012 and Haryo Wibowo in Jakarta, 9 May 2016). Darusman was later replaced by Baharudin Lopa for a short period of time.[8] Lopa died unexpectedly while on pilgrimage, only three months after his appointment as Attorney General, and was replaced by one of Wahid's confidants, Marsillam Simanjuntak.

In the years following 1998, the Attorney General's background was a topic of considerable debate. It mattered a great deal whether the Attorney General was a career prosecutor or had a non-career background from outside the office because the Attorney General's roles were central—yet political—in pursuing the reform agenda on rule of law issues such as elimination of corruption and human rights accountability. Some people suggested that career prosecutors should hold the position as they could be more professional and had more experience in actually carrying out prosecutions; others argued that outsiders would potentially have a stronger commitment and independence in settling major cases especially

8 After Darusman was dismissed, he returned to Komnas HAM and later became a member of parliament in period of 2004–2009.

those involving human rights and corruption.[9] After all, Kejagung had been deeply politicised under the New Order, and the office had also been deeply implicated in the webs of corruption and patronage that underpinned the regime.

Whether the Attorney General himself (or herself) was a career prosecutor or outsider was thus in fact largely beside the point; in fact the problem was structural and lay in the merging of the function of the government's chief lawyer, which was a political role, and that of public prosecutor, which was notionally independent of government.[10] Lindsey (2007: 18) identified two complications. The first was that political skills were institutionally more favoured than technical expertise in the Office, and the second was that the Office could hardly respond to pressure to prosecute prominent members of the New Order elite for cases of human rights abuses and corruption because of its close integration into New Order power structures.

Such complications occurred when President Megawati assumed office in July 2001 and appointed a career prosecutor, M.A. Rachman. Rachman took office during the time of the investigations for the ad hoc human rights trials. His appointment was controversial especially among victims. Rachman was not a prominent figure and had not shown any commitment to human rights prior to his appointment. He led Kejagung's joint investigation teams into both the East Timor and Tanjung Priok cases, and as previously explained, the indictment these teams produced did not include senior military officers named in Komnas HAM's inquiries. When the investigation for the Tanjung Priok case started, Rachman was the Junior Prosecutor for Special Crimes (Jampidsus). During the whole period of the investigation and before the trials, Rachman offended victims several times. On one occasion, around 15 victims of the Tanjung Priok repression, including AM Fatwa and Beni Biki, came to the Kejagung to enquire about the schedule for the first trial. Rachman as Jampidsus made a provocative statement to the victims, and Lopa as the Attorney General had to defuse the tense situation (interview with Beni Biki in Jakarta, 16 May 2012). Unlike Rachman, victims felt Lopa was very professional and committed to bringing the case to justice. Unfortunately, Lopa died a week later of a sudden heart attack.[11]

9 See, for example, on "Select outsider to Reform AGO", *Jakarta Post*, 17 September 2010. http://www.thejakartapost.com/news/2010/09/17/select-outsider-reform-ago-says-exprosecutor.html. Accessed 6 June 2016.

10 Until 1959, the role of Kejagung was ambiguous. Its resources came from the executive and it was subordinated under a particular Ministry or Deputy Prime Minister (during the period of parliamentarism in Soekarno's period), but its jurisdiction was placed under the authority of the Supreme Court.

11 Many people found his death unnatural, including his family, because he was very healthy and never had any heart problems. Rumors spread around after his death, leading to speculation that he was murdered due to some serious cases he had been handling including the Tanjung Priok and East Timor trials.

Tempo magazine, in a special edition published in August 2001, speculated that Rachman's appointment was a compromise. Megawati had to make with the military, including Wiranto and Hendropriyono, corrupt business actors, and civilian political leaders allegedly involved in corruption, including Megawati's own husband, Taufik Kiemas. Rachman enjoyed close relationships with these elites.[12] Lawyers for the accused military officers, however, denied any link between the military and Rachman's selection (Mizuno, 2003: 140).

In fact, Rachman also failed to rigorously pursue corruption cases including those against Soeharto, his son Tommy Soeharto, and prominent heads of conglomerates such as Samsul Nursalim and Prajogo Pangestu, and various BLBI (*Bantuan Likuiditas Bank Indonesia*, Bank Indonesia Liquidity Support) cases.[13] To make matters worse, Rachman himself became implicated in a corruption case when the KPKPN (*Komisi Pemeriksa Kekayaan Penyelenggara Negara*, Commission for Monitoring of the Wealth of State Officials) reported him to the police for indications of corruption and dishonesty in his wealth report (*Tempo*, 16 December 2002). At the institutional level, Rachman failed to continue internal reform of Kejagung. This failure stood in stark contrast to improvements in judicial competence that were being made around this time (Lindsey, 2007: 19). One obvious result was the poor performance and unprofessionalism of prosecutors during the Tanjung Priok and East Timor trials.

The judges for the ad hoc human rights trials all had non-career and independent backgrounds. Following the enactment of Presidential Decree No. 53/2001 under President Wahid and later revised by Decree No. 96/2001, a Supreme Court team led Benjamin Mangkoedilaga, a Supreme Court judge, recruited 30 both career and non-career human rights judges between September and November 2001. All of the judges for the ad hoc human rights courts were university professors who specialised in human rights. Rudi Rizki, one of the judges in the East Timor trials, was a prominent law professor well known for his stance in support of human rights. Many observers praised him as the key actor in ensuring wrongdoers were held accountable for what happened in East Timor (Cohen, 2003). In the Tanjung Priok trials, despite the inconsistencies of the judges' verdicts, two particular judges received much credit and praise—Komariah E. Sapardjaja and Kabul Supriyadi. Komariah was one of a small number of women judges with a solid academic background. Her main interests and concerns have been the rights of women and children. Supriyadi, like Rizki and

12 See *Tempo* Magazine. Jaksa Agung Titipan Tentara? (No. 22/XXX/30 July–5 August 2001).

13 In 1998 during the economic crisis, Bank Indonesia (BI) granted Rp 145.5 trillion in loans to help 48 troubled banks deal with the massive cash runs they experienced. However, around 95 per cent of the disbursed money was eventually embezzled. In 2002, Megawati issued "release and discharge" letters to 21 banking tycoons, freeing them from any obligation to pay their debts. See Liputan6.com. http://news.liputan6.com/read/2932794/korupsi-blbi-cerita-tak-tuntas-2-dekade-lalu. Accessed 24 February 2018.

Sapardjaja, also came from an academic background as a professor of law at a state university. After he finished his term as an ad hoc judge, he was selected as a commissioner for Komnas HAM.

If the quality and performance of these judges was a factor that helped to ensure that fair trials were held for both the East Timor and Tanjung Priok cases, the prosecutors' substandard performance was one of the flaws in the process and helped to generate the disappointing results of the trials. The inappropriateness of the indictments they prepared, and their failure to present reliable and relevant evidence, were noted by many observers.

In addition to such legal flaws, there were also non-legal flaws in the process, including failures to provide security for witnesses and judges. Many of the victims and judges were intimidated both directly and indirectly during the trials. Direct intimidation involved targeting of certain individuals. One of the judges in the Tanjung Priok trial, Kabul Supriyadi, for example, experienced terror and intimidation directed at him and his family:

> After I got selected as the judge for Tanjung Priok, yes, there were threats through phone calls to my home, my family, and my cell phone. In the end I even challenged them one day to meet in person. 'You are a man, not a woman, let us meet face to face,' I said (interview with Kabul Supriyadi in Jakarta, 10 March 2012).

The identity of the callers was not known, but to deal with this kind of intimidation, Supriyadi had to strategically plan his trips and activities. For example, when he had to travel to another city, he preferred to travel by train than by plane and did not book his tickets and accommodation in advance in order to avoid other parties tracing his travel plans. This was a new experience for him in his career as a judge.

One of the Tanjung Priok victims interviewed in this research also admitted that she and some other witnesses and their families were constantly intimidated and watched by intelligence officers (interview with Wanma Yetti in Jakarta, 2 September 2012).[14] Most of the time victims and their families were followed and watched; on a few occasions, these officers talked to them and made death threats (*Tempo*, 23 September 2003). The victim believed such intimidation was one reason why some witnesses changed their testimonies and when in the courtroom contradicted what they had said in the police investigation reports (Berita Acara Pemeriksaan, or BAP) recorded prior to the trials. For example, a witness named Mokhtar Dewang, who in his BAP testified that he was shot in the leg and illegally detained for 10 days in Guntur Police Prison, denied

14 See also interview with a victim who was also former political prisoner and later became active in the Tanjung Priok movement, Yusron Zaenuri, in Tabloid DeTAK No. 83 Tahun ke-2, 29 Februari-6 Maret 2000.

this testimony in the trial. He told the judges that he had made the testimony because he wanted revenge and that during the trial he felt that he could forgive and forget what happened to him. Instead of asking follow-up questions in cross-examination, the prosecutor gave Rp 20,000 to the witness and his two other friends after the trial concluded that day—as reported in the media (Hukumonline, 19 November 2003).

Intimidation also occurred indirectly when soldiers created psychological fear in the courtroom. During the Tanjung Priok sessions, Kopassus mobilised soldiers to attend and occupy seats inside the Jakarta Court building during the trial of Sriyanto Mumtrasan, a commander of the Kopassus special force. The military also 'secured' the trials by surrounding the court with trucks and a large number of military personnel. Similar behaviour occurred in the East Timor trials, especially during the trial of Adam Damiri. A Kopassus soldier shouted to Rudi Rizki, one of the judges, "Rudi Rizki, you are dead!" He identified Rizki as the judge responsible for handing down four guilty verdicts in trials before Damiri's case (Cohen, 2003: 28).

Other than intimidation, the *islah* agreement offered by Try Sutrisno also had an effect on the process and results of the trials (Junge, 2008: 25; Sulistiyanto, 2007: 87). The *islah* and, more to the point, the benefits offered as part of it, prompted some witnesses to change their testimonies. Dewi Wardah, Amir Biki's wife, was one of the victims who agreed to this arrangement. After three years of struggle to get justice from the state, she decided to accept the compensation being offered by Sutrisno. As with Wardah, many of the victims lived in poverty and had suffered from discrimination ever since the killings took place (interviews with Wanma Yetti in Jakarta 2 September 2012 and Beni Biki in Jakarta, 4 September 2012). An amount of Rp 1.5 to two million (around $150) per person was a large sum of money for many victims (Junge, 2008, pp. 23). Beni Biki was also approached by Sutrisno to agree to accept *islah*. He testified:

> After I met MA Rahman (the Attorney General), someone from the Office drove me home, on the way he stopped and I was asked to come to Try Sutrisno's house. One of the men said, "Here's the deal. You read the draft, if you agree, sign it, if not just cross out the clauses you don't agree with … Just come and see for yourself." I did not want to go to Try's house because I was tired and it was late. The two Attorney General Office intelligence officers were upset, "What do you want, facilities, positions, money, we'll get them for you. You are the only one left, others have signed … Note this, you won't win in the trial!". I said "I don't care about winning or losing, as long as trials do take place." And then I got out of the car and took a taxi (interview in Jakarta, 4 September 2012).

The flaws, both legal and non-legal, in the trials had implications for the outcomes of the trial processes. As mentioned in the first chapter, I assess the outcomes by looking at several points: the numbers of perpetrators punished, whether truth was established or records of the violence created and whether there was acknowledgement and reparations for victims. Cassese (1998a: 6), reflecting on the International Criminal Tribunal for former Yugoslavia (ICTY), added two other achievements that trials can have: they can help the dissipation of calls for revenge and promote reconciliation of victims with their tormentors. Other than those aspects, I also look for the unveiling of command responsibility.

The first and most basic outcome—were wrongdoers found guilty and punished?—was not achieved. As mentioned above, the trials in each case found some of the wrongdoers guilty, but they all appealed to higher courts and were acquitted. As a result, the trials failed to bring accountability and end impunity in Indonesia.

The second outcome—whether the trials produced documents and evidence that could be used to establish a public record of the violence—was also not met. In both sets of trials, much of the evidence and documents were not made accessible to the public, and therefore the final judgements failed to establish public acknowledgement of the violence. Evidence of great inconsistency on this score can be found in the trial judgements themselves. In the Tanjung Priok trials, the court made two final judgements that totally contradicted each other (ELSAM, 2004a). The first judgement, on Butar-Butar and Sutrisno Mancung, confirmed that crimes against humanity had occurred; the second judgement, on Sriyanto and Pranowo, held there was insufficient evidence to prove crimes against humanity.

The third outcome assessed in this chapter is acknowledgement of and reparations for the victims. Article 35 of the 2000 Law on Human Rights Court provides for reparations for victims in the form of compensation, rehabilitation, and restitution. However, such reparations can only be granted if there are binding legal decisions. This is also stipulated in more detail in Government Regulation No. 3 year 2002 on compensation, rehabilitation, and restitution for victims of gross human rights violations. Reparation in any of these forms was not included in the court's decisions on the East Timor cases. However, the judges in the Tanjung Priok case decided that the Indonesian government and the perpetrators had to provide compensation to 13 victims or their descendants.[15] This was a breakthrough, even though the judges had to debate among themselves on the issue (interview with Kabul Supriyadi in Jakarta, 10 March 2012). However, because a higher court annulled the decisions made in the ad hoc Human Rights Court, the compensation was also cancelled. Later on, this became another

15 See the list of the names and amounts of compensation in ELSAM, *Final Progress Report Pengadilan Tanjung Priok: Gagal Melakuakn Penuntutan yang Efektif*, 2004. http://lama.elsam.or.id/downloads/1268369271_Final_Progress_Report_Pengadilan_HAM_Tanjung_Priok.pdf. Accessed 5 June 2016.

issue of conflict among the victims because some of them thought compensation should still be paid even though the ad hoc decision had been overturned.[16]

Two of the positive effects of trials mentioned by Cassese (1998a), the dissipation of revenge and reconciliation, also did not fully take place. For the East Timor victims, it was difficult to relate to the trials at all since they were not involved in them, and they took place in a very remote location. For the Tanjung Priok victims, revenge had never been their motivation for seeking justice.[17] Instead, most of them wanted the trials to give them a sense of justice and, for some, information about what had happened to their loved ones. In Wanma Yetti's words:

> I watched a film on reconciliation in South Africa. There was a scene where the perpetrator met and apologized to the family of the victims. I expected the trials would result in a similar outcome. I wanted the perpetrator to come to me. It's not that I wanted revenge, or for them to say sorry. I just want them to come and tell me where my father was murdered, why he was murdered, and where they dumped his body (interview with Wanma Yetti in Jakarta, 2 September 2012).

Meanwhile, victims who signed the *islah* with Sutrisno did not find the agreement satisfying. On 21 September 2001, three days after the second *islah*, Dewi Wardah and two other victims announced their withdrawal from the agreement (*Liputan6*, 21 September 2001). The *islah* divided victims into two groups: those who were for and against it. During the trials, these two groups were often involved in direct and even physical conflicts; many of the members of the pro-*islah* group, facilitated by the military, used violence and intimidation towards members of the other group to get them to change their testimony (Akmaliah, 2014: 180). However, over time the division became weak and many of those who took part in the *islah* came to join the anti-*islah* group in advocating for their rights (interview with Wanma Yetti in Jakarta, 2 September 2012).

Because justice was not fulfilled and perpetrators were not found guilty, the trials failed to achieve reconciliation between victims and perpetrators. As mentioned by Yetti, even though victims wished to experience reconciliation such as that which had occurred in South Africa, in the end no victims and perpetrators were even recognised because all the decisions were annulled by the higher court. In other words, impunity closed the door to reconciliation.

16 KontraS even made a calculation of the amount of money each victim should receive from the compensation decision and proposed the Kejagung include the amount in the investigation and follow up with judges for other cases in the court. See http://www.kontras.org/tpriok/data/surat%20kontras%20untuk%20permohonan%20kompensasi,%20restitusi%20dan%20rehabilitasi.pdf. Accessed 8 February 2015.

17 See some of their testimonies in Subhan SD and FX Rudi Gunawan. *Mereka Bilang Di Sini Tidak Ada Tuhan*. KontraS: Jakarta, 2004. Also interview with Wanma Yetti in Jakarta, 2 September 2012.

Conclusion

The implementation of ad hoc human rights trials for the 1999 violence in East Timor and the 1984 Tanjung Priok massacre was the government's response to international and domestic pressures for human rights accountability. Habibie's and Wahid's response to the international call for the Indonesian government to take responsibility for the serious crimes that took place in East Timor during and after the 1999 referendum stimulated demands domestically for a similar response to other cases of past abuses under Soeharto's regime. Victims of the 1984 massacre garnered particular sympathy from the new political elite because it involved and implicated influential figures who had been engaged in semi-opposition under the New Order regime.

Even though one trial was a response to international pressure and the other was conditioned by domestic pressures, there was no significant difference in terms of implementation and outcomes. Both trials suffered legal flaws, and were politically influenced to produce outcomes that mostly benefited the perpetrators rather than delivering justice for the victims. Even so, the trials served certain purposes for the government. They helped it to gain support and legitimacy from both the public and from the international community, and helped it to manage opposition within key political institutions, especially in the parliament.

Both trials were partially successful in procedural terms, but they failed to provide justice and truth for the victims. Moreover, they ultimately reinforced impunity, and high ranking military personnel responsible for the past crimes were found to be innocent.

Chapter 4

The adoption and annulment of the Law on the Truth and Reconciliation Commission

Introduction

The previous chapter discussed the adoption and implementation of one of the key mechanisms associated with transitional justice—prosecutions. In this chapter, I discuss another mechanism which is a commonly used in the transitioning countries: a Truth and Reconciliation Commission (TRC). In 2004, the Indonesian House of Representatives passed the UU KKR (*Undang-Undang Komisi Kebenaran dan Rekonsiliasi*, Law on the Truth and Reconciliation Commission), after 17 months of discussions various institutions and social groups.

I argue in this chapter that, like the trials, both the replacement and transplacement aspects of Indonesia's democratic transition facilitated the processes of drafting and legislating of the Law. The creation of the Law on the TRC was the only legislation which was based on something close to a consensus among the executive and legislature, human rights groups and politicians, and political elites themselves on how best to resolve past injustices. As it turned out, however, a desire to achieve substantive justice for victims of human rights abuses was not one of the main objectives of the TRC law.

I argue in this chapter that the goal of establishing a TRC, rather than being set up to achieve transitional justice objectives, instead largely served the interests of the new political elite, many of whom had been involved in semi-oppositional activity during Soeharto's New Order, as well as the interests of the elements from the New Order regime who were in attempting to retain their positions of political influence. It was the opportunity for the new elite to gain social legitimacy without losing support from elements supporting the status quo, especially the military. Unlike the human rights court, the idea of a TRC was enthusiastically welcomed by a wide range of political actors, as was obvious during the process of drafting the Bill. The legislative process started in 2000 even though the idea of having a truth and reconciliation commission had been promoted from the beginning of *reformasi* in 1998.

However, the broad political support that eventually came together for the TRC bill tells us a story of unreconciled understandings and conflicting interests in truth, and throws light on how truth relates to reconciliation. There were big gaps between those who advocated the TRC from the start, notably human rights groups and Komnas HAM, and those members of the political elite who eventually supported the idea. For human rights groups, including victims, the TRC was a mechanism aiming at truth-seeking, political acknowledgement of past injustice, and reparation for victims. For the political elite, the TRC was above all a vehicle for reconciliation, which was in turn aimed at ensuring national integration and unity. Many in the political elite did not consider truth to be a significant goal, but they did aim at reconciliation, along with amnesty for perpetrators. This seemed to many of them to be a convenient option for closing the book on stories of past injustice. Blanket amnesty would provide win-win solution, helping to ensure political consolidation among both old and new elites.

The first part of this chapter looks back at the discourse of 'truth' and 'reconciliation' in the early years of *reformasi*. Different actors had different understandings of the term 'reconciliation', and thus of the roles of 'truth'. Komnas HAM and human rights groups proposed a view of reconciliation embedded in recognition of truth and acknowledgement of past human rights abuses, based on the experiences of victims. Many politicians, government officials and military officers, in contrast, promoted a version of political reconciliation as a means for consensus among the elites, both old and new, and as a means to promote the nationalist ideology of NKRI under which social harmony was valued, above all. Truth, for some advocating this view, was partial and political, and could only be achieved when amnesties were granted. In contrast, civil society groups and Komnas HAM demanded a mechanism similar to South Africa's TRC to deal with past abuses through a restorative justice approach.

The second part of the chapter explores the process of adopting and implementing the TRC. I look at the dynamics of the political transition and how these affected the TRC. The preparation of the law in parliament was a lengthy and complex process. After four years of legislative process, the result was a problematic law—a law with substantial flaws if viewed through a transitional justice framework in part because it privileged reconciliation and amnesties over truth-seeking. When it was time to implement it, the parliament had already changed its composition, and power was concentrated in the executive under the new president, Susilo Bambang Yudhoyono. The implementation of the law was painfully slow under Yudhoyono's leadership, and several civil society groups lodged a case for judicial review of the law, objecting to several articles within it. Unexpectedly, the Constitutional Court decided to annul it.

The third section of the chapter evaluates the TRC Law, both in terms of procedures and outcomes. I reflect on how civil society groups and elites had differing aims and understandings of the mechanism and its purposes. I also discuss the implications of the eventual *absence* of truth and reconciliation mechanisms in Indonesia's democracy. Many human rights and other civil society activists saw the annulment of the law as a significant setback for democracy. Towards the end of this section, I assess both the positive and negative consequences of this outcome. I argue that the biggest impacts have been the absence of a nationally recognised deliberative process to discuss the legacies of the old regime and the absence of a nationally recognised political judgement about that regime and its shortcomings.

Discourse on truth and reconciliation in the early years of political transition

On 21 October 1998, a large number of students in Jakarta rallied to demand that the MPR recommend what the formation of what they called a 'Badan Rekonsiliasi Nasional' or a National Reconciliation Body (*Kompas*, 22 October 1998). Students were not the only civil society group to demand around this time the adoption of a mechanism to address past human rights abuses. Human rights groups, most notably Komnas HAM, also made similar calls. The idea of having such a mechanism emerged following the establishment of a number of truth-seeking mechanisms under Habibie's leadership. These included the Joint Fact-Finding Team (*Tim Gabungan Pencari Fakta*) on the May Riots and Komnas HAM's team of inquiry examining the military operations in Aceh. Numerous human rights advocates believed it was important to move beyond such case-based inquiries and launch systematic investigations into past abuses. As a result, from the end of 1998–1999, the demand for a national reconciliation body mounted. However, there were different and competing discourses on the term 'reconciliation' itself, and on the mechanisms that would be best to pursue it. Human rights advocates and political elites, in particular, often had very different views on these matters.

From relatively early on, several prominent human rights organisations and activists came with own proposals for the establishment of a truth and reconciliation mechanism. These included Institut Sosial Jakarta, or the Jakarta Social Institute, an organisation associated with Tim Relawan untuk Kemanusiaan or the Volunteer Team for Humanity which conducted its own investigation into the May Riots (Zurbuchen, 2002: 574). Prominent figures such as Abdurrahman Wahid, who later replaced Habibie as President, proposed a KINKONAS (*Komisi Independen Pencari Kebenaran untuk Rekonsiliasi Nasional*, Independent Truth Commission for National Reconciliation) in January 1999.

The most widely known model was that of TRC in South Africa. Not only was it popular with prominent activists such as Adnan Buyung Nasution[1] and Abdurahman Wahid, but it was also a model for Komnas HAM's proposal for a TRC. Komnas HAM discussed the proposal for a TRC with the Ministry of Foreign Affairs and the Australian Human Rights and Equal Opportunity Commission, also inviting a commissioner of the South African TRC, Glenda

1 Nasution met with Bishop Desmond Tutu and started to promote the South African model of TRC for Indonesia. "Perlu dibentuk Komite Rekonisliasi Nasional", *Kompas,* 1 September 1998.

Wildschut, to Jakarta to discuss the institution (*Suara Pembaruan*, 3 December 1998). ELSAM, an NGO that came to lead the main civil society initiative to formulate plans for a TRC, also referred to the South African model in its proposal.

ELSAM, which was an important human rights NGO formed in August 1993 by some prominent human rights activists such as former Komnas HAM commissioner Asmara Nababan, Abdul Hakim Nusantara, and current commissioner Sandra Moniaga, campaigned hard for the formation of a TRC between 2000 and 2004 organising many conferences and workshops on the idea, promoting the concept in the national media and lobbying for it with politicians and within wider civil society networks. Because it was the civil society organisation promoting that did most to promote the formation of the TRC, ELSAM's views on the purposes of such an organisation are worth considering. As it explained much later, ELSAM defined truth by adopting the philosophical approach of Habermas (1984) and seeing it as having three integrated aspects (Kasim, 2000b). First, truth has to be a fact that really happened. Second, it is normatively based on a judgement from what we experience. Lastly, truth is what is expressed in an accurate and proper way. According to ELSAM, these three aspects of truth about Indonesia's violent past had to be fulfilled if the rights of victims to know about their past experiences were to be fulfilled.

According to ELSAM, the basic function of a TRC should be to fulfil this basic 'right to know' for victims, but the TRC would also deliver to victims a right to reparations in the form of compensation or restitution as stated in the UN's Declaration of Basic Principles of Justice for Victims. Finally, ELSAM considered reconciliation to be a goal of a TRC: by enabling victims to know the truth about what had happened to them and loved ones it would allow for. In these ways, ELSAM argued, a TRC would help to guarantee freedom from political violence. Its main goal was the creation of peace and a stable democracy for the nation. It would achieve this goal only with difficulty:

> bearing painful injustice, individuals, groups, and the state have to forget what happened. Thus reconciliation means the willingness to forgive and forget for the sake of creation of democratic political order in the future (Kasim and Terre, 2003a: 5).

Having said that, for ELSAM, a TRC was primarily a strategy for dealing with the difficult transition from an authoritarian to a democratic regime. ELSAM leaders recognised that the sheer volume of past human rights abuses and the ever-present dangers of authoritarian backsliding meant that it would be preferable for perpetrators of human rights abuses to acknowledge the truth of what they had done and so allow for reconciliation to take place. They believed that the TRC should be established within this frame to help maintain stability in what was still a young and vulnerable democracy (Kasim and Terre, 2003a: 10).

For some other groups and activists, the plan for a TRC was problematic. Some groups opposed the formation of a TRC; others accepted it with reservations. Mostly, those who opposed it did so because they saw the emphasis on truth-telling, forgiveness, and reconciliation inherent in the TRC—and the possibilities it opened for amnesties—as potentially undermining the goal of holding human rights abusers accountable for their crimes. During the process of formulating a plan for a TRC that was led by ELSAM, certain debates kept recurring. Rachland Nashidik of the NGO Imparsial rejected the proposal for a TRC. According to him,

> Some people prefer just reconciliation instead of carrying out prosecutions. The emphasis is on balancing and truth-seeking ... If we choose reconciliation, the question is: reconciliation between who? If this means reconciliation between victims and perpetrators, it ignores the sense of justice for victims ... what we need is not to stop violence, but to make sure what happened in the past will not be repeated, so what we need is justice and not reconciliation (Kasim and Terre, 2003b: 53–54).

Meanwhile, Rudi Rizki, a human rights lawyer, recognised the TRC as being complementary but also secondary to prosecutions and trials. For him,

> A TRC cannot fulfil the need for justice as a whole; therefore the search for justice is only through prosecutions. However, to be able to get justice from prosecutions, the first step is total legal reform ... a TRC has a temporary nature; in the future, it has to be through prosecutions (Kasim and Terre, 2003b: 67).

Meanwhile, for Komnas HAM, the choices between truth-seeking and prosecution were merely about the appropriate strategy to achieve larger goals of justice. As Marzuki Darusman pointed out,

> This is about a debate between sequencing or prioritization of TRC and trials. In my opinion, there is no need to debate because the end goal is to end impunity. We can have reconciliation first but it should aim at legal resolution. This was a debate [on sequencing or prioritization] in the 80s and 90s. It's a matter of strategy. […] The problem is pragmatism, as if the easiest path is the right one. There won't be a settlement if either truth-seeking or prosecution are absent (interview with Marzuki Darusman in Jakarta, 4 May 2012).

In fact, the most notable proposal came from Komnas HAM. Many hoped that Komnas HAM, as a state institution, would be able to push the agenda for truth and reconciliation most effectively. Many civil society activists regarded Komnas HAM as the only state institution they could trust to protect human rights and strive for justice in cases of past abuse, including when Komnas HAM proposed a mechanism to settle cases of past human rights abuses through establishing a

Komisi Nasional Rekonsiliasi (National Reconciliation Commission) in August 1998 (*Kompas*, 14 August 1998). The proposal was received by President Habibie through his Minister of Law Muladi, who later became a commissioner in Komnas HAM himself. The initial meeting between Komnas HAM and the government to discuss the adoption of such a mechanism took place on 4 September 1998. The discussion subsequently dragged on for months until the end of President Habibie's term, and the proposed mechanism was never realised. Members of Komnas HAM revealed that there were some disagreements between them and President Habibie. Among the disagreements were the names to be used for the mechanism: the President insisted on using the name National Consolidation Forum instead of National Reconciliation Commission. They also had different interpretations of '*makar*' or treason as stipulated in Indonesia's Criminal Law, a topic which was also to be included in the mandate of the institution to be established (*Kompas*, 17 October 1998). Instead of approving the mechanism, Habibie freed political prisoners on 31 December 1998 (*Kompas*, 8 January 1999).

It is reasonable to believe that Habibie's unwillingness to establish such a body was closely linked to the military's reaction during that time, as evidenced by his statement that "the military had had an objection" to the idea (Aswidah, 2005: 38). As I explained in Chapter 2, the push for state accountability for violations of human rights was mainly targeted at the military because of their role in committing violence and past abuses. When the idea of a reconciliation commission was voiced by human rights groups and victims, attracting attention of the international community, military leaders did not oppose the proposal in public. The main response to human rights pressures from the military as an institution, as Honna (2003) explains, was to review its security and political (*dwifungsi*) roles. However, some individual military personnel publicly gave their opinions on the reconciliation mechanism proposal in the early months of the transition. For instance, General Agum Gumelar, the governor of the National Security Agency (Lemhanas), said he had no objection to the idea but would prefer to have a '*rembug nasional*' or national gathering instead of institutionalised reconciliation. Hendropriyono took a further step by initiating *islah*, which as we have seen was a kind of traditional reconciliation mechanism used in Muslim communities, with victims in the massacre case in Talangsari where he had been in charge. These kinds of 'informal' settlements, as argued by Akmaliah (2014: 1–34), contributed to cultural impunity in the post-Soeharto era, in part because they directed people's attention away from formal and institutionalised processes.

In general, the political elite's interpretation of 'reconciliation' was vastly different from that of human rights advocates. Unlike the human rights groups, politicians regarded reconciliation as a tool for political consolidation in the new democracy. An illustration of the disconnectedness between the two understandings of reconciliation is a full three-hour meeting that was held between Komnas HAM representatives and President Habibie on 4 September 1998.

Habibie dominated the first hour of conversation by explaining his new idea of 'synergy-plus'—a strategy for working together with all political groups—before eventually allowing Komnas HAM to talk about their proposal for a truth and reconciliation mechanism. This proposal, said M. Sadli, "was welcomed by Habibie and it was decided to form a 'National Reconciliation Team'". However, reconciliation was understood by Habibie and most of the political elite then as an initiative for:

> Everyone to gather (*silaturahmi*), similar to Ied al Fitr [the Muslim celebration at the end of the fasting month], to forgive each other, and join hands together to solve the economic crises and develop democracy ("Rekonsiliasi Nasional" in *Business News*, 28 September 1998).

When they talked about reconciliation, political elites often talked in such terms, emphasising the need for national unity and for past wrongs to be put aside. Human rights groups criticised this and similar notions of reconciliation as misleading and deviating from the meaning of reconciliation as advocated in standard transitional justice approaches, where reconciliation is seen as being inseparably connected to open investigation into and recognition of the truth of past injustices.

Whereas Komnas HAM approached Habibie and various ministries directly, human rights groups advocated a TRC mostly with the MPR. At that time, in the first two years of the democratic transition, the MPR held supreme authority in Indonesia's political system.[2] The executive and legislature were subordinated to the MPR. Not surprisingly, therefore, NGOs tried to lobby the MPR to take part in settling cases of past injustice. Moreover, at that time, the MPR was more accessible to civil society groups than the executive or parliament. Around 30 per cent of the 500 MPR members had backgrounds in NGOs or as professionals, representing *utusan golongan* (group representation) (interview with Nursyahbani Katjasungkana in the Hague, 19 September 2013). The MPR eventually responded, in December 1998, by drafting a decree on strengthening national unity which included a clause on reconciliation, stating that reconciliation was a precondition for national unity. Abdul Hakim Garuda Nusantara, the leader of ELSAM and a senior human rights lawyer and activist, later gave his impression about the time when he was invited by the MPR to discuss this decree. He said,

> I don't know what the politicians in MPR were thinking when they formulated Tap MPR no. V of 2000 … My question is whether they really understood it? Considering that their common understanding was only focusing on national reconciliation (Kasim and Terre, 2003b: 67).

2 Undang-Undang Dasar 1945, Article 1(2).

Whether politicians in the MPR had the same understanding as human rights advocates or not, from the time 'reconciliation' was presented in the MPR decree in 2000 in terms of the role it could play in strengthening of the unity of the nation, the proposal for a reconciliation mechanism became very appealing for many members of the political elite because they saw it primarily as a means of pacifying political conflicts which had arisen in the wake of the tumultuous collapse of the Soeharto regime.

When the DPR began to discuss legislation to establish a TRC in 2004, many key political actors continued to view the idea of reconciliation as acceptable so long as it did not entail revenge directed at perpetrators but instead meant closing the book on the past and offering a new beginning. In other words, the goal was to forgive and then forget. Akbar Tandjung, the DPR speaker and one of the key figures of *reformasi*, said reconciliation aimed at forging an 'Indonesia Baru' or New Indonesia, which is "not the Indonesia that is chained by its past with a tendency to blame each other easily and pursue unnecessary revenge" (Tanjung and Thohari, 2003: 44). Thus, often the term 'reconciliation' was defined not in relation to truth about past human rights abuses but as form of consensus among political actors, even as an effort to pursue democratic consolidation.

For the military, reconciliation meant defending the principle of the NKRI. Still smarting from 'losing' East Timor after the referendum and also dealing with secessionist movements in places like Aceh. Military leaders plus some sympathetic nationalist politicians—presented 'reconciliation' as an alternative to secession or federalism and as a win-win solution in which all elements of society, including discontented people in Aceh and Papua, could sit together and come up with a new national consensus, even if the details of this consensus were only hazily defined.

Overall, we can conclude that the idea of a TRC eventually gained support from a wide part of the political elite, both old and new, because it allowed multiple interpretations of what reconciliation might mean. For many members of the political elite, reconciliation was appealing for it could be understood and institutionalised as a way to close the book on past injustices and facilitate consolidation of a new political order in which all the major groups—including those implicated in past human rights abuses under the New Order—could find a place. Many human rights groups had a very different view, seeing a TRC and the idea of reconciliation as potentially giving them the opportunity to push a wider agenda of transitional justice.

Getting to a TRC

When Wahid became Indonesian president after the 1999 election, the window of opportunity for establishing a mechanism for truth and reconciliation was wide open. As previously explained, Wahid was known as a prominent human rights campaigner and activist, and he maintained a close relationship with many pro-democracy and pro-human rights activists and scholars. As mentioned earlier, he was very active in promoting the idea of a truth and reconciliation commission, which he called KINKONAS. In his proposal, this non-official commission would work to "find and acknowledge the truth regarding major issues and incidents, such as the issue of East Timor, Irian Jaya, and Aceh, with the purpose of formulating ways to resolve these issues and allow Indonesians to learn from the past so that similar mistakes would be avoided in the future".[3] Aside from this proposal, he was also active in promoting 'reconciliation' in the political sense, bringing together a wide range of political forces from both the old regime, political parties, and civil society into his 'rainbow coalition' government.

Through the Ministry of Law and Human Rights, Wahid's government responded to calls that a mechanism for truth and reconciliation be established by inviting human rights groups to draft a Law on the Truth and Reconciliation Commission. ELSAM welcomed the invitation and took the lead in the process of formulating and drafting the proposed law. The organisation submitted an outline to the government in 2000, after a series of public seminars and discussion involving activists and scholars, and after it also invited international experts and practitioners, including ICTJ members and former commissioners of the South African TRC. Wahid took the opportunity to visit South Africa where he met with President Thabo Mbeki on 9 April 2000 to discuss the possibility of adopting South Africa's TRC as a model for Indonesia (*Kompas*, 10 April 2000). However, when Wahid had to step down from office in 2001, the draft law had not yet been completed.

The government of Wahid's successor, Megawati Soekarnoputri, continued finalising the draft. After several extensions, the Ministry of Human Rights finally submitted the draft TRC Law to the House of Representatives on 26 May 2003. In less than two months, on 9 July 2003, the parliament set up a Pansus (*Panitia Khusus*, Special Committee) to start preparing the draft Law. The Pansus consisted of 50 Members of Parliament from all nine fractions (*fraksi*) and was led by Sidharto Danusubroto of the PDIP.

The composition of the Pansus (see Table 4.1) is important in explaining why and how the draft law on the TRC was discussed during the legislative process. Members of Megawati's party constituted the largest group in the Pansus, followed by members of Akbar Tanjung's Golkar party. Akbar Tanjung was then the DPR speaker; together with some leading politicians such as Amien Rais and others from Poros Tengah, he instigated the impeachment against President Wahid and supported Megawati succeeding him as President. As a result, the majority of the Pansus was aligned with the government.

With the majority of members of the Pansus supporting Megawati's government, the legislative process within it did not give rise to serious debate or

3 Quoted in Zurbuchen, 574, from typescript document "Independent Truth Commission for National Reconciliation" dated 19 February 1999.

Table 4.1 Composition of DPR Pansus on the TRC Law, 2004

Factions	*Number of Members*	
Coordinators	4	FPDIP (chair), FPG, FPPP, FKB
FPDIP	14	
FPG	11	
FPPP	5	
FKB	5	
FReformasi	4	
FTNI/POLRI	4	
FBB	1	
FKKI	1	
FPDU	1	

Source: *Keputusan* DPR RI, Parliament Decision No. 49A/DPR RI/IV/2002-2003 on the establishment of Special Committee on Draft Law of Truth and Reconciliation Commission.

opposition. Most of the opposition to, or critical arguments concerning, the TRC idea came from smaller groups in the Pansus, including TNI/POLRI. At that time, TNI/POLRI still had the right to be represented in the DPR without having to compete in elections, as one lingering legacy of Soeharto's military regime and its military doctrine of *dwifungsi*. However, although it had clear interests in preventing scrutiny of its past human rights record, the military was also under intense public scrutiny at this time for its role in many past human rights abuses (Honna, 1999: 77–126, 2003), and its representation in the DPR was also being questioned. Therefore, it would not have been advantageous for the TNI/POLRI representatives to openly oppose transitional justice initiatives within parliament. Throughout the process, TNI/POLRI representatives thus objected to various elements in the new law, but in the end they agreed to it, albeit with reservations.[4]

The Pansus held public hearing meetings for two months between January and February 2004 involving 58 organisations and individual invitees that included relevant government officials, legal and human rights NGOs, religious organisations, military veterans, victims' organisations, academics and researchers from various universities and other institutions, and ambassadors from other

4 In their final opinion (*pendapat akhir*) on the draft Law on the TRC, the TNI/POLRI fraction accepted the law with three reservations. Firstly, there should be a guaranteed that truth-seeking processes guarantee would not give rise to any new problems that could threaten the unity of the nation. Secondly, the findings and outputs of TRC should not be used to justify acts of subversion. Lastly, Indonesian nationalism and national unity should be the underlying spirit in implementing the TRC. *Risalah Rapat* RUU KKR, or Minutes of Meeting of the TRC Bill, 18 February 2004.

countries. The meetings aimed at gathering inputs from a wide range of elements in society on whether Indonesia needed a TRC and what form it should take. The Pansus also organised a field study to South Africa to learn directly about the country's experience with its TRC. From all these processes, the fractions came up with an DIM (*Daftar Inventarisasi Masalah*, inventory list) which itemised 190 problems to be discussed in finalising the draft law proposed by the government.[5] After months of intensive meeting with government representatives and others, the committee finally came up with a Law on the TRC consisting of 44 clauses. It was passed by the DPR on 7 September 2004, eight months after the institution had begun discussing the idea.

During this lengthy legislative process, two issues attracted a great deal of public attention because of their controversial nature: the relative value of truth-seeking versus reconciliation, and the place of an amnesty for human rights abusers. Let us discuss each of these issues in turn.

Truth versus reconciliation

In the last session discussing the in which the Law on the Truth and Reconciliation Commission in the DPR, the then interim Ministry of Justice and Human Rights, M.A. Rachman, representing the Indonesian government, said in his speech:

> By settling cases of gross human rights violence followed by revealing the truth, admissions of guilt, forgiveness, peace, rule of law, provision of compensation, rehabilitation and restitution, and amnesty, peace will be fostered as well as reconciliation and national (Sekretariat DPR, 2004b).

The statement encapsulates the whole idea and purpose of setting up a Truth and Reconciliation Commission in Indonesia. At first glance, the understanding expressed in the minister's remark is consistent with how human rights groups understood the purposes of a TRC. However, it also points to two significant points of contention: the first is on the role of reconciliation and its relation with truth; the second is the use of amnesty to achieve goals of reconciliation.

Even though everyone seemed to agree on reconciliation as an ideal, agreement on the term 'truth' was far more difficult to achieve. During the legislative process, for example, a definition of 'truth' was debated among committee members as well as between the representatives of state and civil society who were invited to the public opinion hearing meetings (rapat dengar pendapat umum or RPDU). Two fractions, the Reformasi group which consisted of members of

5 Only one fraction, a small Islamic party, *Partai Daulat Umat*, did not submit any list because it objected to the establishment of a TRC in Indonesia. *Risalah Rapat* RUU KKR, or Minutes of Meeting of the TRC Bill, 18 February 2004.

two Islamic parties and the TNI/POLRI fraction, proposed to eliminate the word 'Truth' from the title of the draft law. The Reformasi fraction proposed to change the title to Law on Accountability and Reconciliation Commission, while TNI/POLRI proposed the name Law on the Reconciliation Commission.[6] In the committee, there were various debates on questions of whose truth was to be discovered by the TRC, the limits of truth, and who would gather and authorise truth. Eventually, all the fractions agreed that 'truth' in question referred to a truthful account of gross violations of human rights. The final clause on this point in the Law is as follows:

> Article 1(1)
> Truth is the truth on an incident that can be revealed in relation to gross human rights abuses, including regarding victims, perpetrators, place and time.

This definition becomes rather problematic and vague when viewed from the transitional justice perspective. Roichatul Aswidah problematises the Law's definition of 'truth' by saying that it only applies to particular *peristiwa* or 'incidents' without any reference or links to the root causes of why such an incident might have happened in the first place (Aswidah, 2005: 48). This contradicts the clause in the Law that stipulates "(t)he commission has an institutional function of a public nature to reveal gross violations". From the transitional justice perspective, the right to know the truth means a right to know "the circumstances of the reasons that led to the consistent pattern of human rights violations" (Aswidah, 2005: 49). Aswidah argues that the establishment of truth has to unveil the machinery which led to violence becoming an administrative practice (Aswidah, 2005: 49). This argument is in line with ICTJ's comments about the Law on the TRC. The organisation criticised the narrow definition of the research to be conducted, "which is limited to a case-by-case investigation, thus precluding the analysis of the context and patterns of the several waves of violence experienced in Indonesian history" (Gonzáles, 2004: 1). In their words, "While the factual truth of *incidents* is essential, a society needs much more than that in order to assess its past including the acknowledgement of victims' stories and an engagement in historical analysis" (Gonzáles, 2004: 5–6).

For the politicians involved in drafting the law, though victims' narratives and historical analysis were important, their function was to achieve the purpose of comprehending what happened, and who was affected, not for any deeper inquiry. They were mostly quite explicit that they did not want the TRC to address substantive questions about the root causes of violence and the systematic ways in which human rights violations took place. In the words of Sidharto

6 *Persandingan Daftar Invetarisasi Masalah* (DIM) RUU KKR, or Comparison of Issues Inventory List of the TRC Bill, Secretariat of Pansus DPR-RI, 2004.

Danusubroto, the chair of the Pansus, in one of the sessions to discuss the definition of truth (item 17 on the DIM),

> we can't be carried away by the questions of why and how with regard to the root causes, but we have to focus on the facts about where, when, what, and who; place, time, perpetrators, victims, etc. ... If we are carried away by the questions of why and how, then we are far from the main issue that we are targeting (Minutes of public hearing meetings (RPDU), Secretariat DPR RI, 2 July 2004).

By avoiding questions about root causes, the DPR designed a TRC that was never intended to address the political motivations and authorities that had led to the crimes. In other words, such a TRC was unlikely to engage in any sort of comprehensive examination or condemnation of the New Order regime, the security apparatus, or its modes of functioning.

Moreover, the Law also missed, or was ambiguous on three significant issues. These were the timespan of cases to be covered by the Commission, and a detailed explanation on the mechanisms for truth-seeking itself (Gonzáles, 2004).

The first problem concerned the timespan to be covered by the TRC. This issue was endlessly debated among human rights groups, and the draft proposed by the government also did not specify this point. During the public hearings held to discuss the draft, almost all invitees discussed this particular clause, with many different suggestions given. Historians such as Asvi Warman Adam of the LIPI proposed Indonesia's independence in 1945 as the starting point of the period to be covered by TRC.[7] Most human rights and victims' groups proposed 1965 as the starting year, which would have allowed the TRC to cover the mass violence that took place during the transition to Soeharto's government. Members of the Pansus had differing views; some believed it should start with the period of Dutch colonialism or Indonesian independence in 1945. In the end, the TRC law did not establish any definitive timespan for its coverage.

The second aspect that was missing from the Law was an elaborate description of the mechanisms or methods to be used for truth-seeking. For example, there was no mention in the law of whether the TRC would use methods such as public hearings, seminars, open dialogue sessions, or symbolic rituals in order to allow it to build transparency into its work and engage in active outreach to victims, which are often adopted as goals by other TRCs around the world. Members of Pansus argued that these aspects did not need to be included in the Law in order to give future commissioners the freedom to decide and agree between themselves on what methods were most appropriate (Secretariat DPR, 2004). This argument reflects the unwillingness of the Pansus to emphasise truth as

7 RDPU with historians, Secretaria 4 July 2004.

the condition for reconciliation. As one of the member of Pansus, Sutidarno Nurhadi from the TNI/police faction, stated: "TRC shall not be the medium to justify subversion against the NKRI, it must not justify betrayal against this nation". (*Tempo*, 7 September 2004). It was obvious that Nurhadi, and some other members of the Pansus, was referring to the truth about the 1965 mass violence (Secretariat DPR, 2004, interview with Firman Jaya Daely in Jakarta, 9 May 2017). In other words, truth was considered secondary to the larger aim of the TRC—reconciliation at any cost.

Debates on amnesty

As a strategy, a TRC was supposed to achieve two somewhat contradictory aims: it would satisfy the rights of victims and citizens at large to the truth about past rights abuses, but it was also supposed to stabilise democracy by facilitating reconciliation. In many transitional justice processes around the world, amnesties for former human rights abusers have been viewed as one pathway to reconciliation. In many cases, such as those in Spain and South Africa, amnesty became a middle way between punishing and forgetting, and was widely seen as a painful but necessary precondition for achieving a peaceful democracy.[8] For Ifdhal Kasim, amnesty was needed in a transitional society:

> The amnesty policy is a necessary evil which must be taken by new governments to fulfil the greater purpose of protecting still-fragile democratic stability that could any time return to the old authoritarian political system (Kasim, 2000a: 6).

Referring to Huntington's *The Third Wave*, Ifdhal seemed to agree that political consolidation should be prioritised more than decisions to punish individual perpetrators. However, he argued that the TRC should not issue a blanket amnesty. Introducing Jose Zalaquette's criterion of amnesty, he explained three conditions that needed to be met: first, truth should be obtained before any amnesty issued; second, amnesty should not to be given for serious crimes including crimes against humanity and genocide; and lastly, amnesty has to reflect 'willingness' on the part of society to go down this path (Kasim, 2000a: 9). For Roichatul Aswidah (2005), a prominent human rights advocate who was also a member of ELSAM, amnesties were justified if they met the three conditions above. As we will see below, these conditions were not included in the final version of the Law on the TRC, prompting human rights groups to lodge a judicial review.

8 See for example on the Spanish case Iosif Kovras, *Truth Recovey and Transitional Justice: Deferring Human Rights Issues*. London: Routledge, 2014, and on the South African case Philip J. Brendese, *The Power of Memory in Democratic Politics*, New York: University of Rochester Press, 2014.

Politicians in parliament were even more keen—and less discriminating—on amnesty, with many of them viewing amnesties as a precondition for reconciliation. The discussions on amnesty during the legislative process mainly focused on procedures rather than substance. Article 1(9) of the Law on TRC defines amnesty as "forgiveness that is given by the President to perpetrator(s) of gross human rights violations after considering discernment presented by the national parliament". The definition was originally proposed in the government's draft of the Law and all members of the Pansus agreed on it. Debates about amnesty mainly focused on Article 29 on procedures. The article ended up specifying that an amnesty must be recommended by the TRC whether or not victims forgive the perpetrators, and is not given only when A perpetrator refuses to admit what he or she did and refuses to ask for forgiveness from victims.[9] The article is inconsistent with the main spirit of restorative justice whereby victims' interests and views should be prioritised as part of the healing process. The fact that amnesties are to be issued regardless of victims' views is especially problematic given that the TRC was supposedly established as a substitute for prosecutions and trials. With little prospect of facing punishment, perpetrators thus had little incentive to appear voluntarily before the TRC and apply for amnesty, unless their names happened to appear in an investigation report produced by the Commission

Based on the previous discussion of reconciliation and amnesty, I conclude that these two issues were inseparable from TRC functions but were interpreted differently by the human rights groups and by the political elite. For human rights advocates, both reconciliation and amnesty should be preconditioned by truth, and linked to requirements for accountability and prioritising the rights of the victims. For the elite, the two concepts were simply a means to political consolidation and a means to satisfy elements of the new and old regimes.

When the law was eventually issued as Law No. 27 of 2004 on the Truth and Reconciliation Commission, Indonesia had elected a new president through the country's first direct presidential election. President Susilo Bambang Yudhoyono did not immediately implement the law by establishing the TRC. The Law stipulated that the executive, i.e., Indonesia's president, had to establish the Commission within one year at the latest of the law being passed. He established a selection committee to recruit commissioners for the TRC through the Keppres (*Keputusan Presiden*, Presidential Decree) No. 7 of 2005. He also issued the Perpres (*Peraturan Presiden*, Presidential Regulation) No. 27 of 2005 on Procedures on Selection Processes and Recruitment of Members of TRC. However, it was only ten months after the Law was enacted that the open recruitment started, and a few months afterwards the recruitment committee came up with a list of 42 candidates from which the president was supposed to select the TRC's commissioners.

9 Article 9(1) (2) and (3), Law No. 27 of 2004 on TRC.

Meanwhile, however, human rights groups were criticising the law. They believed that conceptually and operationally, the law suffered from various flaws that could potentially damage the outcomes of truth and reconciliation. These included its mandates, processes, and outputs. In particular, human rights groups rejected the idea that for reparations and justice for victims could only be provided once amnesty had been granted to perpetrators. Dissatisfied with the potential damage to victims, human rights NGOs and victims' rights groups lodged a challenge to several aspects of the law with the Constitutional Court in 2005.

In December 2006, the Constitutional Court made a surprise ruling by annulling the entire law rather than dismissing specific disputed provisions.[10] The problematic provisions, according to Jimly Asshidique, the then Chair of Constitutional Court, were "at the heart of the law that obliterates the whole logic of the law ... Not only were they against the constitution but also against international laws" (interview with Jimly Asshidique in Jakarta, 2 May 2012).[11]

Following the decision, the Court recommended two options for the future: the passage of a new law or reconciliation efforts through policies of rehabilitation and amnesty.[12] Later on, the Ministry of Law and Human Rights chose the first option by re-drafting a new bill on the TRC and submitting it to the DPR for further discussion during the 2010–2014 parliamentary period. The drafting took more than three years, involving legal scholars led by Harkrituti Harkrisnowo, the General Director for Law and Human Rights of the Ministry of Law and Human Rights, who was also a senior scholar at the University of Indonesia. The drafting involved both government officials and civil society groups, and consultations with representatives from Aceh and Papua. The new draft contained some positive changes, particularly with regard to the exclusion of amnesty provisions (which was the main source of controversy in the previous

10 The decision states, "Whereas although the petition granted is only related to Article 27 of the TRC Law, however, as the overall implementation of the TRC Law depends on and must pass via the aforementioned article, the declaration that Article 27 of the TRC Law is inconsistent with the 1945 Constitution and does not have binding force renders all the provisions of the TRC Law unenforceable" Constitutional Court Decision No. 6/PUU-IV/2006, 24 (2006). http://www.mahkamahkonstitusi.go.id/public/content/persidangan/risalah/risalah_sidang_Risalah%20Perkara%20006.PUU-IV.2006,%20dan%208%20Desember%202006%20Putusan.pdf.

11 For a more detailed analysis of this decision and its implications, see ELSAM, *Ketika Prinsip Kepastian Hukum Menghakimi Konstitusionalitas Penyelesaian Pelanggaran HAM Masa Lalu: Pandangan Kritis atas Putusan Mahkamah Konstitusi dan Implikasinya bagi Penyelesaian Pelanggaran HAM* [When the Principle of Legal Certainty Undermines the Constitutionality of Resolving Past Human Rights Violations: A Critical View of the Constitutional Court's Decision and Implications for Resolution of Human Rights Violations].

12 See Summary of Constitutional Court Decision No. 006/PUU IV/2006 on the Law No. 27/2004 on the Truth and Reconciliation Commission, Constitutional Court, 7 December 2006.

law). The draft was eventually submitted to the parliament to be turned into a law. However, there it stagnated: at the time of writing this research, the draft has not yet been listed as priority for legislative action in parliament.

Evaluating the processes and outcomes of the adoption of the TRC Law

Having discussed the formulation and implementation of the Law on the TRC, we are now in a position to assess the processes and outcomes. First of all, I argue that, conceptually, the TRC as a transitional justice mechanism emphasises restorative justice, and thus has certain limitations. The case of the TRC Law in Indonesia reflected this situation. Second, I discuss the aspects derived from the nature of Indonesia's democratic transition that hindered the TRC mechanism from producing any substantive outcomes.

Acknowledging the limits of restorative justice

Controversies around the problematic clauses in the law and the ultimate failure to establish a TRC at all reflect the limitations of the restorative justice approach as a means of achieving transitional justice. The limitations derive mainly from the basic assumption that such a mechanism aims above all to heal the suffering of victims.

Human rights groups, including Komnas HAM, emphasised the basic restorative or healing principle in their proposals for a truth and reconciliation mechanism. In April 2006, human rights NGOs and representatives of victims successfully requested a judicial review of the 2004 TRC law, claiming that three provisions violated victims' constitutional right to remedy: (1) the TRC's power to recommend amnesties for perpetrators of serious crimes; (2) a provision that stated that cases dealt with by the TRC could not be prosecuted in court, and; (3) the requirement that victims would only receive compensation if the perpetrator of the crimes against them was given amnesty.[13] Human rights groups rightly argued that the law could potentially restrict the opportunities for achieving truth and justice for victims by preventing punishment, obscuring the truth, and providing total amnesty.

A deeper particular problem was that that TRC was designed in such a way to place the emphasis on victims' individual experiences and their need for healing, assuming that achieving these goals could be done impartially and independently from political influences. This approach had the potential to gain

13 For a more in-depth analysis on the weaknesses of this law, see Comment by the International Center for Transitional Justice on the Bill Establishing a Truth and Reconciliation Commission in Indonesia, http://www.ictj.org/static/Asia/Indonesia/050603.ICTJ.IndoTRCComment.eng.pdf.

social legitimacy and political support for the TRC and its processes, but at the cost of obscuring the political and historical context under which past human rights crimes had occurred. It left out the most innovative idea of a truth commission, namely the goal of evaluating past wrongs in order to make a political judgement about the regime that allowed them to occur. Such an evaluation should address the root causes of violence incorporating a clear-eyed evaluation of the political machinery and systematic violence of Indonesia's repressive New Order regime. No human rights group criticised the law for failing to make the achievement of such a political judgement a core objective of the TRC, though this in my view was one of its chief weaknesses. Achieving a political judgement and publicising that in the community is the foundation for one of the aims of transitional justice: the non-recurrence principle. The goal of any TRC should be to produce a reflective and critical history of the nation, uncovering the causes of past abuses, and in this way set moral standard for peace and accountability for the future democracy. For this reason, I argue that a TRC *should* be political, the processes involved in truth-seeking and its outcomes *should* be politicised, precisely because making a political judgement about what happened in the past needs to be a core goal of a TRC. The TRC needed to acknowledge a broader truth beyond the victims' individual suffering and their needs for healing, and could do that only by paying attention to the political dynamics and contexts of past abuses.

Of course, emphasising truth only with the goal of achieving victims' healing and reconciliation was a much more appealing goal for the politicians. It allowed them to avoid confronting the realities of Indonesia's violent past and its legacies in the post-Soeharto political landscape. It masked the power compromise that had been achieved between elements of the old repressive regime and the new post-1998 reform elite. Little wonder that these efforts to form a TRC failed to challenge the denial of past injustices—most obviously but not exclusively with regard to the 1965–1966 mass violence—which continued to made by many leading politicians, government officials, religious leaders, generals and other members of the political elite throughout this period.

Making a political judgement about the sources of past violence would help citizens to determine whether the new regime was indeed fully 'new', a regime that was born from a political break with the Soeharto period. Of course, the discussions and meetings held during the preparation of the law did not touch on such matters. The choice to not specifically define the temporal jurisdiction of the TRC was one indication that the designers of the Commission were steering away from making political judgements about the past regime. As explained above, the law did not stipulate the exact period of time to be covered by its investigations. The ICTJ pointed to this omission as one of the main challenges the TRC would face in establishing truth. According to them, "completion of the commission's mandate would be a daunting task, given that victims, witnesses, and evidence of the earliest violations would likely be unavailable" (Gonzáles, 2004: 9). Especially if the TRC wanted to investigate abuses that had occurred in the first two decades of Indonesia's history, its task would have been enormous.

Human rights abuses took place in various places against various backgrounds during the Soeharto regime. Some of them did not seem to even have any relation to one another. It is necessary, however, to set up a temporal jurisdiction based on important historical and political events to lead to a better explanation of the root causes of violations and to explain how the repressive regime worked in the past to wield its terror and repression. In the case of the New Order, the temporal jurisdiction should start from 1965 and run until 1998. In fact, human rights abuses have never been separated from the political dimension. This is especially true for gross human rights abuses, including genocide and crimes against humanity. Such crimes always involve the abuse of power by those in charge of state authority. By only focusing on individual experiences and reconciliation, members of the political promoting the TRC were trying to depoliticise the truth of past injustices, with the goal of maintaining 'national unity'. Not explicitly including 1965 in the temporal jurisdiction, suggests the drafters were not interested in seeking accountability from the old regime, the so-called New Order.

In the case of Indonesian TRC Law and its outcomes, the argument that victims' sufferings and justice were universal and thus should not be politicised as argued by NGOs such as KontraS and ELSAM fit well with the consensus among politicians that reconciliation was the priority for Indonesia. The aim of this consensus was not to agree to confront the evils of the past but to close the book on them and move forward as a nation and new regime. Human rights groups and politicians shared a common language of reconciliation and they even shared a similar definition of reconciliation and agreed on the same path for achieving it, namely amnesty. However, for the victims and human rights groups, amnesty should be granted only when certain conditions about truth-seeking and victims' rights had bene met. Politicians were only really interesting in granting an amnesty, which for them would be unconditional, and then to move forward to what were for them more important tasks of regime and nation building.

Transitional justice and the transplacement nature of democratisation

As already explained earlier, during the process of drafting the TRC politicians seemed to avoid emphasising the pursuit of truth. The discussions and meetings during the preparation of the law rarely touch on this goal. Stressing and defining truth in a comprehensive way would have meant revealing three things: the root causes of past violence, the political machinery used to carry out that violence, and the identities of the authority holders involved in decision-making and execution of violence. In other words, it would expose the repressive nature of the Soeharto regime and of the military. By avoiding trying to define this truth politicians revealed that they did not wish to make a clean break with the repressive regime. The legacies of the Soeharto regime remained strong precisely because, as I have repeatedly stressed throughout this book, there was a strong element of transplacement in Indonesia's political transition, which led to strong elements of continuity linking the new governments to the old authoritarian system.

One of the factors that leads to this conclusion is of course the presence of the military faction in the parliament. Between 1999 and 2004, the retained be representation in parliament as a result of the *dwifungsi* principle created by Soeharto. The members of parliament from the military faction represented their institution in all parliamentary decision-making processes. As the part of the institution that was the main perpetrator of past human rights abuses, it seemed to be impossible for these MPs to take a position to supporting truth-seeking as understood from the transitional justice perspective. Under pressure from civil society on the need for military reform and accountability, these members did not openly oppose the TRC legislation, but their comments and inputs during the process reflected that they sought to dampen its potential to dig out the truth about past events.

Aside from the role of the military in parliament, two other factors help explain why the TRC process veered away from confronting the truth of Indonesia's violent past. These were, first, the central role of presidential leadership and, second, the collusion among parties for the purposes of gaining access to power. On the first point, it was clear that the proclivities and interests of the president influence the decision and processes to establish TRC. This reflects the positive response to the initiative on the TRC. The Law was first drafted and most enthusiastically discussed during Wahid's presidency, which is not surprising given that Wahid was personally enthusiastic about the initiative. The process of legislating became slower when Wahid was impeached and Megawati, who was far more sympathetic to the military and more suspicious of human rights ideas, succeeded him. The process became even slower when it was time to implement the TRC under Yudhoyono's presidency. Yudhoyono did not seem to be interested in the TRC. He became even more disinterested when international attention focused on Indonesia in regard to the murder of Munir, the prominent human rights activist, on his flight to Amsterdam in September 2004. Suh (2012, 172) maintains that the shift of focus to Munir's case was one of the main reasons for the stagnation in the settlement of past cases of injustice through transitional justice mechanisms under Yudhoyono.

The second factor was collusion of power among parties, or what Slater (2004) refers to as the cartelisation of Indonesian politics. According to Slater, Indonesian parties in the post-Soeharto period exist in a symbiotic relationship with the state, estranged from society and dominated by public office-holders. The adoption of a *koalisi pelangi* (rainbow coalition) pattern in cabinet formation and the lack of effective oppositions in the DPR were indication of this practice. All three presidents after Habibie sought to maximise party involvement in their governments to ensure that their positions were secure and stable.

This situation made it hard to deal with past human rights abuses, as each presidential coalition contained elements that supported impunity. Wahid, for example, was known for his support for reconciliation through formal mechanisms such as a TRC and for promoting administrative reparation such as by rehabilitating ex-political prisoners and political exiles. However, the main opposition to such policies came from inside his own cabinet. Yusril Ihza Mahendra, for example, the then Ministry of Law, was known to be a strong opponent of any idea of reconciliation with anyone accused of being a PKI member. He was also reluctant to implement Wahid's policy to bring home 1965 political exiles. Mahendra was blunt in his opinion on the limits of the idea of reconciliation:

> That people have to forgive each other, that is humane and ethical. But 'reconciliation' with PKI figures and members, in a sense of national reconciliation to share power for the state's and society's interest, has no urgency now. There is no rationale for that ...What happened was that the PKI was the losing party. Its power was crushed. The teachings of Marxism and Leninism were strictly forbidden. This was a constitutional decision. Marxism and Leninism are principally against the state philosophy of Pancasila. Communists are anti-democratic. In the democratic system adopted under the 1945 Constitution, anti-democracy groups have no rights to live (Mahendra, 2004: 93–94).

Similar dynamics also influenced the implementation of the Law during Megawati's and Yudhoyono's presidencies, each of which with their cabinets also involving a large representation of strongly anti-communist Islamic leaders, Golkar politicians, former military officers, and others with personal connections to the New Order regime.

The absence of a truth mechanism and its implications for Indonesia's democracy

What did it mean for Indonesia's democratic transition that the country ended up without a TRC? Three implications stand out, which we can address now in turn.

The absence of political judgement

In my view the critical consequence of the failure of the TRC in Indonesia was that the country was deprived of the most obvious and convenient means to form a collective political judgement about the past. By political judgement I mean a definitive moral and analytical assessment about just what it was in the past political system, institutions, values, and behaviours that authorised systematic violence and abuse. Such a judgement is needed in Indonesia, as in other countries transitioning away from violence, in order for the nation to agree to avoid repetition of violence in the future and agree upon new systems, institutions, values and behaviours that will help it achieve that goal.

In my view, one of the limitations of the human rights approach to transitional justice in general is that it emphasises victims' sufferings and needs above systemic change. Remedies, or reparations, rightly aim at healing individual victims, and to help them to survive in their daily lives, to overcome their trauma, and to integrate back into their own society. This approach is important, but it is not enough. In this view, truth and justice should not be politicised because justice is pure—there has been some debate about this (Humphrey, 2008; Meister, 2002). In fact, systems of justice are never separate from politics. This is especially true for a transitioning country like Indonesia.

The absence of deliberative space to reflect history and moral standards

One of the innovative aspect of restorative justice is that it emphasises both process and values, with the goal of restoring, or healing, the damage caused by a crime. The core of the process is inclusion of every party involved in the wrongdoing, including victims, perpetrators, bystanders and so on. The meeting of all these parties forms part of the healing process. It allows everyone to tell their stories and to engage in dialogue with each other in an equal setting. The best options for reparations often arise from such a process, reparations that not only the meet the victims' needs but also reinforce to the perpetrator the wrongs in what they did. Such processes can also thus potentially help create new values of justice and humanity among those involved.

Agus Widjojo, a former military general whose father was among the six generals murdered on 30 September 1965 said during an interview,

> I was also a victim, the first victim. I lost my father very early in the morning of the 30th of September. So who's included as a victim? ...What we need now is to have more spaces where we can have a dialogue on the past, on what happened and what we experienced. There is no single truth. But from there we can learn each other (interview with Agus Widjojo in Jakarta, 1 May 2012).

A TRC could serve as the space he referred to, because it would allow a series of deliberative meetings where truth can be presented in the form of dialogues. Such participatory involvement of many parties fulfils the aspect of deliberation in restorative justice not only in terms of process but also in terms of value generation because it facilitates "mutual understanding and expressions of remorse, compassion, apology and forgiveness, which may lead to reparative agreements and feelings of respect, peace, and satisfaction" (Walgrave, 2011: 95). The absence of a TRC has greatly narrowed the space for such value generation in post-Soeharto Indonesia.

Local TRCs

Even though the annulled Law on the TRC did not specifically mention the adoption of TRCs at local levels, other laws did for provide for the adoption of such institutions in the major conflict areas of Aceh and Papua.[14] In an attempt to resolve division and conflict in these regions, the Special Autonomy Law for Papua passed in 2001 and the Law on Governing Aceh (LOGA), passed in 2006, provided for the establishment of local TRCs, although a TRC has never been set up in neither of these places.

In 2001, when the Law on the TRC was still in the drafting stage in the executive, both the DPR and government committed to the Papuans that they would deal with human rights abuses that had occurred in the in the territory. The commitment was integrated in Law No. 21 of 2001 on Special Autonomy for Papua which mentions three mechanisms: establishment of a representative office of Komnas HAM in Papua, the establishment of a human rights court in the territory, and the formation of a TRC there. The adoption of a TRC is mentioned in Article 46 of the Law, which stated that it was to be established to “conduct historical clarification” aimed at strengthening the nation’s unity within the NKRI and also to achieve reconciliation through truth-seeking, apologies, forgiveness, peace, amnesties, and reparations. The ‘historical clarification’ mentioned here was an allusion to the 1969 *Pepera* (*Penentuan endapat rakyat*, Act of Free Choice), by which Papua was formally integrated into Indonesia, and which remains controversial among Papuans in terms of both its legality and the human rights violations that accompanied it. According to the law, the formation of a TRC would be proposed by the Governor of Papua.[15]

In 2006, between the time of the implementation of the TRC Law and the process of judicial review, the Indonesian parliament and government issued Law

14 Another TRC, the CAVR, was also established to look into human rights abuses in East Timor. The UN established this commission under its truth-seeking mandate in the newly independent Democratic Republic of Timor-Leste. As such, it was not an Indonesian transitional justice mechanism, although its findings significantly implicated Indonesian institutions and leaders in abuses in East Timor. For a more specific discussion of the CAVR, see Priscilla Hayner. *Unspeakable Truths: Transitional Justice and the Challenge of Truth Commissions* (2nd Ed., pp. 39–42). New York: Routledge, 2011).

15 Indeed, there is confusion on the jurisdiction of the Law that implicates to the realisation for establishment of TRC. The Law acknowledges Papua Province, headed by a Papuan governor. However, in 2003 President Megawati enacted President’s Instruction (Inpres) No. 1 year 2003 on the establishment of West Papua Province, following the Law No. 45 year 1999 on the dissolution of Papua Province. The Law was opposed by Papuan leaders, and no less than a hundreds of Papuan leaders (Tim 100) met President Habibie to urge for referendum as they opposed the Law. Following Megawati’s Inpres, some Papuan figures opposed it and appealed the Law to the Constitutional Court. The Court annulled the Law, but ironically Jakarta still acknowledged West Papua Province. Despite of the unsettled controversies among the Papuans, the West Papua Province now has its own governor, parliament, and people’s council (Majelis Rakyat Papua or MRP).

No. 11 of 2006 on Governance of Aceh (LoGA). The law was implemented the 2005 Memorandum of Understanding (MoU) signed by the Indonesian government and the Free Aceh Movement in Helsinki to end the three decades of conflict in the territory. Article 229 of the LoGA mentions the adoption of an Aceh-based TRC with the goals of seeking truth and conducting reconciliation. Unlike Papua, the law states that Aceh's TRC will be integrated in the national TRC. That provision meant that the annulment of the national TRC Law placed obstacles in the way of the formation of a TRC in Aceh. However, human rights groups and victims' rights groups in Aceh had a different interpretation of the article. They saw the article as referring to the administration of the institution and not affect its legal base. In 2006, NGOs formed a civil society coalition called KPK (*Koalisi Pengungkapan Kebenaran*, Coalition for Truth-seeking) and over subsequent years organised various meetings and consultations before proposing their draft for a TRC in Aceh to both Aceh's parliament and executive in 2008. After a long process, the local parliament eventually passed a *qanun* or local bylaw on an Aceh TRC in December 2013. After that, implementation was slow, but in 2016, three years after the *qanun* was passed, seven commissioners were selected by an independent committee and inaugurated by the local government. The execution of their mandate remains a problem as the Qanun was considered weak by both national and local government due to the legal problem mentioned earlier.[16]

Conclusion

In this chapter, I have discussed the adoption and implementation of Indonesia's TRC Law, prior to the annulment of that Law by the Constitutional Court. Truth and reconciliation had become important topics of public debate from the beginning of the political transition in 1998. Human rights advocates and students regarded a mechanism for truth and reconciliation as a suitable option by which to require the state and its officers and officials to acknowledge past injustices and to serve as a basis for other transitional justice mechanisms including reparations and prosecutions.

The political elite adopted the idea, but it was far more interested in the idea of reconciliation than truth, let alone prosecutions. Members of not only the new, emerging political elite but also holdovers from the Soeharto era responded to mounting public pressure to adopt such a TRC mechanism. In doing so, they promoted a different sort of public discourse, one in which reconciliation was given a different meaning, implying a process of forgetting and forgiving that would close the door on past conflicts and thus encourage unity among Indonesians. What they actually implied in that notion of reconciliation was an

16 This analysis is based on meetings with several commissioners of the Aceh TRC, especially Afridal Darmi and Evi Zain, between February and May 2017 in both Aceh and Jakarta.

opportunity for political reconciliation between the elements of the New Order and the new democratic regime.

This understanding of truth and reconciliation dominated the process of drafting of the Bill on the TRC. Unlike the preparation of the Law on Human Rights and Human Rights Courts, which took only a few months, the preparation of the TRC bill dragged on for four years, involving various elements including human rights groups, academics, and even representatives of other countries in their public consultations. When it passed, it finally included safeguards that were designed to ensure the TRC would not lead to punishment of officials for past human rights abuses, leading to its eventual demise before the Constitutional Court. With so much time passed since the collapse of the New Order, the regime's political legitimacy crisis had faded, there was less public pressure to deal with past human rights abuses, and so the idea of a national TRC quietly died.

Chapter 5

Human rights groups and transitional justice initiatives

> We [human rights activists] tend to want everything to be put in place. Prosecutions, truth commissions, and everything else, all at the same time, without acknowledging the political dynamics within the transition itself (interview with Ifdhal Kasim in Jakarta, 22 September 2014).

Introduction

The previous two chapters discussed state-sponsored transitional justice mechanisms that were problematic in terms of their implementation and resulted in failure in terms of their outcomes. This chapter elaborates on the role played by civil society groups in promoting the transitional justice agenda during the political transition, and their strategies for advocating the adoption and implementation of mechanisms by the new governments as well as demanding state accountability for past human rights violations. My aim is to understand how such mobilisation affected the successes and failures of transitional justice implementation.

Civil society groups, which will be recalled from Chapter 1 that Aspinall (2005) described as a *proto-opposition*, played a significant role in Indonesia's democratisation. They set the democratic agenda by popularising the idea of transitional justice during the early years of political transition and keeping that agenda alive throughout that time. Suh (2012) argues that the human rights NGOs were the main factor that influenced the government to adopt human rights measures and policies, including the ratification of international human rights laws and the drafting of domestic laws related to transitional justice mechanisms. Despite the fact that Indonesia was a latecomer democracy and was so able to benefit from practices of transitional justice pioneered elsewhere and had support of international organisations and donors, she argues that human rights NGOs play important roles as norm entrepreneurs. They helped to drive these changes by changing the way the public felt about human rights and by pushing the state to change its behaviour.[1]

1 Suh adopted the concept of normalisation and norm entrepreneurs from International Relations theory, especially work produced by Finnemore and Sikkink (1998).

I argue in this chapter that the human rights groups found that their interests converged with the interests of the new political elite in the early years of the political transition. Human rights groups tried to push for a thoroughgoing change of the political system, so thorough that it would have amounted to a regime replacement. However, the strong elements of continuity with the former authoritarian regime hindered their achievement of their goals, while the semi-oppositional groups, moving into positions of power themselves, adopted and adjusted the transitional justice agenda as part of their bargaining with old regime elements. Further, I argue that human rights groups failed to anticipate or identify the change that occurred from a replacement to transplacement style transition, shortly after the 1999 election, which later caused the failure of implementation of transitional justice. From this time on, pressures from below for radical change began to dissipate, and members of the new political elite moving into the DPR and other positions of political power became increasingly interested in making peace with holdovers from the old regime, rather than challenging them.

As I have briefly mentioned in Chapter 1, both NGOs and victims of human rights abuse often acknowledge that the nature of Indonesia's political transition was a factor affecting transitional justice outcomes. But they often merely paid lip service to political analysis rather than integrating it into their understanding of what must and could be achieved. Their miscalculation about the nature of Indonesia's political transition caused them to miscalculate what they could achieve and this led them to make poor decisions. Moreover, human rights groups also lacked leadership and coordination, allowing different and conflicting strategies and approaches to frustrate their common objectives. Bu their failures of achieving their objectives in terms of state-sponsored transitional justice led human rights groups to focus on strengthening and intensifying advocacy at the grassroots level.

The first part of the chapter discusses Indonesian civil society and shows how various NGOs and activist groups *politicised* the human rights agenda during the Soeharto regime. For them, human rights was not merely a legal, let alone a technical issue, but a large issue that raised fundamental problems about the nature of the political system and which led them to see the need for large-scale political transformation. The second section looks at the role of civil society and the human rights movement during *reformasi* and beyond. A third section discusses the approaches and strategies used by these groups in promoting different, sometimes conflicting, transitional justice agendas and strategies. Unlike other studies on this particular topic, I focus on the engagement (or disengagement) of the human rights groups with elements of the political elite. I divide my discussion into two parts: approaches and strategies used during the early years of transition (the period of momentous change) and the period after that (of stalled reform). I also assess how the adoption of such approaches and strategies contributed to the overall poor results of transitional justice implementation. Finally, the chapter ends with a conclusion.

Human rights movements before *reformasi*

To understand the roles played by human rights groups in Indonesia's democratisation, we need to look back at their emergence and the roles they played in criticising the government and promoting human rights discourse in the late New Order years. Human rights groups, as part of a larger network of civil society groups, constituted what Aspinall (2005: 9) refers to as a *proto-opposition*: groups which had fundamental criticisms of the regime but which had limited and partial practical aims, trying to achieve short-term goals, including concessions, policy changes, and greater state accountability rather than engaging in frontal assaults on the regime or trying to overthrow it. These organisations were relatively independent from state structures, but they avoided confrontation with the state and often presented themselves as 'complementary' to the state. However, they were *proto-opposition* groups, because

> despite their partial aims, civil society organizations can become a refuge for many and varied oppositional impulses (...). They can harbour individuals who aim to transform, even overthrow, the authoritarian regime (Aspinall, 2005: 9).

Human rights groups as such did not exist in the early years of the nation's independence. In fact, human rights were not elaborated by the new country's leaders when they drafted the constitution. However, the constitution acknowledged basic freedoms of speech, association, religion, equality before the law and rights to work. Simpson (2013: 188) notes there was from the start a tension between a pro-western conception of human rights adhering to individuals and promoted by people such as the country's first vice president, Hatta, and an 'integralist' approach based on "the doctrine of the family principle, not on the doctrine of individualism" associated with other leaders such as Soekarno and Soepomo. During the early post-independence period, he further notes, the constitutions of 1949 and 1950 drew upon Western European constitutions and integrated many articles from the Universal Declaration of Human Rights (UDHR) that covered more explicit human rights protections (Simpson, 2013: 188).

Liberal voices on human rights grew louder during the debates about establishing a permanent constitution in Indonesia's first constituent assembly (Konstituante) that was elected in 1955 and sat between 1956 and 1959. The Konstituante agreed on a list of 22 civil and political rights to be integrated into the constitution from the UDHR, including articles that accommodated demands from women's groups and Chinese Indonesian organisations that sought acknowledgement of individual rights such as equal marriage and minority rights, despite some members arguing that such rights were incompatible with Indonesia's notion of collective rights and the status of Islam as the majority religion (Simpson, 2013: 188).

Internationally, during this period various postcolonial countries were insisting in the UN and other forums that the right of self-determination should be treated as a basic human right. Indonesia was also a strong supporter as the country needed international acknowledgement of its struggle for independence. Indonesian diplomats not only argued against inclusion of a so-called colonial clause limiting the reach of the UDHR in non-self-governing territories, they also endorsed self-determination as "a prerequisite for the full enjoyment of all fundamental human rights" (Simpson, 2013: 189).

In 1959, Soekarno ended parliamentary democracy and inaugurated the period known as "Guided Democracy",[2] limiting space for political debates on human rights. The president also introduced restrictions on freedom of speech and the press. Such policies were associated with his promotion of an ideological output which claimed to be based on the adaptation of traditional values, and which viewed human rights as a set of 'family rights' rather than individual rights. H.J.C. Princen, a human rights activist who had been a Dutch soldier but defected in order to fight on the Indonesian side, was imprisoned for criticising Soekarno's authoritarianism and his regime's restrictions on freedom of speech and the press (Simpson, 2013: 189).

Even though human rights were restricted under Guided Democracy, as Simpson (2013: 189) explains, throughout the 1949–1965 period human rights issues were central to public debate, and mass movements as well as organisations invoked them in the context of popular mobilisations such as those promoting land reform. This situation changed after 1965 and the transition of power from Soekarno to Soeharto.

Some scholars have acknowledged that members of the public, including students and other groups who favoured the transition to a New Order, demanded human rights accountability during the early Soeharto years. Todung Mulya Lubis (1993) notes that in the early New Order years, many people opposed Soekarno's Guided Democracy and saw Soeharto's leadership as allowing a revival of human rights. The new elite in parliament expressed their commitment to human rights while accusing the ousted government of responsibility for various human rights abuses (Lubis, 1993: 127–128). These elite appealed to the aspirations of Muslim groups who had been excluded during Soekarno's time, and in some cases had experienced human rights violations, and yet had participated in the 1965–1966 mass killings because they saw taking action against Communists as an opportunity for revenge (Boland, 1971).

2 Soekarno believed that parliamentary democracy was derived from the West and was not appropriate for Indonesia as it resulted in political instability. He opted for a system based on the traditional village system of discussion and consensus, and proposed a threefold blend of nationalism (*nasionalisme*), religion (*agama*), and communism (*komunisme*), into a cooperative "nasakom" government.

These dynamics motivated a series of discussions and seminars in the early years of the new regime whose participants demanded inclusion of human rights provisions in the blueprints for the new regime. These events included a Persahi (*Perhimpunan Sarjana Hukum Indonesia*, Indonesia's, Lawyers Association) national congress, which passed a resolution calling for the adoption of the Universal Declaration of Human Rights by the MPRS. The government responded by requesting the MPRS to establish guidelines that included provisions on human rights in accordance with Pancasila and the 1945 Constitution. As quoted in Lubis (1993: 129), the then Chair of the MPRS A.H. Nasution stated that the MPRS was going to establish a Human Rights Charter. The drafting of the Charter was completed in a year, led by Adnan Buyung Nasution, a human rights lawyer who was a member of parliament. The draft was titled *Piagam Hak-hak Asasi Manusia dan Hak-hak Manusia serta Kewajiban Warga Negara*, or the Charter of Human Rights and the Rights and Responsibilities of Citizens, and, unlike most human rights charters, integrated both rights and responsibilities of every citizen.

Even though there was no disagreement about the importance of the Human Rights Charter, the Charter was abandoned and not passed by the MPRS when it convened in 1968. This outcome was a big disappointment for supporters of human rights, especially those who were involved in drafting the Charter. In Lubis's words, this was "a devastating defeat which will not be forgotten" (Lubis, 1993: 144). Two dominant pro-government factions, the military and Golkar, opposed the Charter. Instead, the agenda of the Assembly was dominated by discussion of the PKI's alleged "illegal attempted coup" in October 1965.

Before long, state officials began to look more negatively on the concept of human rights and saw it as potentially subversive of the state's authority. Human rights were acknowledged in general and abstract terms, but their implementation was regulated and limited by the state. This approach derived from the organicist state ideology promoted by the regime (Bourchier, 1996) which viewed the state as a family where everyone was an insider and partner. The state was seen as the embodiment of the entire people, serving as the father or guardian. The view was initially proposed by Soepomo but also voiced by Soekarno and later Soeharto. In such a worldview, the state was the source of all rights, and individual rights could only be recognised if the state allowed and endorsed them. In the following years, legal products and policies were developed to deny the very concept of individual rights.

Soeharto maintained his power by using the security forces to ensure stability and development, which basically meant suppressing basic rights of freedom of expression and association. The military, especially the army, frequently exercised its power to crush any opposition, using violence when necessary. Denial of human rights was made systematic and justified in the name of development and stability, the core slogan justifying the regime's agenda of military-led modernisation.

Although popular mobilisation was repressed during the New Order period, lawyers, former student activists and others were able to form non-government organisations (NGOs). NGOs started to be recognised in the early 1970s and later experienced significant growth by connecting their activities to the development programmes carried out by the Soeharto government (Aspinall, 2005; Eldridge, 1995, Hadiwinata, 2003, Uhlin, 1997). Until the 1990s, Indonesian NGOs had different foci and approaches. Aspinall (2005) divided them into NGOs that focused on development, adopting more practical approaches to empowering poor communities, and 'rights-oriented' NGOs which focused on more specific topics such as the promotion of the rights of farmers, workers, women, and consumers. In the early 1990s, with growing numbers of critical middle-class intellectuals, limited space for them in the formal political institutions and the growing authoritarianism in the New Order, NGOs became more critical of government policies (Antlöv, Ibrahim, and van Tuijl, 2006: 4; Aspinall, 2005: 88–89). NGOs began to be seen as anti-government institutions.

Human Rights NGOs and their transnational networks had long been engaged in criticising Soeharto's policies and the New Order regime in general. As discussed in Chapter 2, the earliest, and the largest, human rights NGO established during the New Order period was the LBH (which later became YLBHI). The organisation, and later followed by other organisations as discussed in Chapter 2, was very critical of the regime. But despite their criticisms, LBH and most other NGOs, and civil society organisations in general, only criticised prevailing political mechanisms without challenging the right of the government to rule. As Meuthia Ganie Rochman (2002: 127) points out,

> For the NGOs, it would be politically naïve to challenge the government, not only because they were unsure about how other social groups would react, particularly in light of the fact that the politically aware middle class and bourgeois institutions, which should have been beyond state control, were in fact weak and subordinated to state control.

When viewed against the broader developments in the international human rights movement, NGOs in Indonesia provide a good example of how transnational advocacy networks can play an active role in shaping both domestic politics and foreign policies. Transnational activism, which includes advocacy, is broadly defined by Piper and Uhlin (2004: 4–5) as social movements and other civil society organisations and individuals operating in networks that cross state borders. In many cases, including Indonesia, transnational activism often plays a significant role in domestic political change.

Jetschke's (1999) study on human rights and security, for example, highlights important periods under the New Order when the Indonesian state was forced to change its policies on human rights as concessions to pressures from transnational advocacy networks and political pressures from western countries and donors. The first case was the release of communist political prisoners in the

1980s; the second was in response to the Dili massacre in 1991 which resulted in the establishment of Komnas HAM as explained in Chapter 2 (See also Jetschke, 2011). The establishment of Komnas HAM set an example of how tactical concessions made by the state to outside pressure could provide opportunities for advancing and institutionalising human rights concerns during the final years of the repressive regime. When the regime eventually collapsed in 1998 and was replaced by a more liberal democratic regime, such opportunities widened greatly. During the democratic transition, the ruling elite needed to make many tactical concessions to maintain or gain legitimacy.

Human rights and the transitional justice agenda during the democratic transition

Human rights groups were part of a much larger civil society which played a significant role during the democratic transition in Indonesia, especially by putting key issues at the heart of the reform agenda including human rights accountability. After Habibie opened up political space and granted basic freedoms of expression and association in 1998, civil society sector grew in size and in the scope of their work (Antlöv, Ibrahim, and van Tuijl, 2006). Civil society organisations included non-governmental organisations, religious organisations, mass-based membership organisations, unions, professional groups, and so on. The BPS (*Badan Pusat Statistik*, Indonesian Bureau of Statistics) noted a massive growth in the number of NGOs from 10,000 in 1996 to 70,000 in 2000 (Setiawan, 2014).

This massive growth of NGOs, however, did not involve major changes in their structure. NGOs maintained their structural independence from the state during the authoritarian period and, because of that, when the old regime collapsed, NGOs were not implicated in its misdeeds. Unlike established political institutions and elites linked to Soeharto, who experienced a legitimacy crisis after the fall of their patron, NGOs expanded their activities and numbers, assisted by new funding from international and private donors. *Reformasi* gave them more space to articulate their criticisms of the old regime and provide inputs to the new regime without having to confront the state or fear its repression. Accordingly, the scholarly literature is generally positive on the roles played by NGOs during *reformasi*. Antlöv, Ibrahim, and van Tuijl (2006: 4), for example, mention that the transition to democracy would have taken longer and been more difficult had it not been for the voluntarism and commitment among the NGOs. Not surprisingly, NGOs played an important role in negotiating and reformulating the balance of power between state and citizens.

Some works discuss the strategies applied by NGOs in the post-Soeharto period. Aspinall (2004), argues that NGOs maintained strategies that were fundamentally similar to what they had done under the New Order: articulating short-term and partial goals of gaining state concessions, policy changes and greater accountability. Most NGOs actively engaged with the state and articulated their interests to the state openly, rather than being estranged from formal political processes, especially at the national level. Aspinall highlights this approach as a main feature of civil society groups in the post-Soeharto period, most of which shared a consensus that the state and social order after 1998 were fundamentally legitimate, and that "the primary aims of politics were conceived as pressuring, lobbying, or otherwise influencing the state to achieve desirable policy outcomes" (Aspinall, 2004:75).

Other observers propose different arguments in regard to the roles and strategies adopted by NGOs under the new democracy. They suggest that during this early period, some of these organisations avoided working with government institutions and chose to be watchdog organisations as an expression of their distrust of the new regime. Instead, they preferred to build solidarity with, and mobilise, victims or the grassroots, ignoring representative bodies including political parties (Farid and Simarmata, 2004; Priyono, Samadhi, and Törnquist, 2007). This refusal to engage with official politics was a feature which differentiates Indonesian approaches from the human rights strategies used by activists in Latin American countries during their post-authoritarian transitions.[3] This approach had two effects, according to Priyono. By focusing only on victims and victims' empowerment, activist groups ensured that issues of past injustice and the need for state accountability would become their exclusive concern, rather than being linked with the general population and their interests. Second, working only with the victims and grassroots communities without making links with formal political institutions undermined the potential of these activists to achieve institutional and legal reforms.[4]

My research indicates that all of these arguments on NGO roles and strategies can be applied to the issue of transitional justice. Both human rights NGOs and victims' groups shared the same approach in relation to the state and in articulating their interests. NGOs worked independently and voluntarily in pushing for a reform agenda through a 'dual-track' strategy—lobbying the upper political elite to influence them to adopt a reform agenda, and working independently from any elite group to empower grassroot communities. During the early years of transition, human rights groups were mostly focused on working with the political elite for the adoption and implementation of transitional justice mechanisms. When that failed, these groups put more emphasis on developing initiatives to

3 See for example the discussion in Teitel, Ruti G. "How are the New Democracies of the Southern Cone Dealing with the Legacy of Past Human Rights Abuses." In N. J. Kritz (Ed.), *Transitional Justice: How Emerging Democracies Reckon with Former Regimes* (pp. 146–153). Washington: U.S. Institute of Peace Press, 1995.

4 Priyono, A.E, *Demiliterisasi dan Keadilan Transisional dalam Proses Demokratisasi di Indonesia* (Demiliterization and Transitional Justice in Democratisation Process in Indonesia). http://www.demosindonesia.org/diskursus/3074-demiliterisasi-dan-keadilan-transisional-dalam-proses-demokratisasi-di-indonesia.html (16), also in an interview on 16 May 2012 in Jakarta.

work 'from below' at the grassroots level. This 'dual-track' strategy was necessary because, as mentioned by Galuh Wandita,

> Unlike during Soeharto's time, after *Reformasi* some of the civil society elements chose to work with or become the new political elite, for better or for worse. But this could be a disadvantage, because it could lead to neglect of the link to the grassroots. Therefore we needed to ensure that civil society used the opportunities at the upper level, working with or becoming part of the elite, but at the same time there should also be organizations that work with the grassroots as well. And organizations working at both levels need to collaborate well. We need to work "dual-track" to ensure the reform agenda works in the new democracy (interview with Galuh Wandita in Jakarta, 12 March 2012).

In this section, I discuss the roles and strategies human rights groups adopted in two different periods: the early years of transition (the momentous change period) and subsequent years (when reform stagnated and then stopped).

Human rights groups, the new political elite, and transitional justice agenda in the early transition

Human rights groups tried to push for a reform of government practices so thorough that it would have amounted to regime replacement. They did this by advocating the achievement of what the Soeharto regime had always managed to avoid: human rights accountability. The politics of the human rights movement was effective in injecting into the transition strong call for such accountability. Human rights groups believed one of the earliest agenda items for the new democracy was to ensure state responsibility for past human rights abuses by way of adoption and implementation of transitional justice. Transitional justice, for these groups, provided the platform for a clean break with the old regime and an agenda for thorough reform.

Komnas HAM did the same by establishing the Surabaya Principles on Transitional Justice in November 2000. The Principles were a result of Komnas HAM's fourth annual national meeting titled "*Transitional Justice Menentukan Kualitas Demokrasi Indonesia di Masa Depan*" or "Transitional Justice Determines the Quality of Indonesian Democracy in the Future" (interview with Enny Soprapto in Jakarta, 29 March 2012).[5] Komnas HAM included elements of both state and civil society in the meeting. The principles were a blueprint for a transitional justice agenda, which included seven commitments: (1) respect for human

5 The meeting was attended by Mary Robinson, the United Nations High Commissioner. The meeting agreed on the establishment of a Transitional Justice Society, a community of experts and practitioners that would work together on the transitional justice agenda. See also Komnas HAM report, *Prinsip-Prinsip Surabaya mengenai Transitional Justice di Indonesia*, Jakarta, 2000.

dignity and to stand with victims of human rights abuses, (2) ensuring victims' participation in efforts on transitional justice policy making and implementation, (3) seeking accountability from the regime and individuals involved in past human rights abuses, (4) public transparency, (5) guarantees of non-recurrence of serious human rights abuses, (6) state and individual acknowledgements in public of past abuses, and (7) reparations for the victims of human rights abuses (Komnas HAM, 2000a). With these commitments, Komnas HAM and human rights group came together to demand a far-reaching transitional justice agenda.

Achieving transitional justice seemed possible after Habibie allowed a referendum in East Timor and established a joint inquiry team to look into the 1984 Tanjung Priok massacre. As discussed in Chapter 3, the investigation of the mass violence during and after the 1999 East Timor referendum triggered domestic demands for a similar investigation into the 1984 Tanjung Priok massacre. In contrast to the weak public and elite support for the East Timor process, there was wide support for investigations and trials for Tanjung Priok. In Chapter 3, I argued that this support was possible because of a contingent meeting of the interests of human rights groups and elements of the new elite. Even though these elite were fundamentally interested in short-term goals and gaining political legitimacy, their support became a push factor for the government to adopt some transitional justice measures. These included the passage of the Law on Human Rights and the Law on Human Rights Courts, with the latter needed to pave the way for trials in both of these cases, and the Law on the Truth and Reconciliation Commission—which was much more delayed, precisely because it stretched into the period of consolidation of the new political order.

It is important to note that NGOs did not establish a platform for working together to achieve their transitional justice goals, nor did they pause to analyse and evaluate the processes and outcomes of their activities. This is a feature identified by Mikaela Nyman (2006), and it reflects the fragmentation of Indonesian civil society. The disunity of the elements within civil society made it difficult to cooperate on day-to-day issues on democratic reform, even though the call to remove Soeharto's regime had previously united them as a movement. When it came to prioritising goals and activities, NGOs had different expectations, and their goals and strategies sometimes clashed. The most notable example was the competing emphases on trials and prosecutions versus truth and reconciliation. On this critical strategic choice, the perspectives of two of Indonesia's most important human rights NGOs diverged: the first approach was advocated by the KontraS (*Komisi Nasional untuk Orang Hilang dan Korban Kekerasan*, National Commission for Enforced Disappearance and Victims of Violence) and the latter was articulated by the ELSAM.[6] During the periods of momentous change and compromised

6 KontraS was established in 1998 as a transformation of KIP-HAM, the Independent Commission for the Monitoring of Human Rights Violations, a coalition of non-governmental organizations concerned on the increased violence by government during 1997 election where there

reform (i.e., the periods of transitional justice between 1998 and 2009 discussed in Chapter 2), KontraS was the lead civil society organisation articulating the position that prosecutions were the best way to settle past human rights abuses, despite the organisation's scepticism about the corrupt and inept legal system in Indonesia (Farid and Simarmata, 2004). When the political elite became concerned about the international attention on human rights accountability for the serious crimes that took place in East Timor, KontraS and particularly its chairperson, Munir, consistently supported the establishment of human rights courts that would deal with various cases of past human rights abuses, especially cases they campaigned on such as Tanjung Priok, Talangsari, East Timor, Aceh and enforced disappearances. Munir was also a member of the drafting of the Human Rights Court Bill established by the Minister of Law and Human Rights (see discussion in Chapter 3).

For KontraS, the goal of having human rights courts was not merely to deprive the military courts of their authority in terms of human rights accountability, but also to put into effect an international standard of criminal justice that could increase possibilities of punishing high-ranking generals and decision makers by taking command responsibility and crimes of omission into account (Suh, 2012: 134). KontraS strongly supported prosecution because there was an opportunity for human rights courts to be effective due to the weakening of the military and the strengthening of demands for human rights accountability (Fernida, email on 1 August 2017).

This stance was debated by some other groups, most notably ELSAM, which argued that truth-seeking, was the first step towards justice, and thus a national truth and reconciliation commission was needed. In addition to its participation in the official drafting team (discussed in Chapter 4), ELSAM prepared its own draft law on the TRC, involving international experts on transitional justice and a series of meetings with victims' rights groups (Suh, 2012: 144–145). Its former director, Ifdhal Kasim, admitted that the South African model inspired their initial conceptualisation of a TRC. However, he added that the Indonesian TRC needed to be adjusted beyond the South African model by learning best practices from other TRCs (interview, 20 September 2004). As I discussed in the previous chapter, Kasim drew the basic idea of a TRC from Huntington, arguing that amnesty was a necessary evil during the political transition (Kasim, 2000b). He later suggested a 'third way' which refers to the complementarity of different transitional justice measures, but he always acknowledged the strong political influences of old regime forces such as Golkar and the military would make transitional justice difficult (Kasim and Terre, 2003a).

had been cases of oppositions such as activists, students, and party members, were forcedly disappeared. See their profile at http://www.KontraS.org/eng/index.php?hal=profile. ELSAM was established earlier in 1993 by some prominent lawyers and human rights advocates, aimed at promoting and protecting civil and political rights of Indonesian citizens. See http://www.ELSAM.or.id/.

Suh (2012) discusses the different approaches of these two NGOs as an example of how NGOs as norm entrepreneurs could pursue plural models of justice adopted from transitional justice practices in other transitioning countries such as Argentina and South Africa. KontraS activists strongly believed that they needed to press ahead in order to assert basic principles of justice during the transition and to establish precedents that could be used to prevent future human rights abuses. ELSAM, by contrast, believed that it was essential to take into account the continuing strength of standpatter, conservative elements in the ruling elite, and move more slowly in promoting human rights protection.

In terms of strategy, all NGOs similarly emphasised the importance of working with elements within the government and political elite. Most of them pursued a strategy of working with government and the new political elite by lobbying for the formal adoption of human rights and transitional justice measures into law and to otherwise take action on past abuses. They actively lobbied both the executive and legislature to seriously deal with cases such as the East Timor abuses, the 1984 Tanjung Priok massacre, the 1998 kidnappings of activists, the Trisakti and Semanggi shootings, and the conflicts in Aceh and Papua. NGOs also contributed directly to the drafting of human rights laws such as the Law on Human Rights and the TRC Law.

Two cases illustrate the success and failure of the adoption of this strategy: the 1984 Tanjung Priok massacre and the Trisakti, Semanggi I and Semanggi II shootings. The leading NGO involved in advocacy on the 1984 Tanjung Priok massacre was KontraS. Initially, KontraS focused on the East Timor violence, especially after its Coordinator, Munir, became a member of the Komnas HAM investigation team that was looking into this case. Some members of the political elite, especially from Muslim parties and groups later criticised KontraS for not paying the same amount of attention to Tanjung Priok (interview with Mugiyanto Sipin in Jakarta, 10 May 2012). In response, Munir and his team in KontraS started their own investigation of the Priok case by approaching the families of the victims. Yetti, one of the victims whose father went missing during the event, remarks:

> I remember one day I saw a pamphlet by KontraS saying that if your family member or anyone you knew was missing from the incident in 1984, you can report it to KontraS or Munir and there was a contact address and numbers that we could call or visit. So I went there together with some others to report on my missing father and some other victims (interview with Wanma Yetti in Jakarta, 23 March 2012).

KontraS and the *Asosiasi Pembela Islam* (Islamic Defenders Association, or API, led by Hamdan Zoelfa of PBB, a member of parliament), worked together in advocating for the victims of the Priok violence. On 27 August 1999, they took 30 victims to the headquarters of the Military Police (Puspom) to report the incident and demand an investigation (*Kompas*, 27 August 1999). Later, these two organisations, together with the YLBHI, the LBH APIK (*Lembaga Bantuan Hukum Asosiasi Perempuan Indonesia untuk Keadilan*, Women's Legal Aid) and the APRODI (*Aliansi Pengacara untuk Demokrasi Indonesia*, Lawyers Alliance for Indonesian Democracy), an organisation consisting of figures affiliated with Islamic political parties) established a coalition called the KPKP (*Koalisi Pembela Kasus Priok*, Defender of the Priok Case Coalition). The coalition was very active in calling for Soeharto to be held accountable for the violence (*Kompas*, 23 September 2000). Furthermore, as I discussed in Chapter 3, Hamdan Zoelva and colleagues from PBB and PPP assisted Beni Biki, the brother of Amir Biki, in lobbying the parliament to address the Tanjung Priok case. The coalition actively monitored the whole trial process, but only KontraS remained active in campaigning on the case and promoting the rights of victims after the trials.

The fact that this coalition succeeded in raising the Tanjung Priok case to the national agenda, and even got trials going, made human rights groups confident that they could successfully lobby and collaborate with elements of the political elite to push forward the transitional justice agenda. Indeed, as I discussed in Chapter 3, the Tanjung Priok case was special because of the commitment and involvement of political elements of the Muslim groups, most notably members of the political parties and prominent political figures, such as A.M. Fatwa, among the victims. NGOs often used special connections with particular politicians in both the executive and legislature to further their lobbying efforts on the case.[7] As Haris Azhar, coordinator of KontraS explained,

> Lobbying through personal contacts is more effective. This is because mechanisms for [institutional] lobbying are either not available or not functioning; access for institutional lobbying is so scarce ... We first need to identify politicians who are on our side, or at least open to accommodate our interests, sort out the reformist ones (interview with Haris Azhar in Jakarta, 11 May 2012).

This strategy of individual lobbying worked well in some cases—the 1984 Tanjung Priok case, for instance—but not so well in others. The Trisakti, Semanggi I and Semanggi II shootings were an example of failure. These cases stemmed from three different incidents that took place immediately before and after Soeharto resigned. The Trisakti shooting occurred on 12 May 1998 in front of Trisakti University where protesting students were calling for Soeharto's resignation. Troops shot dead four Trisakti students—Elang Mulia Lesmana, Heri Hertanto, Hafidin Royan, and Hendrawan Sie—and injured dozens of others. The Semanggi shootings occurred during two separate incidents of student protest

7 According to Indria Fernida, some of the individual member of parliament they often lobbied, or had good relationships, were Nursyahbani Katjasungkana of PKB, Eva Sundari of PDIP, Wila of PDIP, Hamdan Zoelfa of PBB, and others (email communication, 1 August 2017).

about Special Sessions of the Parliament, in November 1998 and September 1999. In the Semanggi I incident, which occurred from 11 to 13 November 1998, 17 people, mostly students were killed. In the Semanggi II incident, on 24 September 1999, one student and 11 others were killed, and more than 200 people were injured. Families of the victims demanded that the state should be held responsible for these deaths and injuries. In June 1998, the military prosecuted in a military court six officials from the Indonesian Police for the Trisakti shooting, and they were sentenced to six to ten months in prison a year later. The second prosecution started in June 2001 and targeted 11 members of Brimob (Police Mobile Brigade) for the Semanggi I case, with nine of them were sentenced to three to six years in prison in January 2002. In June 2003, another military court also sentenced a soldier from the Army Strategic Command (Kostrad), Buhari Sastro Tua Putty, for the shooting of Yun Hap at Semanggi II.[8]

These military court trials did not satisfy the families of victims mainly because they only prosecuted low-ranking officers, without targeting the main perpetrators higher up the chain of command (interview with Maria Sumarsih in Jakarta, 12 May 2012). The families, TRK and KontraS paid visits to and lobbied state institutions including Komnas HAM, the Jakarta Military Command, the Ministry of Defence, and Presidents Habibie and Wahid, seeking their support for proper justice processes on behalf of the victims. They also lobbied the DPR through some individual members, a strategy that was also adopted in the Tanjung Priok case. As Sumarsih, whose son was killed in the Semanggi I shootings, explained:

> We lobbied individuals in parties and parliamentary factions so that the DPR as an institution that is supposed to monitor the executive could demand that the government resolve the cases (Sumarsih in Andalas, 2008: 163).

Sumarsih was quite confident the lobbying would work. Prior to the shooting of her son, Wawan, Sumarsih had worked in the DPR secretariat for more than ten years as a civil servant, and she knew some of the politicians personally (interview with Sumarsih in Jakarta, 12 May 2012). She was hopeful that the DPR could play a role in pushing the government to settle the case. She and other family members of victims did not anticipate the fact that the military and police still retained the privilege of having their own faction in parliament and therefore were able to wield significant influence in decision-making in the DPR (Andalas, 2008: 163).

8 Little information is information available on these trials, except in a book written by former Army Strategic Commander (Pangkostrad) Djadja Suparman, who was in charge when the Semanggi II incident took place. In his book, Suparman mentioned that the trial prosecuted an Army soldier, Buhari Sastro Tua Putty, for shooting Yun Hap (Suparman 2013: 186). Even though it was proven in the Court that the bullet which killed Yun Hap had come from Putty's weapon, Suparman suggests in his book that the weapon might have been used by an unknown party.

After a mixed response from parliamentarians to the lobbying, in 2001 the parliament agreed to set up a Pansus (*Panitia Khusus*, Special Committee) to investigate the three cases and give a recommendation to the government on how to deal with them. The Pansus was headed by Panda Nababan, a senior politician from PDIP, the party which won the largest vote share in the 1999 election. After experiencing internal deadlock a few times, on 9 July 2001, when the prosecution of the six police officers in the military court was still on-going, the Committee presented its report and recommendations on the cases to a plenary session of the DPR. The party factions in the Pansus were divided. Two factions (PDIP and PDKB) concluded that the series of shootings were a case of gross human rights violation and that the president should set up an ad hoc human rights court to try the perpetrators. One faction (PKB) also concluded that the cases were a gross human rights violation but it recommended reconciliation as a form of non-judicial settlement. The other seven factions concluded that gross human rights violations were not proven, and thus the shootings should be continued to be dealt with through the military courts (Andalas, 2008: 164–165). During voting in the general session this final group won, and the cases were declared closed.

This outcome was not anticipated by the families of victims and human rights groups. It clearly showed that their lobbying efforts had not been successful. There were two reasons for this result. The first and most obvious was that members of parliament lacked interest in these cases. The TRuK (*Tim Relawan untuk Kemanusiaan*, Voluntary Team for Humanity) argued that the outcome was due to the failure of the members of the Pansus to take their job seriously. The average attendance by members' presence in the Pansus meetings was very low, at only 27 per cent. Out of 50 members, 11 of them never showed up at all (TRuK, 2001: 2). An interview with Firman Jaya Daely of the PDIP, one of the most active members of the Pansus, confirms:

> To be honest, I found that most of the members did not find the case 'sexy' or interesting; during that period there were lots of other issues and meetings that they were also involved in (Firman Jaya Daely, interview in Jakarta, 9 May 2017).

Daely was one of the MPs who supported human rights. He was approached and lobbied by the human rights groups and was also invited to be on the advisory board of IKOHI. Other MPs who were lobbied including the Pansus Chair Panda Nababan, also of PDIP, and Effendy Choirie of PKB. Some of the Pansus members were open to meeting and discussing the case with human rights groups, but the two members from TNI/Polri faction, Suwadji and Ronggo Soenarso, did not give a positive response.[9]

9 Email communication with Indria Fernida, former vice coordinator of KontraS, 1 August 2017, and interview with Daely, 9 May 2017.

It could be that such laxness was partly due to ignorance and lack of a human rights perspective among most members of parliament, but a second reason for the outcome was indeed political. The Pansus worked between January and July 2001, a period when Wahid's leadership as president was undergoing a crisis as he lost support in the parliament and opposition to him was mounting. He had to deal with opposition not only in parliament, but also within his own ministries. In March 2001, he dismissed Yusril Ihza Mahendra of the PBB and Nurmahmudi Ismail of the PKS, parties that had supported Wahid's candidacy against Megawati. On 20 July 2001, Amien Rais, then the Speaker of the MPR, declared that a Special Plenary Meeting of the MPR would be held on 23 of July to impeach the president. Wahid responded by issuing a decree dissolving parliament, but this decree did not get support from a majority of the members of parliament, and he was impeached. The meeting also decided that Megawati would replace Wahid as the fifth president of Indonesia.

The political landscape changed significantly after Megawati took over the presidency. As discussed in Chapter 2, the year 2001 marked the start of the period of 'compromised mechanisms', exactly after Wahid was impeached. Indonesia's new ruling elite, consisting of members of formerly semi-oppositional parties and organisations, was increasingly consolidating its position through the distribution of patronage and power-sharing arrangement in cabinet and elsewhere. Most of its members saw little value in a confrontation with the security forces over abuses that had occurred during the transition that had elevated them to power.

Human rights groups failed to recognise or acknowledge this shift. With the families of victims, they adopted a strategy that was similar to what they had successfully used in the Tanjung Priok case—personal lobbying of party elites. But unlike in that earlier case, few parliamentarians had a personal interest in or connection to the Trisakti or Semanggi shootings. After the 2004 election, activists lobbied the new members of parliament especially members of Commission III (in charge of law and human rights issues) to annul the Pansus report and set up a new Pansus instead of following up on a Komnas HAM investigation into the cases, the report of which had been released in March 2002.[10] Supported by the PDIP, PKS, and PDS factions, Commission III agreed to urge the DPR to annul the Pansus recommendations. However, the DPR leadership did not agree to include the issue failed in the agenda for its plenary session. In other words, the

10 NGOs and families of victims had lobbied Komnas HAM, resulting in the establishment of an investigation team shortly after the DPR announced its own report and recommendation in July 2001. A year later, on 21 March 2002, Komnas HAM launched its report, announcing that gross violations had taken place in the three incidents, and named 50 high and middle-low ranking military and police personnel as having been involved in the incidents. The Attorney General's Office announced it was refusing to follow up on the report in March 2003, saying that the cases had already been pursued in the military court. See the chronology in http://www.bbc.com/indonesia/berita_indonesia/2015/05/150512_indonesia_trisakti_1998. Accessed 10 April 2017.

Trisakti and Semanggi cases were closed for further discussion in the parliament (see also discussion about this in Chapter 2).

From the two cases explained above, we can conclude that the strategy of personal lobbying as adopted by KontraS, or other NGOs in general, was not always successful in producing the desired outcomes. This strategy was intensively used by human rights groups especially during the period of momentous change between 1998 and 2001, and it continues until today, though generally with much less success The different results on lobbying on the Tanjung Priok massacre and on the Trisakti and Semanggi shootings show that the dynamics within the political elite are what determines outcomes, much more so than the strategies and resources used by the human rights groups themselves.

Transitional justice from below: human rights strategies after *reformasi*

The advocacy efforts on the 1984 Tanjung Priok massacre and the Trisakti and Semanggi cases show how human rights groups collaborated with individuals who had backgrounds in semi-oppositional groups in the late New Order but had moved into new positions in the political elite once the transition began. Such collaboration was possible due to the replacement element of the political transition whereby opposition groups had mobilised mass demonstration in order to overthrow the Soeharto regime. Human rights accountability was one of the major issues raised by these mass mobilisations, and semi-oppositional organisations used it to gain power in the aftermath of the collapse of Soeharto and his regime. At the same time, international attention on Indonesia's human rights record was mounting after the 1999 East Timor referendum, resulting in much pressure on Indonesia to comply with human rights norms.

In the meantime, the reformers from the old regime had to balance their positions with the standpatters by engaging in negotiations with the opposition and civil society groups. This led to the transplacement elements in Indonesia's transition. This situation meant there was often space for negotiations, formal and informal, with NGOs including human rights groups. Wide-ranging negotiations between varieties of actors were thus normalised as part of the distinctive pattern of Indonesian democratisation. On the one hand, these negotiations stabilised Indonesia's political transition and consolidation (see discussion in Chapter 1). On the other hand, human rights accountability was compromised by leaders of the elite through such negotiations in the service of their own agendas. Moreover, the lobbying of individual members of the new elite by the human rights groups often only had limited influence because the individuals they had access to were not the top leaders of the political parties. Bringing human rights and transitional justice into the formal political system thus had limited impact.

Another significant challenge for human rights groups was that they had compete with other pro-democracy groups in raising the issue of past human rights abuses to the national agenda, alongside issues such as corruption, social and economic rights, the environment, and many other issues facing the country. Quoting research produced by the democracy research institute DEMOS (Democracy Research Institute), AE Priyono explained:

> Indonesia has many problems and thus it is very difficult to consolidate because of fragmentation. From the fourteen issues we (DEMOS) identified, each sector has different issues and different solutions. For example, land, the problems of the urban poor, and so on. Therefore it's a big challenge for the human rights sector to compete with other sectors in order to promote their transitional justice agenda. Because all other sectors are also being promoted and groups are demanding solutions to them, especially during a time of transition, everyone compete for their own agenda (interview with A.E. Priyono in Jakarta, 16 May 2012).

Apart from this challenge, unfortunately, there was not much agreement among human rights groups on which issues they should prioritise in their advocacy work. Ifdhal Kasim, former director of ELSAM and Commissioner of Komnas HAM from 2007 to 2012 explained that lack of coordination among human rights groups on strategies was one of the biggest hurdles in promoting transitional justice during the early period of the political transition:

> During *reformasi* everyone wanted to promote their issues: corruption, development, and so on. We (ELSAM) promoted transitional justice as an answer for human rights accountability. One of the options was prosecution, but this would have had an impact on real politics because democracy was vulnerable and political change involved elements of the old regime, the TNI/Polri faction was still in parliament, and all the New Order parties were also still in parliament: Golkar, PPP, and PDIP even though PDIP was also a victim. The second option was amnesty, but amnesty would upset people and delegitimate the political transition. So we offered the model of a Truth and Reconciliation Commission. [...] Among the NGOs, however, there were always disagreements. For example, I was said to be always opposed to Munir, because Munir preferred prosecution. [...] [I believed] we needed to sequence the options: first was the right to know, and then the right to justice, later we could have the rights to reparation. But not everything at the same time (interview in Jakarta, 20 September 2014).

Even though human rights groups failed to work out a consensus on their strategies and priorities, they did over time maximise their 'dual-track' approach by not only continuing elite lobbying but also intensifying their bottom-up work, encouraging initiatives for transitional justice within communities at the local level (Lundy and McGovern, 2008), including strengthening collaboration with and involvement of communities of victims. Human rights groups were blocked from making significant progress at the national level, but found they could move forward at the local level. Such opportunities were much greater in the context of the far-reaching decentralisation of political power brought about by Habibie at the start of the *reformasi* period. The next chapter discusses in detail human rights groups' initiatives in working with local government on transitional justice measures as decentralisation gave them the opportunity and the space to do so.

Meanwhile, NGOs also mobilised victims and initiated empowerment programmes with them, including assisting victims to establish their own organisations. Victims' groups were deeply involved in the various efforts to promote transitional justice. After the fall of Soeharto, the opening of political space allowed victims of past human rights abuses, including the 1965–1966 repression, to form a variety of associations. Victims' organisations such as the YPKP 65 (*Yayasan Penelitian Korban Pembunuhan 65*, Research Foundation for Victims of the 1965–1966 Killings), the Pakorba (*Persatuan Korban Orde Baru*, Association of Victims of the New Order), the LPKP 65 (*Lembaga Penelitian Korban Peristiwa 65*, Research Institute for Victims of the 1965 Tragedy), the LPK 65 (*Lembaga Pembela Korban 65*, Institute for the Defenders of 1965 Victims), the LPRKROB (*Lembaga Perjuangan Rehabilitasi Korban Rezim Orde Baru*, Organization for Rehabilitation Struggle for New Order Victims), the KKP HAM 65 (*Komite Aksi Korban Pelanggaran HAM 1965*, 1965 Human Rights Victims Action Committee),[11] the IKOHI (*Ikatan Keluarga Orang Hilang Indonesia*, Association of Families of the Enforced Disappeared) as well as individual victims, took some initiatives in conjunction with other civil society groups, including human rights activists, researchers, scholars, teachers, and community leaders. Most of the victims involved in these organisations were former political prisoners detained under the post-1965 purge which helped establish Soeharto's rule. In almost all of these initiatives, NGOs involved victims' rights groups and individuals. Such involvement conveyed a clear message to the wider public about the need to understand victims' perspectives and to provide them with solidarity. Victims saw their involvement in civil society initiatives as necessary. As Bedjo Untung, head of YPKP, said:

> NGOs have to open widely the space for victims to be involved in all forums available ... because they (victims) are the ones who experience the injustice, therefore they are the one who can tell what injustices are (interview with Bedjo Untung in Jakarta, September 2012).

11 Some of these organisations claim to have hundreds of members and branches throughout the country. Some draw exclusively on the former members of the PKI, but others include non-PKI affiliated figures and/or family members such as PAKORBA or IKOHI. See short profiles of some of these organisations in Farid and Simarmata (2004: 36–38).

The 'dual-track' strategy of lobbying government officials and engaging the grassroots applied in almost all areas of work organised by human rights groups. An assessment by the International Center for Transitional Justice (ICTJ) in 2005 noted that at least 200 activities related to issues of past injustice in Indonesia were carried out by these groups between 1999 and 2002. Activities ranged from truth-seeking (documenting victim testimonies, exhumation of bodies, publications, and memorialisation) to filing cases for criminal justice, from lobbying for reparations for victims to promoting reconciliation (Farid and Simarmata, 2004).

At the local level, civil society groups used grassroots or community-based activities especially since 2000, mainly organising around documentation, exhumation, memorialisation, commemoration, and reconciliation as well as organising public seminars. These local organisations have worked with victims and grassroots communities. Some have also collaborated with the local governments. The next chapter of this book discusses one example of this approach in Palu City.

Since 2000, victim organisations have not only been involved in the human rights groups' initiatives, they have also been very active in documenting their own stories and in organising or getting involved in various truth-seeking and reconciliation initiatives alongside NGOs. In the early years after *reformasi*, victims—whether as individuals or affiliated with organisations—were not so much engaged in NGO initiatives nor did they organise their own initiatives. As Nurlaela Lamasitudju, the Coordinator of SKP HAM Palu (Solidarity for Victims of Human Rights Violation in Palu) explained,

> In Palu, when I met former political prisoners for the first time, LPKP 65, LPR KROB, already existed but their activities were mostly underground ... They only met secretly ... They came to NGO events, joined in advocacy activities on land issues and some other topics. At that time they did not speak within a human rights framework ... We convinced them that if many people told their stories, then we could see the picture of what happened to them (interview with Nurlaela Lamasitudju in Jakarta, 8 May 2012).

The tendency of victims—especially victims of the 1965–1966 repression—to be apprehensive about engaging in open associational activities during that early period of the political transition was understandable because of the fears and trauma that persisted after long years of oppression. For many of them, this was also a period when they were still in the process of building solidarity (Farid and Simarmata, 2004). Thus, even though the public was starting to acknowledge their experience, as Zurbuchen notes, being identified as a 1965–1966 victim still carried risks in a society still polarised by the events of those years and by anti-communist sentiment (Zurbuchen, 2002: 580–581).

Indeed, it would have been difficult for victims' organisations to run their own activities without the support of NGOs or other elements in civil society.

Sekber 1965 (*Sekretariat Bersama 1965*, Joint Secretariat for 1965 Tragedy) in Solo was one local victims' organisation that was quite active and often organised its activities in public by involving various elements including student organisations, academics, local government officials, members of parliament, journalists, as well as Islamic groups. Helped by a local legal aid organisation called the LPH-YAPHI (*Lembaga Pengabdi Hukum-Yekti Angudi Piyadeging Hukum Indonesia*, Institute of Dedication for Law-Yekti Angudi Piyadeging of Indonesian Law), the group started in 2005 with ten members and later became very active in recruiting hundreds of victims around Solo and Central Java to join its activities. The group held regular internal meetings, cooperated with other civil society groups, and established good relationships and networks with other elements in society as well as local state authorities, with the result that they received public acknowledgement and support. Since 2010, Sekber 1965 has provided public access to its activities including commemorations and reconciliation events, which have been widely covered by local media.[12] The only resistance to their activities came from the Central Java Military Command which warned the public to be wary of the 'revival of communism' and threatened to 'abolish' such attempts (*Solopos*, 17 December 2012).

In most local communities, the positive outcomes of these initiatives were also determined by the backgrounds of the actors driving the processes. The coordinator of SKP HAM Palu, Nurlaela Lamasitudju, came from a family with a strong Islamic background. Her father was a prominent *ulama* who owned his own traditional religious school or *pesantren*. Though she never associated her activism with the family's fame and influence, she was advantaged by her background, especially when meeting and gaining trust from anti-communist Islamic leaders.

As well as personal background, in some areas, organisational affiliation was also a central factor in determining the positive outcomes of such grassroot initiatives. Syarikat in Central Java, for example, successfully organised what they called as 'cultural reconciliation' between victims of the 1965 violence and several perpetrators from their communities, including religious leaders from the Nahdlatul Ulama (NU). Between 2001 and 2004, Syarikat held gatherings in 18 cities and districts around Central Java and Yogyakarta. Members of Syarikat were mostly *santri* (pupils) and young leaders of the NU. Their main reason for organising these events was the involvement of many NU members and leaders in the 1965 mass violence (interview with Rumekso Setyadi in Jakarta, 10 May

12 In 2009, Sekretariat Bersama 1965 (Sekber 1965) commemorated International Human Rights Day by organising a big public event with traditional art performances such as *wayang* and dance, and a dialogue forum involving victims, public officials, members of parliament, Muslim groups, and student organisations. Hundreds of victims came to the event, which was also attended by members of a right-wing Islamic organisation. The media covered the event and newspapers such as *Joglosemar* and *Solopos* wrote a series of profiles of several victims.

2012). The gatherings were well attended, as participants shared their experiences of decades of trauma and potential tension within their communities. As Sulistyanto and Setyadi explain,

> In the absence of a national truth-telling forum, victims have nowhere to go except to participate in victims' forums like the one organized by Syarikat, hence the importance of these grassroots initiatives is that they can act like an unofficial truth commission because they provide a forum in which victims and perpetrators can exchange their personal stories (Sulistiyanto and Setyadi, 2009: 207).

Other than working at the local level with victims, human rights groups also adopted a more comprehensive approach by combining both advocacy and campaigning at national and local levels. A coalition of NGOs called KKPK (*Kelompok Kerja Pengungkapan Kebenaran*, Working Group for Truth-seeking) is an example. Initially the KKPK was set up by activists in 2008 to advocate on, and monitor, processes then taking place in the government in relation to the drafting of Law on the Truth and Reconciliation Commission, several transitional justice mechanisms for Timor Leste (the ad hoc Tribunal and the Commission for Truth and Friendship) and related justice policies. At first led by former Komnas HAM commissioner Asmara Nababan, in 2010 the group changed its name to *Koalisi Keadilan dan Pengungkapan Kebenaran* (Coalition for Justice and Truth-Seeking) and was now led by Kamala Chandrakirana, former commissioner of Komnas Perempuan. The new name meant that the coalition did not limit its mandate to truth-seeking but also aimed at promoting various initiatives for justice, both retributive and restorative.[13] The coalition consisted of more than 30 national and local organisations, including NGOs, victims' rights groups, as well as individuals concerned with human rights issues.

In 2012, the coalition launched a truth-seeking and reconciliation project called the Year of Truth. This initiative sought to document 100 cases of past human rights abuses in Indonesia, ranging from civil rights violations to economic and socio-cultural rights violations by the state. One of the activities held during this year was what they called the DK (*Dengar Kesaksian*, Testimonial Hearings), which were also intended to promote public education. These hearings were inspired by and modelled on the truth commission philosophy and involved hearings organised in open spaces so the public would have the chance to listen to the personal histories, or testimonies, of victims. They were widely covered by the national and local media.[14] Prominent public figures facilitated the process as 'commissioners' organised in what was called a 'People's Council'

13 See KKPK's website, http://kkpk.org/tentang-kkpk/. Accessed on 5 July 2014.

14 Some videos of this initiative are available on YouTube and have been widely distributed worldwide. See the website http://kkpk.org/.

or Dewan Warga. Testimony Hearings were organised in three locations: Palu, Solo, and Kupang and gained much attention from local communities, especially when victims testified on the 1965 tragedy.

This new wave of civil society 'bottom-up' initiatives produced some achievements in terms of truth and reconciliation, though mostly only at the local or community level. The initiatives contributed to wider local acknowledgement of cases of past human rights abuses and of victims' experiences of injustice. Thus, such initiatives were also important in terms of promoting victims' agency and self-healing. As Net Markus, who lost eight members of her family, including her father, brother, and younger sister, to executions in 1965–1966, said before her testimony in the hearing in Kupang:

> Only by telling all the truth of what happened, can we really be free from the trauma of the past ... We deserve the truth about the history of this nation, and a guarantee from the state that these [injustices] will never happen again.[15]

The shift of strategy to local-level hearings and activities was partly a consequence of the failure to achieve meaningful results at the national level. The next chapter elaborates on how the bottom-up approach was also pursued in collaboration with local authorities. By taking Palu City as an example, I expand the positive achievements challenges of such local-level transitional justice objectives.

Conclusion

This chapter has discussed the roles played by human rights groups in promoting transitional justice measures in Indonesia. I have argued that, as part of a broader 'proto-opposition' under the Soeharto regime, human rights groups' campaigning helped to influence the popular demands for Soeharto's dismissal. The transition occurred in a context in which demands for better protection of human rights were an integral part of the movement pushing for democratic reform. The element of replacement in the political transition—the societal mobilisation, the legitimacy crisis experienced by authoritarianism and the sudden nature of the regime transition—gave many opportunities for these groups to collaborate with individuals who had previously been involved in semi-oppositional institutions in the late New Order. Later, in the period of momentous change, these individuals moved into parliament and other state institutions, where they had considerable influence over political developments. Habibie's decision to allow a referendum among the East Timorese in 1999, meanwhile, scaled up pressure from the international community for state human rights accountability. It also increased domestic pressure for accountability for the 1984 Tanjung Priok case.

15 See her story in a KKPK video at http://kkpk.org/vlcsnap-15910137/. Accessed 5 July 2014.

The state responded with concessions by ratifying international conventions and passing a Human Rights Law and Human Rights Court Law which later became the basis for prosecutions in both the East Timor and Tanjung Priok cases.

However, as I argued in Chapter 2, the political transition also involved a large element of transplacement and negotiations between old regime forces and the new rising party elites. This element became a major challenge for these human rights groups. Though there was momentum for better human rights protection, it was counterbalanced by the political dynamics arising from the negotiations and compromises taking place between elements from the old authoritarian regime and the new party leaders and emerging elite. Meanwhile, human rights groups lacked a common strategy to push through the changes they were aiming for. The result was the impunity I discussed in Chapters 3 and 4.

With the state's top-down mode of delivering transitional justice failing to achieve either justice goals or even basic acknowledgement of past human rights abuses, human rights groups adopted a 'dual-track' strategy, continuing to advocate for change at the national level, but with little success, and at the same time working from below at the grassroots with victims' groups and local authorities. This second strategy produced some positive achievements in terms of local acknowledgement and local reconciliation but also faced challenges. The next chapter examines local transitional justice efforts in greater detail.

Chapter 6

Transitional justice at the local level

The case of Palu, Central Sulawesi

> It is better to settle this [the 1965 mass violence] in partial ways in the regions, [because] there is still a deep wound at the national level. PKI made *agitprop* [agitation and propaganda] that hurt lots of people ... If the PKI was crushed, well, that's how it was. People were punished, but the punishment was beyond reasonable ... You know, it's all about the political game. One time we won, another time we lost. That's the way it is (interview with Rusdy Mastura in Palu, 26 September 2014).

Introduction

In previous chapters, I have discussed and assessed several mechanisms and initiatives of transitional justice, at the state and civil society levels. This chapter looks at another approach to transitional justice, which took place at the local, or district, level. It focuses on policies on reparations for the victims of the 1965 mass violence which were adopted as one transitional justice mechanism in Palu City, Central Sulawesi. I refer to this regional level measure as a 'margin-to-centre' approach to transitional justice. Unlike the bottom-up approaches discussed in the previous chapter, which were basically civil society initiatives, the margin-to-centre approach combines collaboration of local-level representatives of the state with local NGOs, while allowing the possibility of even wider local participation. Though local state officials and political elites played an important role, it should be recognised, in fact, that it was mostly civil society elements, including NGOs and victims, who initiated, and sometimes led, these processes. These initiatives thus look like a successful local-level version of the 'dual-track strategy' that was adopted by human rights groups at the national level.

I argue in this chapter that decentralisation provided space for transitional justice initiatives at the local level. It was the key enabling factor for local experiments in transitional justice. Indonesia started the process of rapid decentralisation in 1999 from a highly centralised government structure under Soeharto's regime. Regional autonomy legislation was passed in 1999 (Law Nos. 22 and 25) and implemented in 2001, focusing on the sub-provincial or district level. As discussed in the previous chapter, the failure to achieve meaningful results at the national level prompted human rights groups to adjust their strategies by intensifying the 'bottom-up' approach. Regional autonomy provided them with space for new strategies aimed at strengthening local groups in collaboration with local governments, at least in some locations.

Even though decentralisation enabled transitional justice, there were other factors in Palu that opened the possibility of addressing the 1965 mass violence in that particular location—and which in fact made it the first and only initiative on transitional justice at the city level in all of Indonesia. One was the leadership of the Mayor, Rusdy Masthura, and his political networks. A second factor was the nature of the violence itself in Palu, while a third factor was the role played by the key local NGO—SKP HAM.

I divide this chapter into four parts. The first section discusses the 1965 mass violence in Palu to provide the context for the transitional justice efforts that occurred there decades later. The second part focuses on the transitional justice initiatives taken by victims and the leading local NGO, SKP HAM, and how they succeeded in convincing the local government of Palu City to develop policies and programmes for the victims of the 1965 mass violence. In the next section, I assess these initiatives by looking at their processes and outcomes. I also examine various factors that enabled them. Finally, I end the chapter by considering the implications of the Palu experiment.

The 1965 mass violence in Palu

Palu is the capital and largest city of Central Sulawesi province, with a population of around 350,000 in 2013. The city reflects the pluralism of Central Sulawesi province, one of the most ethnically and religiously diverse area in Indonesia (Diprose, 2007: 38).

From the late 1950s until 1965, the PKI was not a significant political force in Palu or in Central Sulawesi. In the 1955 election, the PKI won fifth place in Central North Sulawesi Province, coming after Masyumi, PSII (*Partai Syarikat Islam Indonesia*, Indonesian Islamic Union Party), Parkindo (*Partai Kristen Indonesia*, Indonesian Christian Party), and PNI (*Partai Nasional Indonesia,* Indonesian National Party), with a total of 33,204 votes or 0.5 per cent of the total (interview with Haliadi in Palu, 25 September 2014). During those years, Central Sulawesi was part of Sulawesi Province. In 1960, the province was divided into South and Southeast Sulawesi Province, and Central North Sulawesi Province which included what became Central Sulawesi province in 1964.[1] The PKI had its General Regional Committee (CDB) based in Palu after 1960, with Daeng Abdurrahman Maselo as its chairperson. The membership was also small,

1 Central Sulawesi only became a province in 1964 with four districts (*kabupaten*): Donggala, Poso, Buol Tolitoli and Banggai. In the 1955 election, PKI won 328 votes in Donggala district and 1,177 votes in Poso district (interview with Haliadi in Palu, 25 September 2014).

less than 1,500 members, a tiny fraction of its membership in Java. Nationally, the party claimed to have one million members in 1960, as well as millions of sympathisers in groups such as BTI (*Barisan Tani Indonesia*, Indonesian Peasents' Front). Some 90 per cent of the party's members were in Java (Ricklefs, 2001: 302). Because the party was small in terms of membership and political influence in Central Sulawesi, the PKI experienced little conflict with other parties in the region. The two most influential parties were Masyumi and PNI. Masyumi had the largest number of members, while PNI was strong within the ruling elite in Central Sulawesi.

When anti-PKI demonstration took place in Jakarta shortly after 1 October 1965, the situation in Palu remained calm as it had always been. Protests and demonstrations only started around the end of October 1965 when students, mostly from the *Amanat Penderitaan Rakyat* (Ampera, or Message of the People's Sufferings), Action Command (KOAMPA), held protests demanding the Communist Party be dissolved. Mass arrests and detentions took place in four waves (Lamasitudju, 2014: 372–373, and interview with Haliadi in Palu, 25 September 2014). The first wave took place from late October to December 1965 as was directed at the PKI and its affiliated organisations in Central Sulawesi. The second wave occurred from 1966 to 1967, and again targeted members and sympathisers of the PKI and its affiliated organisations. The third wave of mass arrests and detentions took place between 1969 and 1971 and was this time directed against military personnel from the Brawijaya Regional Command, specifically Battalion 711, who were based in Palu. Some of them had just returned from their mission in West Papua associated with the 1969 Act of Free Choice. There is no clear information on why they were arrested. Finally, the last wave of arrests took place in 1975. These were known as arrests of the 'PKI Gaya Baru' or 'the New Style PKI'. The arrests targeted local figures who were critical of the government and bureaucracy in Central Sulawesi.

As with other cases on the 1965 mass violence in various places in Indonesia, information on the exact number of victims killed in Palu is very limited. Compared to other places in Sulawesi, much less is known about what took place in Palu and the numbers of casualties there. However, according to SKP HAM that has been working on documenting victims as well as perpetrators' testimonies on what happened in that period, dozens of people died during the first wave of violence (Lamasitudju, 2014: 74). Two Military Regional Commands (Kodam)—the XIII Merdeka Kodam in Manado and XIV Hasanuddin Kodam in Makassar—were responsible for security in Central Sulawesi. Joint teams from both Kodams carried out arrests and investigations. SKP HAM's documentation identified dozens of fatalities, hundreds more cases of people being tortured and enslaved, and four PKI members who disappeared (including Daeng Maselo).

Based on interviews and victims' testimonies, SKP HAM identified forced labour as the dominant form of violence for both men and women detainees in Palu. The total number of cases in their documentation is 793 out of a total of 1,210 cases. Seven men died while on forced labour. The detainees had to build public infrastructures not only in Palu, the capital city of Central Sulawesi, but also in Donggala and Poso districts. Because Central Sulawesi had only recently been established as a new province, the focus of the new government was to build infrastructures. As the military was responsible for implementing these projects, the detainees were forced to work without payment. The infrastructure they worked on included an airport, bridges, military housing and compounds, and government offices. Asman Yodojolo, aged 72, a former detainee who was arrested for leading the IPPI (*Ikatan Pemuda Pelajar Indonesia*, Indonesian Youth Student Association) told his story:

> I had to join forced labour, the first time was in 1966 in Palu river [...] building a bridge, we got the stones from Buluri, Bronjong, hundreds even thousands [of stones., and after that in 1968 I worked building a road from Palu to Parigi for a year [...] It was tough because there were often landslides, hundreds of cubic meters of landslides, and the work was done only with human hands, no equipment at all, only shovels. We worked until night, many of us got dysentery [...] We didn't get paid, we got beaten ...".[2]

The forced labour took place in the period between 1966 and 1981. The governor then was Anwar Majo Datuk Basanan Kuning, and the Head of the Korem (*Komando Resor Militer*, Military Resort Command) 132 Tadulako was M. Yasin.

The four people who disappeared were leading figures of the PKI's Regional Committee (CBD). They were Abdul Rahman Daeng Maselo, the first secretary of the CBD and periodical Chair of the Front Nasional (National Front); Hairi Ruswanto, the second secretary and member of Central Sulawesi's parliament; Sunaryo and Zamrud, both CBD officials. Maryam Labonu, Maselo's wife, who was a member of Gerwani and was also detained for a year with her three children, is still looking for the whereabouts of her husband. In 2000, another victim who was detained with her husband said that she saw human bones and remains in the Korem post in Palu. A denture was found in the location, and it was believed to be Maselo's (*Antara News*, 27 December 2012).

Most of the male detainees were imprisoned in Mahesa while the women were detained in a house in Sedap Malam Street in Palu city. They were released in two waves. The first wave was during the period of 1977 to 1979, and the rest of the prisoners were released between 1981 and 1984 (interview with Haliadi in Palu, 25 September 2015). After they were released, most of them were stigmatised in society. For years, up until early 2000, they had to regularly report to the local police or military post. Many of them also lost their property, such as land or houses.

2 See his testimony video clip in KKPK's website, http://kkpk.org/tag/dengar-kesaksian-palu/. Accessed 3 April 2015. Some of the information were also re-told to me in a meeting with victims in Palu, September 2014.

One victim mentioned that his land was used to build a primary school in his village (discussion in Palu, 26 September 2014). Victims and their families lived in poverty, and the stigma continued against their children and grandchildren.

The historical context, and the nature of the 1965 violence in Palu were factors that helped contribute to the success of attempts to deal with the legacy. Compared to most locations in Java, or even in other parts of Sulawesi, the scale and intensity of violence in Palu was much less. This means that far fewer civilian vigilantes were involved in the killings and fewer local people benefited from them, reducing some of the local-level incentives for resistance to later truth-seeking and reconciliation efforts.

SKP HAM, victims' mobilisation, and local government responses

The mobilisation of victims' rights groups at the national level was expanded to Palu after the 1998 *reformasi*. In 2002, several people who had been victims of the post-1965 reprisals against the left in Palu joined two national victims' organisations: the LPKP 65 and the LP-KROB. Both organisations were based in Jakarta and established in the early years of *reformasi* by former political prisoners who had been detained in the post-1965 anti-communist purge. LPKP was established in April 1999 with the purpose of investigating the mass killings in 1965–1966 (Farid and Simarmata, 2004: 36–37). Initially, it was set up as a foundation (*yayasan*) but it later became an institute when its members decided to divide into two groups: the YPKP 65 and the LPKP 65 (interview with Bedjo Untung in Jakarta, September 2012). Meanwhile, the LP-KROB was formed in May 2001. Its main programmes focused on obtaining reparations for victims and re-writing history. The institute also developed income-generating activities and *arisan* (rotating savings groups) to respond to the needs of many of its members who were suffering economically as a result of discriminatory practices (Farid and Simarmata, 2004: 37). Both organisations had local branches in various regions, including Palu, and claimed to have hundreds of members all over the country. However, as with victims' groups in other parts of Indonesia, their activities and mobilisations were limited due to limited capacity and resources.

In Palu, victims were mainly active in participating in various meetings organised by students and NGO activists. They sometimes held meetings among themselves, but not openly as the fear and effects of stigmatisation were still ongoing in their communities. Their mobilisation and activism only became public after a local NGO called SKP HAM started to organise some initiatives involving victims, especially truth-seeking and reparation activities.

SKP HAM was established on 13 October 2004 by KontraS, IKOHI, and a local institute called the LPS-HAM (*Lembaga Pusat Studi Hak Asasi Manusia*, Institute for Human Rights Study) after a three-day workshop in Palu. The meeting was organised as a response to the recent Poso conflict—a protracted inter-religious conflict that had broken out in and around the nearby town of Poso and had lasted for four years. The purpose of the meeting was to at gather victims, not only those who had suffered in the Poso conflict but also others, including victims of the 1965 mass violence, and empower them to take action to address their own problems (interview with Netty in, 28 September 2004 and Nurlaela Lamasitudju in Palu, 26 September 2014). In its platform, SKP HAM aimed at organising, strengthening and empowering victims of human rights abuses in Central Sulawesi, prioritising work on the 1965 mass violence. The organisation applied an inclusive strategy to gain support from the local community and local authorities and to facilitate processes of empowerment and reconciliation among victims as well as with the wider public and the state at the local level (interview with Nurlaela Lamasitdju and discussion with some staff in Palu, 26 September 2014). By 'inclusive', SKP HAM meant that it works always involved local authorities and other elements of Palu's civil society, including students. The organisation also involved younger generation activists and younger members of the families of victims.

Using the inclusive strategy, the organisation started to reach out to more 1965 victims and engaged with a wider variety of groups at the grassroots level. The outreach to victims resulted in a documentation project. Nurlaela Lamasitudju, the chair of the organisation, and other members collected names and identities of 1965 victims in a simple format, and later developed this format into a human rights database. They managed to collect and compile archival documents, photographs, audio-visual materials, and 1,028 testimonies of victims.[3] From this documentation, they identified a total of 1,210 victims in Central Sulawesi during the 1965–1966 violence, spread out in four areas: Palu, Sigi, Donggala, and Parigi Moutong (Lamasitudju, 2014: 378). The organisation then identified a need to engage other members of society, especially the local authorities, in discussing truth and reconciliation on the 1965 abuses. They started with village-level meetings with local villagers, door-to-door visits, and later also meetings with village leaders (*lurah* and *camat*) as well as religious leaders in order to discuss issues related to human rights. The topics included national laws related to human rights, the truth and reconciliation commission, and later more specifically on the 1965 mass violence (interview with Nurlaela Lamasitudju in Jakarta, 8 May 2012). They called this programme *Diskusi Kampung* or village discussions.

The *Diskusi Kampung* were successful in part because of the SKP HAM leader, Nurlaela Lamasitudju. Nurlaela came from a family with a strong Islamic background. Her father was a prominent local *ulama* who owned his own traditional school or *pesantren*. She and her family survived the Poso conflict. Having an educational background in accounting, she became interested in human rights after the Poso conflict and when Munir's death was widely broadcasted on television. She participated in the victims' meeting in October 2004 and accepted the appointment as SKP HAM's chairperson. Even though she never used the family's reputation and influence to promote her activism, her background gave

3 See their website: http://www.skp-ham.org.

her an advantage, especially since her work involved meeting and gaining the trust of Islamic leaders who were opposed to communism.

The *Diskusi Kampung* continued to develop into city-level advocacy and campaign projects. Nurlaela approached prominent figures with political influence in Central Sulawesi to gain their support and engage them in discussion about human rights and the 1965 victims. One of these influential figures, Ince Mawar, admitted that she was not aware about the 1965 victims from the human rights perspective before she met and had discussions with Nurlaela. As with many other Indonesians around the country, she knew about what happened in 1965–1966 but believed those who were arrested deserved it because they were communists (interview, 26 September 2014). Coming from a politically influential family, Ince supported SKP HAM in linking with high officials and parliament members in Palu. When SKP HAM organised public events, some of her networks also became involved, giving these events much-needed publicity.

The first big event took place in 2011, in the form of a book launch to present an edited volume by Putu Oka Sukanta, writer and former political prisoner, called *Memecah Pembisuan* (Breaking the Silencing). A speech from the Governor of Central Sulawesi was read at the event by his deputy, Sudarto. In the speech, the governor admitted that mass violence took place in Central Sulawesi in 1965–1966, and the deputy acknowledged the practice of forced labour in the subsequent years (Lamasitudju, 2014: 380). The launch and the book convinced Palu Mayor Rusdy Mastura to accept SKP HAM's invitation to an event on 24 March 2012 to commemorate the International Day for the Rights to Truth Concerning Gross Human Rights Violation and for the Dignity of Victims, where he delivered an apology to victims as follows:

> The State at the time conditioned the situation where many of its people were arrested, murdered, jailed. It was mass provocation [...] resentment because of different ideologies. But we cannot continue to be like that anymore now, therefore nothing is more appropriate for me to say than to apologize, personally [... and on behalf of the local government of the city of Palu, to all the victims of the 1965 tragedy in Palu and Central Sulawesi (Lamasitudju, 2014).

Rusdy considered himself complicit in the violence. According to him, he and many other civilians in the 1960s were convinced that the PKI was evil. Only 16 years old and still in high school in October 1965, he 'guarded' Gerwani members who were detained in the house mentioned above in Palu. He also believed the PKI committed acts of violence against Islamic groups and parties. However, the punishment of the PKI members, he now said, was beyond comprehension, and he realised that the victims had suffered discrimination their whole lives. This was his personal reason for the apology (interviews with Rusdy in Palu, 26 September 2014). He repeated the statement a few times at some other events in Palu and elsewhere, including during the KKPK's Public Hearing in Palu and Year of Truth Launching in Jakarta in 2014.

Palu's reparation programme

The Mayor's apology spurred SKP HAM and victims to step up their efforts for truth and justice for victims of the 1965 mass violence. SKP HAM followed the event by lobbying local authorities in Palu to plan reparation programmes for the victims. After months of lobbying and working closely with relevant government sectors, the Mayor issued Bylaw No. 17 of 2013 on Action Plan on Human Rights. Initially, reparations for victims under the decree specifically targeted the 1965 victims, but eventually, the government widened its scope to include more general human rights victims as the beneficiaries to avoid strong resistance from various stakeholders in Palu City government offices as well as members of parliament (interview with Nurlaela and Muliati, in Palu 26 September 2014). The bylaw consisted of three aspects: it advanced six main programmes for implementation of human rights in Palu, include a local action plan that aimed to fulfil ten basic rights, and presented mechanisms for implementing the programmes and plans.

The six main programmes were as follows: (1) strengthening of the institutions implementing the Ranham (*Rencana Aksi Nasional HAM*, National Action Plan for Human Rights), (2) introduction of programmes on human rights education, (3) provision of communication services for the public, (4) implementation of human rights norms and standards, (5) harmonising drafts and evaluations of local and national legal products with human rights perspectives, and, (6) conducting evaluation, monitoring, and reporting for each of the programmes mentioned.

The first programme, institutional strengthening, included the establishment of eight Pokja (*Kelompok Kerja*, Working Groups) on human rights education, social protection and improvement of welfare, family guarantees, human rights-based law enforcement and protection, environmental protection, religious pluralism and tolerance, protection of women and children, and lastly a specific working group on human rights for victims of the 1965 human rights violation. A Mayoral Decree No. 180/561/HKM/2014 regulated specific tasks and terms of reference and provided a list of members for each of these working group. Nurlaela was appointed as the chair of the *Pokja* on human rights for the victims of the 1965 human rights violation, leading the group of six members who consisted of both government officials and persons with civil society backgrounds.[4]

The Bylaw No. 17 of 2013 also set the legal basis for cooperation between the local government and SKP HAM and a national NGO, ELSAM, in developing programmes and activities for dealing with the 1965–1966 human rights violations, including violations of the right to education. A Memorandum of Understanding (MoU) was signed in Jakarta on 20 October 2014 by representatives of

4 See the Mayoral Decree or Keputusan Walikota Palu No. 180/561/HKM/2014 on Second Amendment of Mayor Decree No. 180/2088/HKM/2012 on the Establishment of Working Groups for City of Palu's Committee on 2011–2014 Human Rights Action Plan.

the government of Palu and ELSAM. The Palu government was also invited to a national coordination meeting between LPSK (*Lembaga Perlindungan Saksi dan Korban*, The Witness and Victim Protection Agency), Komnas HAM and Komnas Perempuan. Other activities include a focus group discussion on local initiatives to settle cases of gross human rights violations with the participation of a member of the President's Advisory Council Albert Hasibuan, Komnas HAM commissioner Roichatul Aswidah, Vice Chair of LPSK Hasto Atmojo Suroyo, and chair of Komnas Perempuan Yunianti Chufaizah.[5] Palu's government also sponsored programmes on human rights on the local TVRI (*Televisi Republik Indonsia*, Indonesian Republic Television) station, inviting national officials and NGO activists to become resource persons for the shows.

By law No. 17 of 2013 also explicitly mandated a reparation programme for victims of human rights violations. Victims of the 1965 violence were the first, and main, target of the programme. Working alongside SKP HAM staff, a group of researchers from the Faculty of Law of the Tadulako University, was assigned to verify a list of victims' names collected by SKP HAM and to identify the forms of reparation needed.[6] The total number of the research population was 580 families in Palu. The verified names were then included in a Mayoral Decree and submitted to Komnas HAM for further verification. The research identified several forms of reparation for victims. They are shown in Table 6.1.

Table 6.1 Palu City Reparation Program for Victims of Human Rights

No	*Identified Program*	*Numbers of Beneficiaries*	*Responsible Local Government Department*
1	Health insurance	41 families	Dept. of Health
2	House renovation	64 families	Dept. of Social Affairs and Workforce
3	Toilet and bathroom	22 families	Dept. of Housing
4	Scholarships	41 persons	Dept. of Education
5	Livelihoods	55 persons	Dept. of Industrial Relations
6	Farming seeds	6 families	Dept. of Farming and Fishery
7	Rice aid	27 families	Dept. of Economy
8	Work and social care	53 persons	Dept. of Social Affairs and Workforce

Source: Mastura (2014: 10).

5 See the release on President's Advisory Council's website, http://wantimpres.go.id/?cat=11&lang=id. Accessed 4 March 2015.

6 The Palu City Regional Development Planning Bureau or Bappeda allocates a budget for planning and research each year. It was under this budget that the research on the 1965 reparation was conducted by a group of researchers from the Law Faculty led by Professor Aminuddin Kasim. The research team developed verification forms, which were then distributed by SKP HAM's staff. Members of the research team interviewed the head of schools, teachers, and health centre officials in the areas of research (interview with Aminuddin Kasim, 25 September 2014 in Palu).

Palu's budget allocated reparations to victims in the form of free education or scholarships, free medical services, and other forms of assistance to an amount of IDR 500,000 for each of the 578 verified victims (*Palunews.com*, 16 June 2014). To support these programmes, a counselling centre was set up within Palu's Anutapura General Hospital to provide free counselling for victims of human rights abuses, victims who suffered from conflict-related trauma, victims of domestic violence, people addicted to drugs, victims of violence in the workplace, and active smokers (Mastura, 2014, 12).

The Bylaw and Mayoral Decree as well as the reparation programmes became one of the achievements of Mastura's leadership. In 2013, the Ministry of Law and Human Rights awarded the City of Palu with the national award as 'City of Human Rights Awareness' (*Kota Sadar HAM*). Palu's government made a declaration, which was signed by the Mayor, the Governor of Central Sulawesi, Longki Djonggala, and the Minister of Law and Human Rights Amir Syamsuddin on 20 May 2013.[7] The ten points of the declaration included points such as rejection of discrimination and violence as well as a promise to "protect and fulfil the rights of the victims of human rights abuses whose rights have been denied, especially their rights for truth, justice, and guarantee of non-recurrence".

Assessing transitional justice initiatives in Palu

Compared to policies and mechanisms taken at the state level in Jakarta, the regional level transitional justice tried in Palu has been more successful and positive both in terms of processes and outcomes. The processes were initiated and led by SKP HAM and victims at the grassroots level, adopting community-based approach at the village level. The strategy started to change, however, when SKP HAM approached and involved local government officials in 2010. Together they sequentially adopted three aspects of the transitional justice paradigm: truth-seeking, reconciliation and reparations. The organisation began with a truth-seeking initiative that involved documenting testimonies and collecting historical materials. Together with discussions at the village level, this initiative led to community reconciliation and social acknowledgement of the victims' narratives of sufferings. All of these initiatives took place at the grassroots level, but also involved local-level officials and religious leaders. When the initiatives were brought to a higher level of authority, the mechanism chosen for settling the 1965 mass violence was through policy and a programme of reparations. The documentation and reconciliation projects became the basis for formal acknowledgement by the Palu City government and for the modest reparations it provided. Other stakeholders were also involved, including local socio-cultural figures, university researchers, and activists.

The process leading to the reparation programme proved a success because the local government utilised data collected by SKP HAM as well as their networks

7 See http://sulteng.kemenkumham.go.id/berita/berita-utama/368-menteri-hukum-dan-ham-r-i-mendeklarasikan-desa-kelurahan-sadar-hukum-dan-kota-sadar-ham. Accessed 2 April 2015.

and grassroots support. This was a mutually beneficial collaboration between SKP HAM and the government. SKP HAM were able to formalise their programmes for victims by achieving state acknowledgement and reparation policies, and the Palu government also benefited from using SKP HAM's data and grassroots networks to deliver services and support from some of the city's most prominent and influential residents.

The success in designing and establishing these measures could potentially lead to successful implementation. Data collected by SKP HAM was later verified by the government and used as a list of beneficiaries who can access the reparation programme in the city's budget. The Mayor's apology gave the victims a sense of relief and acknowledgement (Discussion with some of the victims in Kayumalue, 24 September 2014). This, in itself, is a form of symbolic reparation for victims.

The main challenge for programme implementation will be to involve the wider public. The policies related to the reparation programme have not been widely promoted to the public, and government staff and officials also have not received much background information. Even though researchers from the Tadulako University conducted the verification for the reparation programme, ironically, the leader of the research team was not aware of the background of the research, which led him to interpret the findings of the research quite differently. Rather than supporting reparations for the 1965 victims, he argued that the research found no discrimination against victims and their families in education and health, and therefore the reparation programme was not necessary (interview with Aminuddin Kasim in Palu, 25 September 2014).[8]

The socialisation started with a few sessions of talk shows on local television and radios. SKP HAM also organised and hosted several events to inform the public on the reparation policies, such as the *DK* as part of the 'Year of Truth' (*Tahun Kebenaran*) project which, as explained in the last chapter, collected hundreds of cases of past human rights violence from 1965 until 2005. Palu was chosen to hold one of the testimony hearings because of the city's record of achievement in reconciliation. During the event, Rusdy once more delivered his apology to victims and announced the reparation programme.

Conditions for transitional justice

The transitional justice initiative in Palu needs to be situated within the context of decentralisation that was implemented from 2001. Under the New Order, Jakarta controlled all decisions and resources in the regions. Faced with the disastrous economic legacy of the Soekarno period, Soeharto's government

8 Different interpretations of the findings came from two different methods used in the research. The first method used forms adapted from SKP HAM and distributed to victims and their families by SKP HAM's staff. The other method used a sample of informants who were interviewed by members of the research team from the university. These informants included the heads of health centres and schools.

prioritised economic development by enforcing 'stability', as opposed to political freedom, as the precondition for growth. This included limiting the regions' roles and centralising authority in Jakarta for the purposes of 'development'. However, the central government's tight control over resources in the regions gave rise to resentment which was widely articulated during the *reformasi* period. While popular movements in Jakarta demanded democratisation, regional movements and local elites demanded autonomy (Aspinall and Fealy, 2003; Erb et.al., 2005; Forrester, 1999; Nordholt and van Klinken, 2007). Some regions, such as Aceh, West Papua, East Timor, and Riau, demanded independence (Pratikno, 2005: 24).

When Soeharto's regime collapsed and had to be replaced by Habibie's administration, the government faced mounting pressure both at the national and local/regional levels. Unlike Soeharto, Habibie yielded to the demands with the aim of gaining political legitimacy and support. Moreover, Habibie's still-ruling party, Golkar, under political fire for its past domination, tried to maintain its power bases in the regions, especially the outer islands, by supporting regional autonomy (Nordholt and van Klinken, 2007: 12). Two laws were drafted and passed quickly and quietly: Law No. 22 of 1999 on local government and Law No. 25 of 1999 on the fiscal balance between the central government and the regions (Rasyid, 2003). The laws significantly changed centre-region relations and had two main implications for local government, greatly increasing the autonomy for district and city governments to manage their own resources, administration, and, to some extent, finances.

Roles of NGOs and victims

The most significant impact of decentralisation in Indonesia was that the policy greatly increased the roles of local actors in political life, both in local government structures and in local civil society. In the Palu reparation policy, the most significant roles were those played by SKP HAM and the executive government led by Mayor Rusdy.

SKP HAM, as discuss earlier, played a major role in initiating and working together with the local government on reconciliation and reparation. Three factors that contributed to the organisation being able to play a leading role were the strategies it used, the backgrounds of the key actor, and the participation of victims in its activities. First, the strategy used by SKP HAM was above all inclusive, in a sense that it included a broad range of actors in their initiatives. The *Diskusi Kampung* started at the village level in remote areas, including an area called Kayumalue that was well known as a former communist base. Many local people in this area were detained and suffered enforced labour in 1965 and afterwards. Discussions were also held in other villages, involving the village and sub-district heads as well as ordinary citizens. The meetings took place mostly in mosques or village meeting halls. Each meeting was attended by a relatively small number of people and started with local rituals such as praying.

Individual leaders of civil society organisations can also play a significant role in determining the success or failure of local initiatives. As mentioned above, the secretary general of SKP HAM in Palu, Nurlaela Lamasitudju, came from a family with strong Islamic ties. Other than Nurlaela, SKP HAM also relied on younger generation activists who were either victims themselves or family members of victims of the 1965 mass violence. These young activists were very active, especially in documenting and verifying data on victims.

The third internal factor was the involvement of victims. In Palu and Central Sulawesi in general, some victims were already members of several national victims' rights groups, such as LPKP, LPRKROB and YPKP, before Sekber 1965 or SKP HAM were established. However, these two new local organisations differed from the other victims' rights groups established by former political prisoners and survivors of the 1965 mass violence not only in organisational structure but also in membership. Although the new organisations involved victims in their decision-making processes, the ideas, and networks as well as resources mostly came from the younger activists who led the organisations. Victims only became active when they were invited to events or other activities such as documentation.

Local political dynamics and the local elite

The other actor that contributed to the success of local transitional justice in Palu was the local political elite. In Palu, and in Central Sulawesi in general, local politics is shaped by an elite identity politics that is largely based on ethnicity and clan connections. Identity politics is central to local political competition and often results in communal and religious conflicts such as the conflicts in Poso, Donggala, Morowali, and some areas in Palu (Aragon, 2007; Diprose, 2007; McRae, 2013).

Identity politics has long been a central issue in debates on regional autonomy in Indonesia, even during the early years of the Republic. Feith (1962: 29) points out that the ethnic groups' communal loyalties existed along with the new identity of 'Indonesia'. However, demands for greater regional economy increased over time due to dissatisfaction over inequitable socio-economic development and over-centralised administration: the regions outside Java felt marginalised socially and politically (Booth, 2000; Harvey, 1977). As early as the 1950s many *pamong praja* (government officials) and military commanders were sent from Java to the regions, prompting discontent in the regions, including in local military garrisons who wanted to be led by 'native sons' (*anak daerah*) (Feith, 1962: 496; Harvey 1977: 9).

Under the New Order, these policies continued and became even more characterised by top-down decision-making and minimum accommodation of local diversity. This included appointing preferred candidates, mostly high-ranking military officers to provincial and district head positions, a policy commonly known as 'dropping' from the centre (Diprose, 2007: 8; Malley, 1999: 76). Over the years, dissatisfaction with this policy grew stronger in many regions, leading to demands for the central government to appoint '*putra daerah*' or native sons to head the regions.

In Central Sulawesi, the local elite resisted 'dropping' in the 1970s. The Kaili are the largest ethnic group in Central Sulawesi but there has long been underlying tension in the province, especially since other ethnic groups have tended to dominate the local government and bureaucracy (interview with Haliadi in Palu, 25 September 2014). The first governor appointed to lead the newly established province in 1964 was Anwar Gelar Datuk Madjo Basa Nan Kuning, a bureaucrat from West Sumatra. He was replaced in 1968 by a police colonel Mohammad Yasin, known as the father of the Brimob. His government was dominated by Christian Bataks and Torajans. To address elite dissatisfaction in the province, Yasin promised to have a *putra daerah* succeed him. However, ethnic tensions intensified when Jakarta appointed A. R. Tambunan, a Batak General from the Armed Forces, to succeed Yasin. The middle-class elite in Central Sulawesi organised a movement to protest against his appointment and leadership. This movement was led by prominent local figures including Saiyid Muhammad bin Idrus Aljufrie, one of the leaders of the most influential Islamic schools in Central Sulawesi, Alkhairaat. As a result of their resistance, some members of the local elite were arrested and detained arbitrarily in 1975. The government accused them of being 'PKI Gaya Baru' or the 'New Style PKI'. This was the fourth wave of arrests mentioned previously in this chapter. They were released in 1977.

Replacing Tambunan was another general from the Armed Forces, Moenafri. Moenafri held the position of governor only for one year from 1978 to 1979. However, he appointed many 'local sons' to government positions. He was temporarily replaced by Colonel Eddy Djadjang Djajaatmadja (1979–1980), also from the Armed Forces, and eventually succeeded by his colleague General Edy Sabara (1980–1981). Sabara proposed a local son, Galib Lasahido, then the Regional Secretary, to replace him. Lasahido became the next Governor from 1981 to 1986, the first local son to lead the region. From then on, *putra daerah*, both from military and civilian backgrounds, have governed Central Sulawesi (Diprose, 2007).

In Palu, the identity politics that matters most is that of the various ethnic Kaili clans. The Kaili was the largest ethnic group in Palu in the past. The census in 2000 showed the Kaili population was at 38.7 per cent followed by Bugis (22.5 per cent), Javanese (9.4 per cent), Gorontalo (2.9 per cent), Buol (1.2 per cent), Balinese (1.1 per cent) and others (24.2 per cent) (Lampe, 2014: 313). Kaili leaders have been dominating political positions in Palu, while other ethnic groups, especially 'pendatang' or migrants, controlled economic resources. Since 1978, Palu's mayors have mostly come from the Kaili ethnic group. Rusdy also had a Kaili ethnic background, as did many other bureaucrats and members of parliament.

There are many clans within the Kaili ethnic group, easily identified by their family names. Some are descendants of local monarchs in the past and have maintained their socio-political influence. The dynamics of local politics in Palu very much depended on the roles of some of these clans, such as Ponulele, Djanggola, Tombolotutu, Lamarauna, Pettalolo, and Lamakarate (Lampe, 2014: 305).

Hailing from a less influential clan, Rusdy was nevertheless elected twice as mayor of Palu. Rusdy's father had been the chair of the Masyumi (*Majelis Syuro Muslimin Indonesia*, Council of Indonesian Muslim Associations) party. However, when Soeharto amalgamated political parties in 1973 and Masyumi was absorbed into Partai Persatuan Pembangunan (Development Unity Party or PPP), Rusdy chose not to join the national party. Instead, as with many other politicians in Sulawesi, he joined Golkar where he gradually built a political career.

From 2005, Rusdy had been establishing his influence through his own political network. He was a senior politician from Golkar and had served as the party's chairperson in Central Sulawesi. He was also the speaker of Palu's parliament for two terms before he ran for mayor in 2005. In the election, he won 70 per cent of the total votes.[9]

Golkar was the majority party in Sulawesi and other eastern parts of Indonesia. The party dominated elections during the New Order never winning less than 82 per cent of the votes in the province. After the 1998 transition, Golkar maintained its position as the leading party even though its share of the votes declined from 54.5 per cent in the 1999 election to only 19.3 per cent in the 2014 national election (see Chart 6.1 below). Local scholars believe this to indicate that party politics is not important for voters, whereas identity politics is (*Kompas*, 23 February 2009).

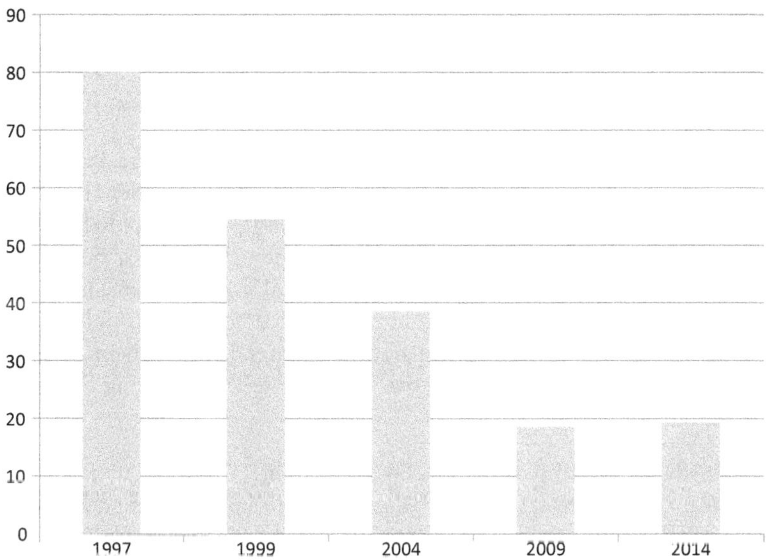

Chart 6.1 Percentage of Votes for Golkar Party in Central Sulawesi in National Election.

9 http://news.detik.com/read/2005/08/01/231736/414093/10/. Accessed 10 April 2015

Other than being ethnically Kaili, Rusdy also had political influence in the PP (*Pemuda Pancasila*, Pancasila Youth), a paramilitary organisation which he led for many years in Central Sulawesi and as Mayor still chaired its advisory board. The PP is a semi-official political group created in 1959 by General A. H. Nasution to support the New Order. Members of the PP are largely recruited from *preman* (the word was originally from freeman, or vreijmaan, referring to semi-official thugs). Officially, the organisation is said to be independent and not affiliated to any political party; however, it channelled members' political aspirations through the Golkar party (Ryter, 1998: 45–69). The PP has always provided security forces, especially the police and the Army as well as government authorities at the national and local levels, with 'security services' in exchange for concessions and control over various formal and informal economic sectors. They have been involved in numerous violent events and criminal acts in Indonesia, including the 1965 killings.[10]

In Central Sulawesi, the PP was also known to have had major influence in local government. Many of the local elite were members of this organisation, including the current Governor of Central Sulawesi, Longki Djanggola, who is also a former Chairperson of PP and a junior to Rusdy in the organisation. Other than Longki, the district heads of Toli-toli, Saleh Bantilan, and of Donggala, Kasman Lasa, were also PP activists. Various head of government departments at the provincial and district levels as well as members of parliaments were also affiliated to PP.[11]

When asked about the articles published in *Tempo* magazine's special edition on the 1965 mass violence in which he was also interviewed for his apology to victims, Rusdy talked about PP and his 'influence' as PP's chair in security matters:

> In Medan the perpetrators [of the 1965 mass violence] were Pemuda Pancasila and the Army. I was the leader of Pemuda Pancasila, but after I talked in *Tempo*, Yapto [the national chairperson of PP] never scolded me ... No one dares to speak against me here. Even when there was a prison breakout, the police had to call me for help. They all stood by me. The prisoners said *eh kak* [oh brother], and I told them to fix (solve the problem) it. The police only stood there and did nothing. Later I asked them "Have you done it?", they said "It's done, Boss. We've "fixed" everything" (Interview, 26 September 2014).

During Rusdy's leadership, there was no major political conflict with any political opposition in the town. Golkar won seats in Palu's parliament and Rusdy was able to manage harmonious relations with the body. He also placed some of his

10 One explanation of PP's involvement in perpetrating the mass violence in North Sumatra is Joshua Oppenheimer's film, *The Act of Killings* (2012). See also Ryter (1998: 55–57).

11 See "Pemuda Pancasila Sulteng Terpandang karena Terdidik", at http://www.metrosulawesi.com/article/pemuda-pancasila-sulteng-terpandang-karena-terdidik. Accessed 10 April 2015.

relatives in the bureaucracy. Anita Mastura, who was the person from Palu City's Regional Development Planning Body who was authorised to lead the verification and implementation of the reparation programme, was Rusdy's nephew.

In his statement quoted at the beginning of this chapter, Rusdy implied two things: one is that it was possible to try to deal with the legacy of the 1965 mass violence partially at the local level, rather than attempting to settle it comprehensively at the national level; and second, that it was difficult to resolve it nationally because the issue was highly political.

Rusdy is surely right. What SKP HAM in Palu managed to achieve shows that despite stagnation of transitional justice at the national level, there was still space for local civil society groups and local governments to address even the most politically sensitive, and the most massive, case of past abuses: the 1965 mass violence. Moreover, positive outcomes of regional initiatives, such as that in Palu, can potentially create 'snowball effects', inspiring other regions to adopt similar measures. Both Rusdy and Nurlaela Lamasitudju of SKP HAM have been promoting these policies and programmes in other regions as well as in Jakarta. Rusdy has established good relations with some numerous government bodies, such as Komnas HAM, LPSK, Komnas Perempuan, the Office of Presidential Advisory Board, and the Ministry of Law and Human Rights. He has also presented his policies in various national events mostly in Jakarta. Meanwhile Nurlaela and SKP HAM have also become active members of the KKPK which works on truth-seeking and restorative justice for cases of human rights violations throughout Indonesia. Nurlaela also maintains strong networks in Palu and has been involved in various national and international events on human rights campaign and advocacy.

National organisations and coalition such as KKPK are also seeking to work with regional governments to encourage and promote similar reconciliation and reparation measures. ELSAM, for example, has since 2013 been working with the Sanggau city government in West Kalimantan on creating human rights-based local bylaws (ELSAM, 2014). Similarly, institutions such as LPSK, Komnas Perempuan and Komnas HAM have also been calling for local groups and regional governments to come up with their own measures to deal with cases of human rights abuses.

However, the second proposition implicit in Rusdy's comment that dealing with the legacies of 1965 is a political challenge is also worth some consideration. Although the truth of what really happened on the night of 30 September remains a subject of endless debate, the mass violence that took place after 1 October 1965 is hardly debatable. The magnitude of the violence points to its systemic roots and its links to the political machine which became the New Order. Nevertheless, discussing the root cause of the violence remains a major challenge since elements of the New Order continue to have a role in the country's political life, including at the local level (see for example Hadiz, 2005).

In Palu, SKP HAM addressed the 1965 mass violence by trying to depoliticise it and its implications for today. Their programmes and activities were built around the language of human rights, detaching them from the political context of the mass violence and politically neutralising the violence by depicting it as a narrative of human tragedy. As a consequence, the group marginalised the systemic and political root causes of the violence from their discussions. As Nurlaela said,

> In Palu, when I met *tapol* for the first time, there were LPKP '65, LPR KROB, but their activities were mostly 'underground' ... They only met secretly ... They came to NGO events, joined in advocacy activities on land rights and some other [issues]. By that time they did not speak using a human rights framework ... We convinced them that if we tell people that the 1965 violence happened to many people, then we can see a clear picture of what happened to them (interview in Jakarta, 8 May 2012).

Nurlaela wanted these victims to speak in a universal language of human rights, rather than to emphasise the political aspects of their experiences. On the one hand, such an approach could help them in gaining sympathy and support from the wider community and from local decision-makers. It opened up more possibilities for healing and reconciliation for victims and for the local community. However, when we remember that one purpose of transitional justice is supposed to be to achieve prospects for the rule of law and democracy under a new regime, it is obvious that such an approach might potentially lead to only a highly localised collective memory, doing little to challenge legacies of violence at national level and effectively sustaining impunity nationwide.

Conclusion

The policies and measures taken by the Palu City's government were an important development in dealing with past injustice in Indonesia. This initiative was made possible because of decentralisation policies. Decentralisation, by giving more autonomy to the regions to handle their own bureaucracies, administration, and finances, often results in more corruption and collusion among local elites, and tension among members of local groups due to politicisation of ethnic identities. In most places, there has been only limited space for victims of past human rights abuses to articulate their narratives.

The Palu case has shown that things can be different. From years of advocacy and documentation work at the grassroot level, SKP HAM brought the narratives of victims of the 1965 mass violence into the public sphere and successfully incorporated them into local government policies on human rights. The popular mayor acknowledged the victims' sufferings in a formal apology on behalf of the Palu government. Moreover, he used SKP HAM's data to provide reparations for victims.

Two of the main factors that contributed to these positive outcomes were the roles of local actors and the dynamics of local politics. SKP HAM and victims had opportunities to work on the issue initially at the community level and achieved considerable success. But it is hard to avoid concluding that the individual leadership of Mayor Rusdy as the head of the government in Palu was critical. For ethnic and other reasons, he enjoyed strong local legitimacy, and was able to mobilise his influence and networks as a senior politician with Golkar and Pemuda Pancasila backgrounds to introduce what, to date, has been one of Indonesia's most remarkable experiments with local-level transitional justice

Chapter 7

Towards Post-Transitional Justice?

In this book, I have aimed to do three things: to assess the record of transitional justice efforts in post-Soeharto Indonesia, explain how this record was shaped by the nature of the country's democratic transition, and to investigate the implications of the transitional justice record for Indonesia's democracy.

My first goal, then, was one of *assessment*. Assessing transitional justice in Indonesia can be problematic. One may argue that Indonesia is a case of successful transitional justice because the country has adopted various policies and mechanisms to promote human rights and state accountability. However, previous assessments of Indonesia's transitional justice experience have mostly found that the outcomes did not meet expectations. By assessing both the procedural and substantive aspects of several mechanisms adopted by the state in Indonesia, my research found that transitional justice in Indonesia was at best a qualified success in its adoption of a variety of mechanisms and their implementation but that these mechanisms completely failed to achieve the broad objectives of transitional justice. My investigation of two examples of state-sponsored transitional justice mechanisms, the ad hoc human rights trials for East Timor and the 1984 Tanjung Priok massacre, and the Law on Truth and Reconciliation Commission, found that both the adoption and design of transitional justice mechanisms, and their implementation, were flawed from the beginning.

In terms of the trials, the flaws started as early as the establishment of their legal foundation and the passage of the Law No. 26 of 2000 on Human Rights Courts. In responding to international pressure for accountability for what happened during and after the 1999 referendum in East Timor, the political elite of the new regime, both in the executive and legislature, issued the law in less than six months. As I reviewed in Chapter 3, the law combined legal and political aspects, representing a fusion of justice goals that complied with at least some of the demands of international law with the political compromises characteristic of Indonesia's time of transition. The mixture of these aspects resulted in a legal foundation for human rights trials that failed to address some of the most important aspects of justice in cases of gross abuses: command responsibility, crimes against humanity, and reparation for victims.

As international pressure in response to the violence in East Timor was mounting, so was domestic pressure for justice on the 1984 Tanjung Priok massacre, with the latter case a particular concern of newly influential Islamic political forces. Both sets of pressure were then accommodated in a 'double package' of ad hoc human rights trials using the Law on Human Rights as their legal foundation. In Chapter 3, I explained in detail how certain elements in these trials gave rise to serious flaws, ranging from the inconsistencies between the Komnas HAM investigations and the Kejagung (*Kejaksaan Agung*, Attorney General Office) indictments, whereby the latter institution seriously watered down the charges against perpetrators, to the serious intimidation of victims, witnesses, and judges in the cases. The courts passed verdicts on several middle- to low-ranking military officers, but they all appealed and were acquitted. In other words, both ad hoc human rights trials were set up to fail and they did just that. The results, as predicted, fell far short of what human rights advocates had hoped for. Not only did impunity remain intact but also the trials also failed to present a comprehensively truthful account of the abuses that had occurred or to provide reparation for the victims.

Another attempt to establish a mechanism of transitional justice that I assessed was the protracted and ultimately unsuccessful process of forming a Truth and Reconciliation Commission. Unlike the trials, which were in large part triggered by international pressure, this initiative got underway mainly in response to domestic pressures for truth and justice for various cases of human rights abuses, including the 1965 mass violence. Initiated by President Abdurrahman Wahid, the drafting and eventual passage of the Law on the TRC took place over four years under the leadership of three presidents. The law was passed just when the members of the first fully post-Soeharto parliament were finishing their term in office in 2004. Subsequently, the new executive under President Susilo Bambang Yudhoyono failed to implement the law. The processes of creating the law itself involved various elements from civil society including victims. However, the decision-making processes were not transparent, and the law suffered fundamental flaws in terms of the objectives and procedures it set out to achieve. One fundamental flaw, as I explained in Chapter 4, was the lack of a mandate to dig out the truth on the systemic roots of violence under the repressive Soeharto regime. In addition, the law would only deliver truth and reparations to victims if perpetrators were granted unconditional amnesties. For this reason, human rights groups lodged a case for judicial review with the Constitutional Court, which decided to annul the entire Law rather than retracting particular articles.

Having assessed the adoption and implementation of transitional justice mechanisms in Indonesia, my attention turned to *causes*. I attempted to explain the factors that led to these outcomes. My investigation focused on the most important contextual factor: the nature of the political transition in Indonesia. Chapter 3 elaborated on this transition and its dynamics, starting in 1998. Borrowing from Samuel Huntington's typology, I argued that Indonesia's political transition combined elements of both replacement and transplacement types of transition.

Replacement-type regime change occurs when an authoritarian regime collapses or is overthrown and replaced by a successor democratic political order. In Indonesia's case, this element of regime change was obvious in the sudden collapse of the New Order's authority in the early months of 1998, and by the inability of the leading elements in the New Order government to overcome the multiple national crises Indonesia was experiencing and regain their former domestic political legitimacy. Their inability to manoeuvre in the face of this crisis left them with reduced power to resist calls for state accountability in various spheres, including human rights. The adoption of transitional justice measures to deal with the human rights legacy of the New Order was a result. Not only could former generals, Golkar politicians, and other elements of the old regime try to regain public confidence by supporting the adoption of transitional justice measures, doing so helped them to distance themselves from Soeharto's regime. In other words, as I argued in Chapters 3–5, transitional justice was largely a *tactical concession* for many important political actors. It did not reflect deep normative transformation or the adoption of a new philosophical outlook on the part of many of the key actors authorising the new transitional justice framework. While this context helped to facilitate the adoption of transitional justice measures, it also helped inject weaknesses into them.

If replacement regime changes are sudden, transplacements tend to take place more gradually and involve protracted bargaining between elements of the old regime and the rising elites of the new democratic order. Especially once Indonesia's new '*Reformasi* Order' began to settle into place, more or less coinciding with the election of a new parliament and the appointment of Abdurrahman Wahid as president in 1999, Indonesia's transition came more and more to resemble transplacement. A new pro-democracy political elite was gaining influence rapidly and demanding reforms in various sectors of politics and governance, but from the beginning, these reformers shaped the direction of the transition in cooperation with elements of the old regime. Negotiations between new and old elements of the political elite were constantly taking place on all aspects of decision-making, including in the design and implementation of transitional justice measures. I thus argued in this book that the problems that arose in the implementation and outcomes of transitional justice were not merely about lack of political will on the part of state leaders—an attitude which is common among human rights advocates in Indonesia—but are better viewed as being products of this constant negotiation of power at the elite level. Overall, justice objectives were compromised in the interests of achieving reconciliation among the political elite.

My third aim in this book was to identify the *impacts* of transitional justice on Indonesia's democracy. Unlike many transitional justice studies, my research was unable to demonstrate that transitional justice measures in Indonesia had any substantial impacts on the rule of law, peace, human rights promotion, or national reconciliation. Instead, implementation of transitional justice in Indonesia resulted in legalising the culture of impunity by acquitting all individuals who committed past human rights abuses. Some of the consequences are visible in the fact that electoral democracy has provided perpetrators of human rights abuses to be elected as candidates in executive and legislative branches of government, at both national and regional levels. By adopting transitional justice policies and mechanisms, Indonesia gained considerable international respectability, but at the same time it failed to significantly improve domestic state accountability by not fully acknowledging past injustices or delivering outcomes that satisfied the victims. More fundamentally, state-sponsored mechanisms failed to acknowledge the systemic roots of violence under the repressive New Order regime and failed to achieve a *political judgement* about past wrongs. Such failures are an indication that the old regime's power is alive and well, and continuing to exercise strong influence.

Although I could not find evidence pointing to strong national-level impacts of transitional justice on Indonesian democracy, I also found that transitional justice in Indonesia is developing in different directions as a consequence of the stagnation of state-sponsored mechanisms. A decentralisation of truth and reconciliation efforts has occurred, with strengthened networks of civil society working on human rights, increased articulation of victims' narrative of sufferings, and the emergence of alternative ways to come to terms with Indonesia's past injustices. I explained these three consequences when I discussed two different non-state-sponsored transitional justice approaches: a bottom-up approach that involved working with communities and a margin-centre approach which involved working through regional governments. These new approaches have arisen in the vacuum created by the failure of national-level programmes.

Reflecting on transitional justice from the Indonesian experience

Indonesia is one example of the many countries that have experimented with transitional justice mechanisms in order to try to deal with the legacies of a repressive regime during a time of political transition. A whole range of approaches and mechanisms, most notably truth-seeking, prosecutions and reparations, were adopted and implemented at the state level during and after the political transition. The expectation was that these measures would strengthen Indonesia's democracy and human rights. Their failure to deliver either the truth about past abuses or justice for victims raised big questions about why it was that these expectations were not met, despite the adoption and implementation of these mechanisms. As I have just summarised, I primarily tried to resolve this puzzle by delving into the nature of Indonesia's political transition. But are there wider implications for the study of transitional justice more broadly?

Most studies of transitional justice around the globe assess the successes and failures of transitional justice based on two aspects: implementation and impacts, often with an assumption that implementing the mechanisms will automatically produce positive impacts on democracy and human rights. The Indonesian experience shows that these aspects do not necessarily correlate since the implementation of various mechanisms has not produced much in the way of positive impacts on Indonesia's democracy or human rights protection.

The problem lies in both the procedural and substantive elements of transitional justice implementation. Within the context of a political transition that had elements of both rupture and negotiation among elites, the design and implementation of transitional justice in Indonesia was above all dictated by the political dynamics of the transition and compromises within the political elite. Transitional justice above all played a role in building legitimacy for the new political order, and it helped rehabilitate some old authoritarian forces.

One lesson learned from this study is thus to the urgency of the question: of whose justice is served by transitional justice? Victims and human rights advocates in Indonesia had very different expectations than their politician counterparts. When the outcomes of these mechanisms did not satisfy victims and human rights advocates, they took up the transitional justice cause where the national government had dropped it, and tried to transplant it beyond the jurisdiction of the central government into communities and regional governments. Scholars of transitional justice, and international advocacy networks promoting it, need to be open to attempts to promote truth and justice both from below and from the margins.

However, my study also showed these alternative approaches posed problems of their own for the achievement of transitional justice objectives. First, one obvious consequence of working for truth and justice at the grassroots or local level is that partial and limited impacts and outreach. It implies the localisation of truth and justice, wherein local abuses are confronted without necessarily relating them to the experiences of other communities or the national context. Such an approach ignores the larger historical and political context of violence, and can thus also detach itself from the systemic roots of violence that served as the foundation of the repressive regime.

Second, victims and human rights advocates working at grassroots and local levels tend to rely on human rights language to frame their critique of past injustices and propose solutions. Partly because of the intimacy of social and political relations at the local level, they tend to avoid politicising past cases of abuse or attributing blame. Their approach reflects Ignatieff's (2000: 292) observation that

> Human rights activism likes to portray itself as an antipolitics, in defense of universal moral claims designed to delegitimize "political," i.e., ideological or sectarian, justifications for the abuse of human beings. In practice, impartiality and neutrality are just as impossible as universal and equal concern for everyone's human rights. Human rights activism means taking sides, mobilizing constituencies powerful enough to force abusers to stop. As a consequence, effective human rights activism is bound to be partial and political.

The depoliticisation of human rights in work of local actors is understandable given that they wanted a strategy to gain public support in the context of an Indonesian society that had long been traumatised by repression. However, an implication of this approach has been widespread inability to comprehend that past violence took place within a political context and that it was produced by a struggle for power and the targeting of particular groups in the interests of achieving and maintain power. Transitional justice needs to acknowledge and address such matters. Without it being related to the political context, transitional justice runs the risk of ending up as a procedural cosmetic covering impunity.

Transitional justice and democracy: investigating the impacts

As transitional justice became a vast area of practice and research worldwide, various analysts have focused on the effects of transitional justice policies and implementation on democracy. An early paper by Thoms, Ron, and Paris (2008) surprisingly reveals that there is insufficient evidence to support proponents' claims that transitional justice measures have positive impacts on reconciliation, human rights promotion, rule of law, or peaceful democracy. However, they also state that there is no strong evidence to support opponents' claims that transitional justice has few positives impacts on these goals. This is despite the fact that for a long-time scholars and practitioners alike not only tended to assume that the different justice mechanisms had particular impacts, and on that basis make recommendations for institutional design in newly transitioning countries. There was a 'templatisation' of transitional justice, which McEvoy says amounted to a 'seduction' (McEvoy, 2007). In fact, much of the early literature on transitional justice was driven by principles rather than empirical data, and sometimes amounted to a sort of 'faith-based' analysis (McEvoy, 2007). However, in the last decade some case-based or comparative studies have been produced on the actual practice of transitional justice and its empirical impacts (Olsen, Payne, and Reiter, 2010).

As noted in Chapter 1, Olsen, Payne, and Reiter (2010) have provided a more optimistic assessment of the positive impacts of transitional justice on democracy. Their dataset, as I mentioned in Chapter 1, suggests that transitional justice is a success when it correlates strongly with improvements in democracy and human rights. They start by breaking countries into four categories based on the transitional justice strategies they adopt. A maximalist approach entails trials; a minimalist approach emphasises amnesties; a moderate approach uses truth commissions; while a holistic approach combines more than one mechanism. Olsen, Payne, and Reiter argue that countries that adopt the final course, combining various transitional justice mechanisms, tend to be more successful at producing positive impacts for democracy and human rights protection. Yet if we were to use this categorisation, Indonesia would fall into this supposedly more successful group of countries, because it tried a range of mechanisms.

Rather than making grand claims about the impacts that state-sponsored transitional justice measures have had on democracy in Indonesia, I have shown in this book that we can demonstrate more modest consequences of the *failings* of those official efforts. My research suggests that some of the main consequences turn out to be alternatives forms of transitional justice, including new decentralised methods of achieving truth and reconciliation, strengthened networks of civil society working on human rights, and increased articulation of victims' narrative of sufferings. These consequences are apparent in the civil society and local government initiatives on transitional justice that have emerged in the shadow of the stagnation and failures of official methods.

By decentralised truth and reconciliation I refer to activities that were held in various local areas in Indonesia.[1] These activities included attempts to achieve reconciliation between victims and perpetrators of the 1965 violence in Yogyakarta, people's gatherings in Solo, memorialisation in Boyolali, Central Java, reconciliation in Palu, Central Sulawesi (the subject of a major case study in Chapter 6), reconciliation in Kupang, Nusa Tenggara Timur, and memorialisation in Aceh. Human rights NGOs and victims' rights groups initiated these activities, involving local government officials, religious figures, and other local leaders. In Solo and Palu, reconciliation meetings were held after the mayors of each city provide an official acknowledgement of and apology for past abuses. None of them attained the support of central authorities for these initiatives (even if in Palu some national links were later made).

Beyond such local impacts, another outcome, but one that is less tangible and more difficult to measure, is changing discourse on human rights in Indonesia, particularly on past human rights abuses and the notion of 'victims'. Human rights has been an increasingly popular topic of public discourse since at least the establishment of the National Commission on Human Rights (Komnas HAM) in 1993. It was very political, and very sensitive, at the end of the New Order regime and during the early years of democratisation. But it was not really until the transition in 1998 that the broader public started to acknowledge specific cases of human rights violations (such as the enforced disappearances of political activists) as being fundamentally different from ordinary criminal acts (such as kidnapping). Moreover, with the emergence of victim communities and

1 The term 'decentralised' transitional justice also appears in some journal articles, referring to strategies or approaches in implementing mechanisms of transitional justice in other countries. I note here Nevin Aiken, 'Learning to Live Together: Transitional Justice and Intergroup Reconciliation in Northern Ireland', in *The International Journal of Transitional Justice*, Volume 4, 2010, and Andrew Illiff, 'Root and Brach, Tree of Life: Sowing the Seeds of Grassroots Transitional Justice', in *Oxford Transitional Justice Research Working Paper Series*, OTJR, 2010. Aiken refers to decentralisation as combining transitional justice with a social learning approach which work on three different 'decentralised' strategies: instrumental reconciliation, socioemotional reconciliation, and distributive reconciliation. Meanwhile, Illiff refers to decentralisation as work on reconciliation, dialogue and accountability at the grassroots and community levels.

organisations, the word ‘victims’ became an important part of the discourse on human rights in Indonesia.[2]

The emergence of victim communities and public acknowledgement of ‘victims’ and their victimhood has helped open up spaces for victims to participate in many aspects of social and political transformation, which I view as an important outcome of transitional justice in Indonesia. This change has been especially significant for the 1965 victims and their family members. Though anti-communist discourse remains an important feature of political life, there have also been signs of progress. In 1999, the parliament passed Law no 3 on Elections that gave ex-political detainees the right to vote. A decision by the Constitutional Court in 2004 removed an article in Law No. 12 of 2003 on Elections (the revised version of the 1999 law) that banned former PKI members from running in elections. This change opened up possibilities for some family members of victims to run for executive and legislative positions, both locally and nationally. More generally, victims have been active in NGOs and their own organisations, advocating for their own interests, speaking up and narrating their own stories of loss and resilience. Such signs of progress may be small, but they show that all the efforts that have been put into transitional justice in post Soeharto Indonesia have not been entirely in vain.

2 This is one of the conclusions of a survey on transitional justice initiatives by International Center for Transitional Justice. See Farid, Hilmar, and Rikardo Simarmata. *The Struggle for Truth and Justice: A Survey of Transitional Justice Initiatives throughout Indonesia* (p. 111). New York: ICTJ, 2004.

Bibliography

Abidin, Zainal. *Pengadilan Hak Asasi Manusia di Indonesia*. Jakarta: ELSAM, 2007.

Akhavan, Payam. "Beyond Impunity: Can International Criminal Justice Prevent Future Atrocities?" *The American Journal of International Law* 95, no. 1 (2001): 7–31.

Akmaliah, Wahyudi. "Islah Sebagai Dalih: Studi Kasus Penyelesaian Konflik Peristiwa Tanjung Priok (1984) dan Talang Sari (1989) Pasca Rejim Orde Baru." *Jurnal Masyarakat & Budaya* 16, no. 1 (2014): 167–190.

Amnesty International. *Amnesty International Report 1997—Indonesia*. Retrieved 1 January, 1997 from http://www.refworld.org/docid/3ae6aa0160.html. Accessed 11 January, 2018.

Amnesty International. *Retroactivity Amendment Regressive for Human Rights*, Press Release, 18 August 2000 from https://www.amnesty.org.uk/press-releases/retroactivity-amendment-regressive-human-rights-0. Accessed 11 January, 2018.

Andalas, Mutiara S. J. *Kesucian Politik Agama dan Politik di Tengah Krisis Kemanusiaan*. Jakarta: Libri, 2008.

Antlöv, Hans, Rustam Ibrahim, and Peter van Tuijl. "NGO Governance and Accountability in Indonesia: Challenges in a Newly Democratizing Country." *NGO Accountability: Politics, Principles and Innovations* (2006): 147–163.

Aragon, Lorraine V. *Fields of the Lord: Animism, Christian Minorities, and State Development in Indonesia*. Honolulu: University of Hawaii Press, 2000.

Aragon, Lorraine V. "Elite Competition in Central Sulawesi." *Renegotiating Boundaries: Local Politics in Post-Suharto Indonesia* (2007): 39–66.

Arthur, Paige. "How Transitions Reshaped Human Rights: A Conceptual History of Transitional Justice." *Human Rights Quarterly* 31, no. 2 (2009): 321–367.

Aspinall, Edward. "Indonesia." In B. Szajkowski (Ed.), *Revolutionary and Dissident Movements of the World* (4th ed., pp. 183–190). Great Britain: John Harper Publishing, 2004a.

Aspinall, Edward. "Transformation of Civil Society and Democratic Breakthrough." In M. Alagappa (Ed.), *Civil Society and Political Change in Asia: Expanding and Contracting Democratic Space* (pp. 61–96). Stanford: Stanford University Press, 2004b.

Aspinall, Edward. *Opposing Suharto: Compromise, Resistance, and Regime Change in Indonesia*. Stanford: Stanford University Press, 2005.

Aspinall, Edward. "Indonesia in 2009: Democratic Triumphs and Trials." *Southeast Asian Affairs* 2010, no. 1 (2010a): 102–125.

Aspinall, Edward. "The Irony of Success." *Journal of Democracy* 21, no. 2 (2010b): 20–34.

Aspinall, Edward. "The Surprising Democratic Behemoth: Indonesia in Comparative Asian Perspective." *The Journal of Asian Studies* 74, no. 4 (2015): 889–902.

Aspinall, Edward, and Greg Fealy. *Local Power & Politics in Indonesia: Decentralisation & Democratisation.* Singapore: ISEAS–Yusof Ishak Institute, 2003.

Aspinall, Edward, and Fajran Zain. "Transitional Justice Delayed in Aceh, Indonesia." In R. Jeffery & H. J. Kim (Eds.), *Transitional Justice in the Asia-Pacific* (pp. 87–123). Cambridge: Cambridge University Press, 2013.

Banto, Tasman. "Pemuda Pancasila Sulteng Terpandang Karena Terdidik." *Metrosulawesi.* October 29, 2014. Retrieved 10 April, 2015 http://www.metrosulawesi.com/article/pemuda-pancasila-sulteng-terpandang-karena-terdidik

Barahona De Brito, Alexandra, Carmen González Enríquez, and Paloma Aguilar (Eds.), *The Politics of Memory: Transitional Justice in Democratizing Societies.* New York: Oxford University Press, 2001.

Boland, Benoit J. *The Struggle of Islam in Modern Indonesia.* The Hague: Martinus Nijhoff, 1971.

Booth, Anne. *The Indonesian Economy in the Nineteenth and Twentieth Centuries: A History of Missed Opportunities.* New York: St. Martin's Press, 2000.

Boraine, Alex. *A Country Unmasked: Inside South Africa's Truth and Reconciliation Commission.* Oxford: Oxford University Press, 2001

Botha, Belinda Megan. *Truth Commissions and Their Consequences for Legitimacy.* Houston: University of Houston, 1998.

Bourchier, David. *Lineages of Organicist Political Thought in Indonesia.* Melbourne: Monash University, 1996.

Brahm, Eric. *Getting to the Bottom of Truth: Examining Truth Commission Success and Impact.* Paper Presented at the International Studies Association Annual Meeting, Honolulu, 2005.

Brahm, Eric. *Truth Commissions and Transitional Societies: the Impact on Human Rights and Democracy.* New York: Routledge, 2010.

Brauchler, Birgit (Ed.). *Reconciling Indonesia: Grassroots Agency for Peace.* New York: Routledge, 2009.

Brendese, Philip J. *The Power of Memory in Democratic Politics.* New York: University of Ronchester Press, 2014.

Budiawan. *Mematahkan Pewarisan Ingatan: Wacana Anti-Komunis dan Politik Rekonsiliasi Pasca Soeharo* [Breaking the Immortalised Past: Anti-Communist Discourse and Reconciliatory Politics in Post-Suharto Indonesia]. Jakarta: ELSAM, 2004.

Burns, Peter. "The Post Priok Trials: Religious Principles and Legal Issues." *Indonesia* 47 (1989): 61–88.

Cassese, Antonio. "On the Current Trends towards Criminal Prosecution and Punishment of Breaches of International Humanitarian Law." *European Journal of International Law* 9, no. 1 (1998a): 2–17.

Cassese, Antonio. "Reflections on International Criminal Justice." *The Modern Law Review* 61, no. 1 (1998b): 1–10.

Cohen, David. "Seeking Justice on the Cheap: Is the East Timor Tribunal Really a Model for the Future?" *Asia Pasific Issue*, no. 61 (August, 2002). Retrieved from https://www.eastwestcenter.org/system/tdf/private/api061.pdf?file=1&type=node&id=31885

Cohen, David. *Intended to Fail: The Trials Before the Ad Hoc Human Rights Court in Jakarta*. New York: International Center for Transitional Justice, 2003.

Collins, Elizabeth Fuller, *Indonesia Betrayed: How Development Fails*. Honolulu: University of Hawaii Press, 2007.

Coppel, Charles A., ed. *Violent Conflicts in Indonesia: Analysis, Representation, Resolution*. London: Routledge, 2006.

Cribb, Robert, ed. *The Indonesian Killings of 1965–1966: Studies from Java and Bali*. Clayton: Centre of Southeast Asian Studies, Monash University, 1990.

Cribb, Robert. "Unresolved Problems in the Indonesian Killings of 1965–1966." *Asian Survey* 42, no. 4 (2002): 550–563.

Crouch, Harold. *The Army and Politics in Indonesia*. New York: Cornell University Press, 1978.

Crouch, Harold. "Indonesia: An Uncertain Outlook." *Southeast Asian Affairs* 21 (1994): 121–145.

Culla, Adi Suryadi. *Rekonstruksi Civil Society: Wacana dan Aksi Ornop di Indonesia*. Jakarta: LP3ES, 2006.

Dancy, Geoff, Hunjoon Kim, and Eric Wiebelhaus-Brahm. "The Turn to Truth: Trends in Truth Commission Experimentation." *Journal of Human Rights* 9, no. 1 (2010): 45–64.

David, Roman. "Lustration Laws in Action: the Motives and Evaluation of Lustration Policy in the Czech Republic and Poland (1989–2001)." *Law & Social Inquiry* 28, no. 2 (2003): 387–439.

Diprose, Rachael. *Passing on the Challenges or Prescribing Better Management of Diversity: Decentralization, Power-Sharing, and Conflict Dynamics in Central Sulawesi, Indonesia*. CRISE Working Paper November 2007, University of Oxford.

Duggan, Colleen. *Show Me Your Impact: Challenges and Prospects for Evaluating Transitional Justice*. Paper Presented at the Annual Meeting of the Canadian Political Science Association on May 29, 2009, Ottawa, 2009.

Duthie, Roger. "Introduction". In A. Mayer-Rieckh & P. de Grieff (Eds.), *Justice as Prevention, Vetting Public Employees in Transitional Societies* (pp. 17–18). New York: Social Science Research Council, 2007.

Eldridge, Philip John. *Non-Government Organizations and Democratic Participation in Indonesia*. Kuala Lumpur: Oxford University Press, 1995.

ELSAM. *Progress Report I on Monitoring of Tanjung Priok Trials*. Jakarta: ELSAM, 2003.

ELSAM. *Final Progress Report Pengadilan HAM Tanjung Priok: Gagal Melakukan Penuntutan yang Efektif*. Jakarta: ELSAM, 2004a.

ELSAM. *Preliminary Conclusive Report Pengadilan Hak Asasi Manusia Ad Hoc Kasus Tanjung Priok*. Jakarta: ELSAM, 2004b.

ELSAM. *Tutup Buku dengan Transitional Justice? Menutup Lembaran Hak Asasi Manusia 1999–2004 dan Membuka Lembaran Baru 2005*. Jakarta: ELSAM, 2005.

ELSAM. *Ketika Prinsip Kepastian Hukum Menghakimi Konstitusionalitas Penyelesaian Pelanggaran HAM Masa Lalu: Pandangan Kritis atas Putusan Mahkamah Konstitusi dan Implikasinya bagi Penyelesaian Pelanggaran HAM*. Jakarta: ELSAM, 2006.

Elster, Jon. "Coming to Terms with the Past. A Framework for the Study of Justice in the Transition to Democracy." *European Journal of Sociology/Archives Européennes de Sociologie* 39, no. 1 (1998): 7–48.

Elster, Jon. *Closing the Book: Transitional Justice in Historical Perspective.* Cambridge: Cambridge University Press, 2004.

Elster, Jon. *Retribution and Reparation in the Transition to Democracy.* New York: Cambridge University Press, 2006.

Erb, Maribeth, Carol Faucher, and Priyambudi Sulistiyanto (Eds.), *Deepening Democracy in Indonesia?: Direct Elections for Local Leaders (Pilkada).* Singapore: Institute of Southeast Asian Studies, 2005.

Farid, Hilmar, and Rikardo Simarmata. *The Struggle for Truth and Justice: A Survey of Transitional Justice Initiatives throughout Indonesia.* New York: International Center for Transitional Justice, 2004.

Feith, Herbert. *The Decline of Constitutional Democracy in Indonesia.* London: Cornell University Press, 1962.

Finnemore, Martha, and Kathryn Sikkink. "International Norm Dynamics and Political Change." *International Organization* 52, no. 4 (1998): 887–917.

Forrester, Geoff, and Ronald James May (Eds.), *The Fall of Soeharto.* New York: C. Hurst & Co. Publishers, 1998.

Ganie-Rochman, Meuthia. *An Uphill Struggle: Advocacy NGOs under Soeharto's New Order.* Depok: LabSosio, 2002.

Gerlach, Christian. *Extremely Violent Societies: Mass Violence in the Twentieth Century.* New York: Cambridge University Press, 2010.

Gibson, James L. *Survey of Truth and Reconciliation in South Africa, 2000–2001: Inter-University Consortium for Political and Social Research (ICPSR).* St. Louis: Washington University, 2005.

Glasius, Marlies. *Foreign Policy on Human Rights: Its Influence on Indonesia under Soeharto.* Antwerp: Intersentia Law Publisher, 1999a.

Glasius, Marlies. *Foreign Policy on Human Rights: Its Influence on Indonesia under Soeharto. School of Human Rights Research* (Vol. 4). Oxford: Intersentia, 1999b.

González, Eduardo. *The Struggle for Truth and Justice.* New York: International Center for Transitional Justice, 2004.

González, Eduardo. *Comment by the International Center for Transitional Justice on the Bill Establishing a Truth and Reconciliation Commission in Indonesia.* New York: International Center for Transitional Justice, 2005.

Guinness, Patrick. "Local Society and Culture." In H. Hill (Ed.), *Indonesia's New Order: The Dynamics of Socio-Economic Transformation* (pp. 267–304). London: Allen & Unwin, 1994.

Habermas, Jurgen. *The Theory of Communicative Action Vol. 1: Reason and Rationalization of Society.* Boston: Beacon Press, 1984.

Habibie, B. J. *Detik-Detik yang Menentukan: Jalan Panjang Indonesia Menuju Demokrasi.* Jakarta: The Habibie Centre, 2006.

Hadiprayitno, Irene Istiningsih. "Defensive Enforcement: Human rights in Indonesia." *Human Rights Review* 11, no. 3 (2010a): 373–399.

Hadiprayitno, Irene Istiningsih. "Food Security and Human Rights in Indonesia." *Development in Practice* 20, no. 1 (2010b): 122–130.

Hadiwinata, Bob S. *The Politics of NGOs in Indonesia: Developing Democracy and Managing a Movement.* London: Routledge, 2003.

Hadiz, Vedi. *Dinamika Kekuasaan: Ekonomi Politik Indonesia Pasca-Soeharto.* Jakarta: LP3ES, 2005.

Harvey, Barbara Sillars. *Permesta: Half a Rebellion* (Vol. 57). Ithaca: Cornell University Modern Indonesia, 1977.

Hasibuan, Albert, Todung Mulya Lubis, Asmara Nababan, H. S. Dillon, Koesparmono Irsan, Nursyahbani Katjasungkana, and Munir. *Ringkasan Eksekutif Laporan Komisi Penyelidikan Pelanggaran Hak Asasi Manusia di Timor Timur*. Timor Timur: KPP HAM, 2000.

Hayner, Priscilla B. *Unspeakable Truths: Facing the Challenge of Truth Commissions*. New York: Routledge, 2001.

Hayner, Priscilla B. *Unspeakable Truth: Transitional Justice and Challenge of Truth Commissions* (2nd ed.). New York: Routledge, 2011.

Hazan, Pierre. "Measuring the Impact of Punishment and Forgiveness: A Framework for Evaluating Transitional Justice." *International Review of the Red Cross* 88, no. 861 (2006): 19–47.

Hefner, Robert W. "Civil Islam: Muslims and Democratisation in Indonesia." *Survival* 44 no. 3 (2002): 153–154.

Honna, Jun. *Military Doctrines and Democratic Transition: A Comparative Perspective on Indonesia's Dual Function and Latin American National Security Doctrines*, PhD Thesis. Canberra: The Australian National University, 1999.

Honna, Jun. *Military Politics and Democratisation in Indonesia*. London: Routledge, 2003.

Horne, Cynthia M. "The Impact of Lustration on Democratization in Post-Communist Countries." *International Journal of Transitional Justice* 8, no. 3 (2014a): 496–521.

Horne, Cynthia M. "Lustration, Transitional Justice, and Social Trust in Post-Communist Countries. Repairing or Wresting the Ties that Bind?" *Europe-Asia Studies* 66, no. 2 (2014b): 225–254.

Horne, Cynthia M. "Reconstructing 'Traditional' Justice from the Outside in: Transitional Justice in Aceh and East Timor." *Journal of Peacebuilding & Development* 9, no. 2 (2014c): 17–32.

Humphrey, Michael. *Human Rights Politics & Transitional Justice*. Paper Presented at the Law and Society Association Australia and New Zealand (LSAANZ) Conference, University of Sydney, 2008.

Human Rights Watch. *Indonesia: Violence and Political Impasse in Papua* (Vol. 2). New York: Human Rights Watch, 2001a.

Human Rights Watch. *The War in Aceh* (Vol. 3, No. 4). New York: Human Rights Watch, 2001b.

Human Rights Watch. *A Return to the New Order?* (Vol. 15). New York: Human Rights Watch, 2003.

Huntington, Samuel. P. *The Third Wave: Democratisation in the Late Twentieth Century*. Oklahoma: University of Oklahoma Press, 1991.

Ignatieff, Michael. *Human Rights as Politics and Idolatry*. Princeton: Princeton University Press, 2000.

International Center for Transitional Justice, and KontraS. *Derailed: Transitional Justice in Indonesia Since the Fall of Soeharto*. New York: International Center for Transitional Justice, 2011.

International Criminal Court. *Rome Statute of International Criminal Court* (1998). Retrieved from http://legal.un.org/icc/statute/99_corr/cstatute.htm

International Crisis Group. *Resolving Timor Leste's Crisis* (Vol. 120). Brussels: International Crisis Group, 2006.

Instruksi Presiden no. 1 2003 tentang Pembentukan Propinsi Papua (President Instruction no. 1 of 2003 on the Establishment of West Papua Province).

Instruksi Presiden Tentang Dukungan Pemerintah dan Pemerintah Daerah untuk Kelancaran Pelaksanaan Pemilihan Kepala Daerah no. 7 2005 (Presidential Decree no. 7 2005 About Government and Local Government Support for Smooth Implementation of Regional Head Election).

Instruksi Presiden no. 50 1993 tentang Komisi HAM (Presidential Decree no. 50 of 1993 on Human Right Commission).

Instruksi Presiden no. 53 2001 tentang Pembentukan Peradilan HAM Ad Hoc untuk Timor Timur dan Tanjung Priok (Presidential Decree no. 53 of 2001 on The Establishment of Ad Hoc Human Rights Courts for East Timor and Tanjung Priok).

Instruksi Presiden no. 129 1998 tentang Rencana Aksi Nasional HAM (Presidential Decree no. 129 of 1998 on National Action Plan of Human Rights).

Instruksi Presiden no. 181 1998 tentang Komnas Perempuan (Presidential Decree no. 181 of 1998 on the National Commission Against Discrimination Against Women).

Instruksi Presiden no. 1 of 2000 tentang Permasalahan Orang-Orang Indonesia yang Berada di Luar Negeri dan Terhalang Pulang ke Tanah Air Sejak Terjadinya Peristiwa G 30 S/PKI. Presidential Instruction no. 1 of 2000 on The Problems of Indonesian People Who Are Abroad and Hindered Returning to Homeland Since Occurrence of Event G 30 S / PKI).

Instruksi Presiden no. 1 2003 tentang Percepatan Pelaksanaan Undang-Undang no. 45 1999 tentang Pembentukan Propinsi Irian Jaya Tengah, Irian Jaya Barat, Kabuoaten Paniai, Kabupaten Mimika, Kabupaten Punjak Jaya, dan Kota Sorong (Presidential Instruction no. 1 of 2003 on the Acceleration of Proliferation of Law No. 45 1999 on the Establishment of Irian Jaya Province, Irian Jaya Barat Province, Paniai District, Mimika District, Punjak Jaya District, and Sorong Municipality).

International Tribunal for the Prosecution of Persons Responsible for Serious Violations of International Humanitarian Law Committed in the Territory of the former Yugoslavia since 1991. *Rules of Procedure and Evidence* (2015). Retrieved from http://www.icty.org/x/file/Legal%20Library/Rules_procedure_evidence/IT032_Rev43_en.pdf

Jeffery, Renée, and Hun Joon Kim. "New horizons: Transitional justice in the Asia-Pacific." In R. Jeffery and H. J. Kim (Eds.), *Transitional Justice in the Asia-Pacific*. New York: Cambridge University Press, (2014), 1–32.

Jetschke, Anja. "Die Aktuellen Entwicklungen in Indonesien und Osttimor." *Antimilitarismus Information* 29, no. 10 (1999): 57–64.

Jetschke, Anja. *Human Rights and State Security: Indonesia and the Philippines*. Philadelphia: University of Pennsylvania Press, 2011.

Junge, J. Fabian. *Kesempatan yang Hilang, Janji yang tak Terpenuhi. Pengadilan HAM Ad Hoc untuk Kejahatan di Tanjung Priok 1984*. Jakarta: KontraS, 2008.

Juwana, Hikmahanto. "Special Report: Assessing Indonesia's Human Rights Practice in the Post-Soeharto Era: 1998–2003". *Singapore Journal of International & Comparative Law* 7 (2003): 644–677.

Kasim, Ifdhal. *Menghadapi Masa lalu: Mengapa Amnesti?* Briefing Paper tentang Komisi Kebenaran dan Rekonsiliasi. Jakarta: ELSAM, 2000a.

Kasim, Ifdhal. Apakah Komisi Kebenaran dan Rekonsiliasi Itu? (2000b). Retrieved 3 March, 2013, from http://referensi.ELSAM.or.id/2014/09/apakah-komisi-kebenaran-dan-rekonsiliasi-itu/

Kasim, Ifdhal, and Edie Riyadi Terre. *Kebenaran vs Keadilan, Pertanggung Jawaban Pelanggaran HAM di Masa Lalu*. Jakarta: ELSAM, 2003a.

Kasim, Ifdhal, and Edie Riyadi Terre. *Pencarian Keadilan di Masa Transisi*. Jakarta: ELSAM, 2003b.

Kenney, Charles D., and Dean E. Spears. *Truth and Consequences: Do Truth Commissions Promote Democratization?* Paper Presented at the Annual Meeting of the American Political Science Association, Washington, 2005.

Kent, Lia. *The Dynamics of Transitional Justice: International Models and Local Realities in East Timor*. New York: Routledge, 2012.

Keputusan DPR No. 49A/DPR RI/IV/2002-2003 atas Pembentukan Panitia Rancangan Undang-Undang (Parliamentary Decree no. 49A/DPR RI/IV/2002-2003 on the Establishment of Special Committee on Draft Law of Truth and Reconciliation Commission).

Keputusan Mahkamah Konstitusi (Constitutional Court Decision) no. 6/PUU-IV/2006. http://www.mahkamahkonstitusi.go.id/public/content/persidangan/risalah/risalah_sidang_Risalah%20Perkara%20006.PUU-IV.2006,%20dan%208%20Desember%202006%20Putusan.pdf. Accessed 26 January, 2018.

Keputusan Walikota Palu No. 180/561/HKM/2014 tentang Pencabutan Keputusan Walikota Palu No. 180/2088/HKM /2012 tentang Pembentukan Kelompok Kerja Komite Kota Palu atas Rencana Kerja HAM 2014 (Mayor Decree of Palu No. 180/561/HKM/2014 on Second Amendment of Mayor Decree no. 180/2088/HKM /2012 on the Establishment of Working Groups for City of Palu's Committee on 2011–2014 Human Rights Action Plan).

Kim, Hunjoon, and Kathryn Sikkink. "Explaining the Deterrence Effect of Human Rights Prosecutions for Transitional Countries." *International Studies Quarterly* 54, no. 4 (2010): 939–963.

Kim, Yong Cheol, R. William Liddle, and Salim Said. "Political Leadership and Civilian Supremacy in Third Wave Democracies: Comparing South Korea and Indonesia." *Pacific Affairs* 79, no. 2 (2006): 247–268.

Kimura, Ehito. "The Struggle for Justice and Reconciliation in Post-Suharto Indonesia." *Southeast Asian Studies* 4, no. 1 (2015): 73–93.

Komisi untuk Penerimaan, Kebenaran dan Rekonsiliasi. *Chega! No More, Stop, Enough*. Dili: Komisi untuk Penerimaan, Kebenaran dan Rekonsiliasi (CAVR), 2006.

Komisi Kebenaran dan Persahabatan Indonesia-Timor Leste. *Per Memoriam ad Spem*. Jakarta and Dili: Komisi Kebenaran dan Persahabatan (KKP), 2008.

KontraS. *Mereka Bilang Di Sini Tidak Ada Tuhan*. Jakarta: KontraS, 2004.

KontraS. *Menerobos Jalan Buntu: Kajian Terhadap Peradilan Militer di Indonesia*. Jakarta: KontraS, 2009.

Kovras, Iosif. *Truth, Recovery and Transitional Justice: Deferring Human Rights Issues* London: Routledge, 2014.

Kritz, Neil J. (1995). *Transitional Justice: How Emerging Democracies Reckon with Former Regimes* (Vol. II). Washington: US Institute of Peace Press, 1995.

Koalisi Keadilan dan Pengungkapan Kebenaran (Producer). (30 April 2013) *Net Markus* Retrieved from http://kkpk.org/vlcsnap-15910137/

Komnas HAM. *Prinsip-Prinsip Surabaya mengenai Transitional Justice in Indonesia.* Jakarta: Komnas HAM, 2000a.

Komnas HAM. *Laporan Tindak Lanjut Hasil Penyelidikan dan Pemeriksaan Pelanggaran Hak Asasi Manusia di Tanjung Priok.* Jakarta: Komnas HAM, 2000b.

Komnas HAM. *Ringkasan Eksekutif Dari Laporan Hasil Penyelidikan dan Pemeriksaan Pelanggaran Hak Asasi Manusia di Tanjung Priok Tanggal 12 September 1984.* Jakarta: Komnas HAM, 2000c.

Komnas HAM. *Ringkasan Eksekutif Hasil Penyelidikan Tim Ad Hoc Penyelidikan Pelanggaran Hak Asasi Manusia yang Berat Peristiwa Talangsari 1989.* Jakarta: Komnas HAM, 2008.

Lamasitudju, Nurlela, and Abbas M. Gagarisman. *Sulawesi Bersaksi: Tuturan Penyintas Tragedi 1965* [Sulawesi Witnesses: Narrations as Told by Survivors of the 1965 Tragedy]. Jakarta: Lembaga Kreatifitas Kemanusiaan and TAPOL, 2013.

Lampe, Ilyas. "Identitas Etnik dalam Komunikasi Politik." *Jurnal Ilmu Komunikasi (JIK)* 8, no. 3, (2014): 299–313.

Laplante, Lisa J. "Outlawing Amnesty: the Return of Criminal Justice in Transitional Justice Schemes." *Virginia Journal of International Law* 49, no. 4 (2009): 915–984.

Leebaw, Bronwyn. *Judging State-Sponsored Violence, Imagining Political Change.* New York: Cambridge University Press, 2011.

Lembaga Ilmu Pengetahuan Indonesia. *ABRI dan Gerakan Reformasi: Reposisi Setengah Hati.* Paper Presented at the Seminar Hasil Penelitian ABRI dan Gerakan Reformasi, Jakarta, 27 Juli 1999. LIPI, 1999.

Liddle, R. William. "The 1977 Indonesian Election and New Order Legitimacy." In *Southeast Asian Affairs* (pp. 122–138). Singapore: Institute of Southeast Asian Studies, 1978a.

Liddle, R. William. "Participation and the Political Parties." In K. Jackson & L. Pye (Eds.), *Political Power and Communications in Indonesia.* Los Angeles: Berkeley University Press, 1978b.

Liddle, R. William. *Ethnicity, Party and National Integration.* London: Yale University Press, 1970.

Lindsey, Timothy. *Law Reform in Developing and Transitional States.* New York: Routledge, 2007.

Linton, Suzannah. "Accounting for Atrocities in Indonesia." *Singapore Year Book of International Law* 11 (2006): 195–259.

Long, William J., and Peter Brecke. *War and Reconciliation: Reason and Emotion in Conflict Resolution.* Cambridge: MIT Press, 2003.

Lubis, T. Mulya. *In Search of Human Rights: Legal Political Dilemmas of Indonesia's New Order, 1966–1990.* Jakarta: Gramedia Pustaka Utama, 1993.

Lundy, Patricia, and Mark McGovern. "Whose Justice? Rethinking Transitional Justice from the Bottom Up." *Journal of Law and Society* 35, no. 2 (2008): 265–292.

MacIntyre, Andrew. "Power, Prosperity and Patrimonialism: Business and Government in Indonesia." In A. MacIntyre (Ed.), *Business and Government in Industrialising Asia* (pp. 244–267). Ithaca: Cornell University Press, 1994.

Mahendra, Yusril I. *Rekonsiliasi Tanpa Mengkhianati Reformasi.* Jakarta: Mizan, 2004.

Mahkamah Agung Republik Indonesia, *Surat Ketua Mahkamah Agung* (Letter of the Chair of Supreme Court), No KMA/403/VI/2003, 12 June 2003.

Malley, Michael. "Regions: Centralization and Resistance." In D. Emmerson (Ed.), *Indonesia Beyond Soeharto: Policy, Economy, Society, Transition* (pp. 71–108). New York: Sharpe, 1999.

Marzuki, Suparman. *The Human Rights Court in Indonesia; Impunity Perpetuates.* Jakarta: Erlangga, 2012.

Mayer-Rieckh, Alexander, and Pablo de Grieff (Eds.), *Justice as Prevention, Vetting Public Employees in Transitional Societies.* New York: Social Science Research Council, 2007.

McAdams, James. *Transitional Justice and the Rule of Law in New Democracies.* Notre Dame: University of Notre Dame Press, 1997.

McDonald, Hamish. *Masters of Terror: Indonesia's Military and Violence in East Timor in 1999.* Canberra: Strategic and Defence Studies Centre, Australian National University, 2002.

McEvoy, Kieran. "Beyond Legalism: Towards a Thicker Understanding of Transitional Justice." *Journal of Law and Society* 34, no. 4 (2007): 411–440.

McRae, Dave. *A Few Poorly Organized Men: Interreligious Violence in Poso, Indonesia.* Leiden: Brill, 2013.

Meernik, James. "Justice and Peace? How the International Criminal Tribunal Affects Societal Peace in Bosnia." *Journal of Peace Research* 42, no. 3 (2005): 271–289.

Meijer, Martha. *The Scope of Impunity in Indonesia.* Utrecht: Netherlands Humanist Committee on Human Rights, 2006.

Meister, Robert. "Human Rights and the Politics of Victimhood." *Ethics & International Affairs* 16, no. 2 (2002): 91–108.

Meister, Robert. "Ways of Winning: The Costs of Moral Victory in Transitional Regimes." In A. D. Schrift (Ed.), *Modernity and the Problem of Evil* (pp. 81–111). Bloomington: Indiana University Press, 2005.

Meister, Robert. *After Evil: A Politics of Human Rights.* New York: Columbia University Press, 2012.

Méndez, Juan E. "Accountability for Past Abuses." *Human Rights Quarterly* 19, no. 2 (1997a): 255–282.

Mendez, Juan E. "In Defense of Transitional Justice." In J. McAdams (Ed.), *Transitional Justice and the Rule of Law in New Democracies* (pp. 1–26). Notre Dame: University of Notre Dame, 1997b.

Mietzner, Marcus. "The Ambivalence of Weak Legitimacy: Habibie's Interregnum Revisited." *Review of Indonesian and Malaysian Affairs* 42, no. 2 (2008): 1–33.

Mietzner, Marcus. *Military Politics, Islam, and the State in Indonesia: From Turbulent Transition to Democratic Consolidation.* Leiden: KILTV, 2009.

Mietzner, Marcus. *Money, Power and Ideology: Political Parties in Post-Authoritarian Indonesia.* Honolulu: Hawaii University Press, 2013a.

Mietzner, Marcus. "Praetorian Rule and Redemocratisation in South-East Asia and the Pacific Islands: The Case of Indonesia." *Australian Journal of International Affairs* 67, no. 3 (2013b): 297–311.

Mietzner, Marcus. "Veto Player No More? The Declining Political Influence of the Military in Post-Authoritarian Indonesia." In M. Kunkler & A. Stepan (Eds.), *Democracy and Islam in Indonesia* (89–108). New York: Columbia University Press, 2013c.

Mizuno, Kumiko. "Indonesian Politics and the Issue of Justice in East Timor". In H. Soesastro, A. L. Smith & M. L. Han (Eds.), *Governance in Indonesia: Challenges Facing Megawati Presidency* (pp. 114–164). Singapore: Institute of Southeast Asian Studies, 2003.

Nalepa, Monika. "Punish All Guilty or Protect the Innocent? Designing Institutions of Transitional Justice." *Journal of Theoretical Politics* 20, no. 2 (2008): 221–246.

Nalepa, Monika. "Infiltration as Insurance: Committing to Democratisation and Committing to Peace." In M. Bergsmo & P. Kalmanovitz (Eds.), *Law in Peace Negotiations, Forum for International Criminal and Humanitarian Law* (Vol. IV) (pp. 121–158). Oslo: Peach Research Institute, 2010.

Nordholt, Henk Schulte, and Gerry van Klinken (Eds.), *Renegotiating Boundaries: Local Politics in Post-Suharto Indonesia*. Leiden: KITLC Press, 2007.

Nyman, Mikaela. *Democratising Indonesia: The Challenges of Civil Society in the Era of Reformasi*. Copenhagen: NIAS Press, 2006.

O'Donnell, Guillermo, and Philippe C. Schmitter. *Transitions from Authoritarian Rule: Tentative Conclusions about Uncertain Democracies*. London: The John Hopkins University Press, 1986.

Olsen, Tricia D., Leigh A. Payne, and Andrew G. Reiter. *Transitional Justice in Balance: Comparing Process, Weighing Efficacy*. Washington: U.S. Institute Peace Press, 2010.

Olsen, Tricia D., Leigh A. Payne, Andrew G. Reiter, and Eric Wiebelhaus-Brahm. "When Truth Commissions Improve Human Rights." *International Journal of Transitional Justice* 4, no. 3 (2010): 457–476.

Parliamentary Secretariat. Summary of Processes of Legislation on Law on Human Rights Court, 2000.

Parliamentary Secretariat. Final Opinion of TNI/Polri Faction on the Truth and Reconciliation Committee Bill, 2004a.

Parliamentary Secretariat. Minutes Meeting of the TRC Bill, 2004b.

Payne, Leigh A., and Kathryn Sikkink. "Transitional Justice in the Asia-Pacific: Comparative and Theoretical Perspectives." In R. Jeffery & H. J. Kim (Eds.), *Transitional Justice in the Asia-Pacific* (pp. 33–60). Cambridge: Cambridge University Press, 2014.

Peraturan Presiden n. 27 2005 tentang Prosedur Proses Seleksi dan Rekrutmen Anggota TRC. (Presidential Regulation no. 27 of 2005 on Procedures on Selection Processes and Recruitment of Members of TRC).

Piper, Nicola, and Anders Uhlin, eds. *Transnational Activism in Asia: Problems of Power and Democracy*. London: Routledge, 2004.

Pratikno. "Exercising Freedom: Local Autonomy and Democracy in Indonesia, 1999–2001." In M. Erb & P. Sulistiyanto (Eds.), *Regionalism in Post-Suharto Indonesia* (pp. 20–35). New York: Routledge, 2005.

Pratikno, Cornelis Lay, et al. *Komnas HAM 1993–1997: Pergulatan dalam Otoritarianisme*. Yogyakarta: FISIPOL UGM, 2002.

Priyono, A. E. *Demiliterisasi dan Keadilan Transisional dalam Proses Demokratisasi di Indonesia*. Retrieved from http://www.demosindonesia.org/diskursus/3074-demiliterisasi-dan-keadilan-transisional-dalam-proses-demokratisasi-di-indonesia.html

Priyono, A. E., Willy Purna Samadhi, and Olle Törnquist. *Making Democracy Meaningful: Problems and Options in Indonesia*. Singapore: ISEAS, 2007.

Rais, Amien, "Menyelamatkan Perjalanan Reformasi." In A. Rais et.al. (Eds.), *Reformasi dalam Stagnasi*. Jakarta: Yayasan Al-Mukmin, (pp. 1–15).

Rasyid, M. Ryaas. "Regional Autonomy and Local Politics in Indonesia." In E. Aspinall & G. Fealy (Eds.), *Local Power and Politics in Indonesia: Decentralization and Democratisation* (pp. 63–71). Singapore: Institute of Southeast Asian Studies, 2003.

Report of the Secretary General on the rule of law and transitional justice in conflict and post-conflict societies, S/2004/6168, August 23, 2004.

Ricklefs, Merle Calvin. *A History of Modern Indonesia Since C. 1200*. London: Palgrave, 2001.

Risse, Thomas, and Kathryn Sikkink. "The Socialization of Internasional Human Rights Norms into Domestic Practices: Introduction." In T. Risse et.al. (Eds.), *The Power of Human Rights: International Norms & Domestic Change* (pp. 1–38). New York: Cambridge University Press, 1999.

Risse-Kappen, Thomas, Stephen C. Ropp, and Kathryn Sikkink, eds. *The Power of Human Rights: International Norms and Domestic Change*. New York: Cambridge University Press, 1999.

Robinson, Geoffrey. "Indonesia: On a New Course?" In M. Alagappa (Ed.), *Coercion and Governance: The Declining Political Role of the Military in Asia* (pp. 226–256). Stanford: Stanford University Press, 2001.

Robinson, Geoffrey. "The Fruitless Search for a Smoking Gun." In F. Colombijn & T. Lindblad (Eds.), *Roots of Violence in Indonesia* (pp. 243–276). Singapore: ISEAS, 2002.

Robinson, Geoffrey. *East Timor 1999 Crimes against Humanity: A Report Commissioned by the United Nations Office of the High Commissioner for Human Rights*. Dili: Commission for Reception, Truth and Reconciliation, 2003.

Robinson, Geoffrey. *If You Leave Us Here, We Will Die: How Genocide Was Stopped in East Timor*. Princeton: Princeton University Press, 2009.

Robison, Richard, and Vedi R. Hadiz. "Reorganising Power in Indonesia: The Politics of Oligarchy in an Age of Markets." *Bulletin of Indonesian Economic Studies* 41, no. 1 (2005): 395–396.

Roichatul, Aswidah. *Dealing with the Past: Challenges Facing the Indonesian Truth and Reconciliation Commission*. PhD diss., University of Essex, 2005.

Rosenberg, Tina. *The Haunted Land: Facing Europe's Ghosts after Communism*. New York: Random House, 1995.

Ryter, Loren. "Pemuda Pancasila: The Last Loyalist Free Men of Suharto's Order?" *Indonesia* 66, no. 10 (1998): 45–73.

Santoso, Budi. *Evaluasi Kritis Atas Kelemahan UU Peradilan HAM*. Paper Presented at the Workshop Merumuskan Amandemen Undang-Undang Peradilan HAM, Yogyakarta, 2003.

Secretariat DPR. *Rapat Dengar Pendapat Umum tentang RUU KKR*, Jakarta, 2 July 2004a.

Secretariat DPR. *Rapat Dengar Pendapat Umum tentang RUU KKR*, Jakarta, 4 July 2004b.

Sekretariat Jenderal MPR RI. *Risalah Rapat Komisi E Sidang Istimewa MPR RI tahun 1998*, Jakarta, 1999.

Setiawan, Bonnie. *LSM sebagai Kekuatan Sosial Baru*. Jakarta: *Kompas*, 17 April 2004.

Setiawan, Ken Marijtje Prahari. *Promoting Human Rights: National Human Rights Commissions in Indonesia and Malaysia*. Leiden: Leiden University Press, 2013.

Shelton, Dinah L. *The Encyclopedia of Genocide and Crimes against Humanity* (Vol. 3). New York: Thomson Gale, 2004.

Sikkink, Kathryn. *The Justice Cascade: How Human Rights Prosecutions Are Changing World Politics (The Norton Series in World Politics)*. New York: WW Norton & Company, 2011.

Sikkink, Kathryn, and Carrie Booth Walling. "The Impact of Human Rights Trials in Latin America." *Journal of Peace Research* 44, no. 4 (2007): 427–445.

Sikkink, Kathryn, and Leigh Payne. "Transitional Justice in the Asia-Pacific: Comparative and Theoretical Perspectives." In R. Jeffery & H. J. Kim (Eds.), *Transitional Justice in the Asia-Pacific*. New York: Cambridge University Press, (2014), 33–60.

Simpson, Brad. "Contested Human Rights Discourses in Suharto's Indonesia, 1968–1980." In S. Moyn & J. Eckel (Eds.), *The Global History of Human Rights in the 1970s* (pp. 186–317). New York: University of Pennsylvania Press, 2013.

Skaar, Elin. "Truth Commissions, Trials or Nothing? Policy Options in Democratic Transitions." *Third World Quarterly* 20, no. 6 (1999): 1109–1128.

Slater, Dan. "Indonesia's Accountability Trap: Party Cartels and Presidential Power after Democratic Transition." *Indonesia* 78 (2004): 61–92.

Slater, Dan. "The Ironies of Instability in Indonesia." *Social Analysis* 50, no. 1 (2006): 208–213.

Snyder, Jack, and Leslie Vinjamuri. "Trials and Errors: Principle and Pragmatism in Strategies of International Justice." *International Security* 28, no. 3 (2004): 5–44.

Stover, Eric, and Harvey M. Weinstein (Eds.), *My Neighbour, My Enemy: Justice and Community in the Aftermath of Mass Atrocity.* Cambridge: Cambridge University Press, 2004.

Stromseth, Jane, David Wippman, and Rosa Brooks. *Can Might Make Rights? Building the Rule of Law after Military Interventions.* Cambridge: Cambridge University Press, 2006.

Suh, Jiwon. *The Politics of Transitional Justice in Post-Suharto Indonesia.* PhD Diss., Ohio State University, 2012.

Suh, Jiwon. "Legacies of International Human Rights Pressure against New Order Indonesia." *The Korean Journal of International Relations (Gukjejeongchinonchong)* 53 no. 4 (2013): 401–432.

Sulistiyanto, Priyambudi. "Politics of Justice and Reconciliation in Post-Suharto Indonesia." *Journal of Contemporary Asia* 37, no. 1 (2007): 73–94.

Sulistyanto, Priyambudi, and Rumekso Setyadi. "Civil Society and Grassroots Reconciliation in Central Java." In B. Brauchler (Ed.), *Reconciling Indonesia: Grassroots Agency for Peace.* New York: Routledge, (2009), 192–213.

Sundari, Eva K. "Parlemen dan HAM: Visi Tanpa Eksekusi." In I. Saptaningrum (Ed.), *Hak Asasi Manusia dalam Pusaran Politik Transaksional: Penilaian terhadap Kebijakan HAM dalam Produk Legislasi dan Pengawasan DPR RI Periode 2004–2009.* Jakarta: ELSAM, 2011.

Suparman, Djadja. *Jejak Kudeta (1997–2005): Catatan Harian Jenderal TNI (Purn) Djadja Suparman.* Jakarta: Yayasan Pustaka Obor Indonesia, 2013.

Suryadinata, Leo. *Nationalism & Globalization: East & West.* Singapore: Institute of Southeast Asian Studies, 2000.

Setara Institute. *Mengukur Komitmen Partai Politik terhadap Hak Asasi Manusia.* Jakarta: Setara Institute, 2008.

Setara Institute. *Indeks Kinerja Penegakan HAM 2011.* Jakarta: Setara Institute, 2011.

Setara Institute. *Indeks Kinerja Penegakan HAM 2012.* Jakarta: Setara Institute, 2012.

Summary of Constitutional Court Decision No. 006/PUU-IV/2006 on the Law No. 27/2004 on the Truth and Reconciliation Commission. 2006.

Tanjung, Akbar, and Hajriyanto Thohari. *Moratorium Politik Menuju Rekonsiliasi Nasional.* Jakarta: Golkar Press, 2003.

Tanter, Richard, Ball, Desmond, and Van Klinken, Gerry (Eds.), *Masters of Terror: Indonesia's Military and Violence in East Timor.* New York: Rowman & Littlefield Publishers, 2006.

TAP MPR No. V 2000 Tentang Pemantapan Persatuan dan Kesatuan Nasional (Decision of the People's Consultative Assembly No. V 2000 on Consolidation of National Unity).

TAP MPR No. XVII of 1998 Tentang Hak Asasi Manusia (Decision of the People's Consultative Assembly No. XVII of 1998 on Human Rights).

Teitel, Ruti G. "How are the New Democracies of the Southern Cone Dealing with the Legacy of Past Human Rights Abuses." In N. J. Kritz (Ed.), *Transitional Justice: How Emerging Democracies Reckon with Former Regimes.* Washington: U.S. Institute of Peace Press, 1995.

Teitel, Ruti G. *Transitional Justice.* New York: Oxford University Press, 2000.

Teitel, Ruti G. "Transitional Justice Genealogy." *Harvard Human Rights Journal* 16, no. 1 (2003): 69–94.

The Act of Killing. Directed by Oppenheimer Joshua. United Kingdom, Denmark, Norway: Det Danske Filminstitut (Denmark) Dogwoof Pictures (UK), 2012. DVD.

Thoms, Oskar N. T., James Ron, and Roland Paris. *The Effects of Transitional Justice Mechanisms: A Summary of Empirical Research Findings and Implications for Analysts and Practitioners.* Ottawa: Centre for International Policy Studies, University of Ottawa, 2008.

TRuK. *Findings of the Joint Fact-Finding Team for the May 1998 Riots.* Jakarta: Tim Relawan untuk Kemanusiaan, 2001.

Ufen, Andreas. "The Evolution of Cleavages in the Indonesian Party System." *GIGA Research Programme: Legitimacy and Efficiency of Political Systems.* Hamburg: German Institute of Global and Area Studies, 2004.

Uhlin, Anders. *Indonesia and the "Third Wave" of Democratisation: The Indonesian Pro-Democracy Movement in a Changing World.* Surrey: Curzon Press, 1997.

Undang-Undang No. 11 2006 tentang Pememrintah Aceh (Law on Governance of Aceh).

Undang-Undang No. 12 2005 tentang Pengesahan Kovenan Internasional Tentang Hak Hak Sipil dan Politik (Law on Ratification of the International Covenant on Civil and Political Rights).

Undang-Undang No. 13 2006 tentang Perlindungan Saksi dan Korban (Law on Victims and Witness Protection).

Undang-Undang No. 14 1970 tentang Ketentuan-Ketentuan Pokok Kekuasaan Hakim (Law on Basic Provisions of Judicial Authority).

Undang-Undang No. 21 2001 Otonomi Khsusu Provinsi Papua (Law on Special Autonomy for Papua).

Undang-Undang No. 23 2014 tentang Pemerintahan Daerah (Law on Regional Governance).

Undang-Undang No. 26 2000 tentang Pengadilan HAM (Law on Human Rights Trial).

Undang-Undang No. 27 2004 tentang Komisi Kebenaran dan Rekonsiliasi (Law on Truth and Reconciliation Committee).

Undang-Undang No. 31 1997 tentang Peradilan Militer (Law on Military Tribunal).

Undang-Undang No. 39 1999 tentang HAM (Law on Human Rights).

Undang-Undang No. 45 1999 tentang Pembentukan Propinsi Irian Jaya Tengah, Irian Jaya Barat, Kabupaten Paniai, Kabupaten Mimika, Kabupaten Punjak Jaya, dan Kota Sorong (Law on the Establishment of Irian Jaya Province, Irian Jaya Barat Province, Paniai District, Mimika District, Punjak Jaya District, and Sorong Municiplity).

Undang-Undang Tentang Pengesahan Kovenan Internasional Tentang Hak-Hak Ekonomi, Sosial Dan Budaya No. 11 2005 (Law on Ratification of International Covenant on Economic, Social, and Cultural Rights).

United Nations. *Updated Set of Principles for the Protection and Promotion of Human Rights through Action to Combat Impunity.* New York: Commission on Human Rights, 2005.

United Nations. *Rule-of-Law Tools for Post-Conflict States—Vetting: An Operational Framework* (p. 4). New York: Office of the United Nations High Commissioner for Human Rights, 2006.

van Klinken, Geert Arend, and HGC Schulte Nordholt. *Politik lokal di Indonesia.* Jakarta: Yayasan Pustaka Obor, 2008.

van Klinken, Gerry. *Communal Violence and Democratisation in Indonesia: Small Town Wars.* New York: Routledge, 2007.

Van Zyl, Paul. *Promoting Transitional Justice in Post-Conflict Society.* In A. Bryden (Ed.), *Security Governance in Post-Conflict Peace Building* (pp. 209–232). Geneva: Center for Democratic Control of Armed Forces, 2005.

Walgrave, Lode. "Investigating the Potentials of Restorative Justice Practice." *Washington University Journal of Law & Policy* 36 (2011): 91–139.

Ward, Ken. *The 1971 Election in Indonesia: An East Java Case Study.* Melbourne: Monash University, 1974.

Weix, Gretchen Garnett. "Resisting History: Indonesian Labour Activism in the 1990s and the 'Marsinah' Case." In B. S. A. Yeoh, P. Teo & S. Huang (Eds.), *Gender Politics in the Asia Pacific Region* (pp. 120–136). London: Routledge, 2000.

Wiebelhaus-Brahm, "Truth Commissions and Other Investigative Bodies", in M. Cherish Bassiouni (Ed.), *The Pursuit of International Criminal Justice: A World Study on Conflicts, Victimization, and Post-Conflict Justice*, (pp. 109–132). Mortsel: Intersentia NV, (2010).

Williams, Jill E. "Legitimacy and Effectiveness of a Grassroots Truth and Reconciliation Commission." *Law and Contemporary Problems* 72, no. 2 (2009): 143–149.

Zalaquett, José. "Confronting Human Rights Violations Committed by Former Governments: Principles Applicable and Political Constraints." In N. J. Kritz (Ed.), *Transitional Justice.* Washington: United States Institute of Peace Press, 1995.

Zurbuchen, Mary S. "History, Memory, and the '1965 Incident' in Indonesia." *Asian Survey* 42, no. 4 (2002): 564–581.

Websites and Newspapers

Australian Broadcasting Corporation. (10 October 2001). Transcript: Xanana Gusmao, Interview: Priorities for the New Nation.

BBC News. (11 May 2015). Hari ini, 17 tahun lalu di kampus Trisakti—BBC Indonesia. http://www.bbc.com/indonesia/berita_indonesia/2015/05/150512_indonesia_trisakti_1998. Accessed April 10, 2017.

Breaking News. (28 September 1998). Rekonsiliasi Nasional. http://www.pacific.net.id/pakar/sadli/0998/280998.html. Accessed January 17, 2017.

Hukumonline.com. (2003). Kasus Tanjungpriok: Saksi Ikhlas Walaupun Disiksa dan Ditembak. Retrieved 16 June, 2016, from http://www.hukumonline.com/berita/baca/hol9208/kasus-tanjungpriok-saksi-ikhlas-walaupun-disiksa-dan-ditembak

Direito Magazine, Yayasan HAK: Dili, 2003.

Kelompok Kerja Keadilan dan Pengungkapan Kebenaran, *Dengar Kesaksian Palu.* Video. http://kkpk.org/tag/dengar-kesaksian-palu/. Accessed 3 April 2015.

Kementerian Hukum dan HAM. (2013). Menteri Hukum dan HAM RI mendeklarasikan desa kelurahan sadar hukum dan kota sadar ham. Retrieved 2 April, 2015, from http://sulteng.kemenkumham.go.id/berita/berita-utama/368-menteri-hukum-dan-ham-r-i-mendeklarasikan-desa-kelurahan-sadar-hukum-dan-kota-sadar-ham

Kompas. (14 August 1998). *Mendesak! Rekonsiliasi Nasional.*

Kompas. (1 September 1998). *Perlu Dibentuk Komite Rekonsiliasi Nasional.*

Kompas. (5 September 1998). *Pemerintah-Komnas HAM Sepakat Bentuk Tim Infromal Rekonsiliasi Nasional.*
Kompas. (17 October 1998). *Pemerintah dan Komnas HAM Masih Beda Pendapat.*
Kompas. (22 October 1998).
Kompas. (27 August 1999).
Kompas. (1999). Korban Peristiwa Tanjung Priok Mengadu ke Puspom. Retrieved 20 April, 2017, from http://www.kontras.org/home/index.php?module=berita&id=245
Kompas. (8 January 1999). *Pembebasan Tapol/Napol Arah Menuju Rekonsiliasi.*
Kompas. (2000). Pembela Kasus Priok Desak Panggil Soeharto. Retrieved 20 April, 2017, from http://www.kontras.org/home/index.php?module=berita&id=430
Kompas. (5 February 2000). *Komnas HAM: Segera Bentuk Komisi Kebenaran dan Rekonsiliasi.*
Kompas. (13 March 2000).
Kompas. (10 April 2000). *Rekonsiliasi Jalan Keluar Bangsa Indonesia.*
Kompas. (16 June 2000). *Kebenaran Tak Mudah Didapatkan.*
Kompas. (23 September 2000).
Kompas. (16 March 2001).
Koran Tempo News. (15 March 2007).
Kusuma, Feri. (December 2007). Jubah Putih di Beutong Ateuh. *Pantau*. Retrieved 20 February, 2018 from https://www.pantau.or.id/?/=d/426
Lamasitudju, Nurlela. (2014). Peraturan Walikota Palu bagi Korban Peristiwa 1965: Jalan Terjal Inisiatif Lokal. *SKP HAM*. Retrieved 12 January, 2016 from http://www.skp-ham.org/588/peraturan-walikota-palu-bagi-korban-peristiwa-1965-jalan-terjal-inisiatif-lokal/
Liputan6.com. (2001). Korban Kasus Tanjung Priok Mencabut Islah. Retrieved 5 June, 2016, from http://news.liputan6.com/read/20404/korban-kasus-tanjungpriok-mencabut-islah
Liputan6.com. (2003). Wiranto: Tuduhan PBB Pembunuhan Karakter. Retrieved 8 February, 2015, from http://news.liputan6.com/read/50225/wiranto-tuduhan-pbb-pembunuhan-karakter
Liputan6.com. (2017). Korupsi BLBI, Cerita tak Tuntas 2 Dekade lalu. Retrieved 24 February, 2018, from http://news.liputan6.com/read/2932794/korupsi-blbi-cerita-tak-tuntas-2-dekade-lalu
Liputan6. (21 September 2001).
Liputan6. (8 February 2015).
Merdeka.com. (2012). Referendum penentu berpisahnya provinsi ke-27 Indonesia. Retrieved 30 June, 2016, from https://www.merdeka.com/dunia/rereferendum-penentu-berpisahnya-provinsi-ke-27-indonesia.html*Republika*. (17 June 2000).
Solopos. (2012). Kodam IV Diponegoro Sinyalir Kebangkitan PKI di Jateng-DIY. Retrieved 20 May, 2017, from http://www.solopos.com/2012/12/17/kodam-iv-diponegoro-sinyalir-kebangkitan-pki-di-jateng-diy-358721/comment-page-1
Suara Pembaruan. (3 December 1998). *Tanpa Rekonsiliasi Kehidupan Bangsa akan Semakin Tercabik-Cabik.*
Tabloid DeTAK. (2000). Interview with Yusron Zaenuri.
Tapol Bulletin, no. 68 (2002).
Tempo. (16 December 2012).
Tempo. (16 December 2002).
Tempo. (23 September 2003).
Tempo. (7 September 2004).

Tempo.co. (2003). KontraS Mengadukan Intimidasi ke Pengadilan. Retrieved 6 June, 2016, from http://nasional.tempo.co/read/news/2003/10/29/05525915/kontras-mengadukan-intimidasi-ke-pengadilan

Tempo.co. (24 July 2003). Retrieved 1 August, 2016, from https://nasional.tempo.co/read/3848/kiki-syahnakri-tak-mungkin-kejaksaan-timor-lorosae-tangkap-saya

Tempo Majalah. Jaksa Agung Titipan Tentara? (No. 22/XXX/30 July–5August 2001).

The Jakarta Post. (7 September 1999).

The Jakarta Post. (22 March 2001).

The Jakarta Post. (28 June 2004).*The Jakarta Post.* (21 February 2005). *Truth, Reconciliation Post Challenge to Government.*

The Jakarta Post. (2010). Select Outsider to Reform AGO. Retrieved 6 June, 2016, from http://www.thejakartapost.com/news/2010/09/17/select-outsider-reform-ago-says-exprosecutor.html

Interviews

Group Discussions with Victims in Talangsari, Lampung, 10 September 2014.

Interview with Kabul Supriyadi in Jakarta, 10 March 2012.Interview with Galuh Wandita in Jakarta, 12 March 2012.

Interview with Patrick Burgess in Jakarta, 22 March 2012.

Interview with Wanma Yetti in Jakarta, 23 March and 2 September 2012.

Interview with Enny Soeprapto in Jakarta, 29 March 2012.

Interview with Agus Widjojo in Jakarta, 1 May 2012.

Interview with Albert Hasibuan in Jakarta, 2 May 2012.

Interview with Jimly Asshidique in Jakarta, 2 May 2012.

Interview with Marzuki Darusman in Jakarta, 4 May 2012.

Interview with Amien Rais in Jakarta, 5 May 2012.

Interview with Mugiyanto Sipin in Jakarta, 10 May 2012.

Interview with Rumekso Setyadi in Jakarta, 10 May 2012.

Interview with Haris Azhar in Jakarta, 11 May 2012.

Interview with Maria Sumarsih in Jakarta, 12 May 2012.

Interview with A.E. Priyono in Jakarta, 16 May 2012.

Interview with Beni Biki in Jakarta, 16 May 2012, and 4 September 2012.

Interview with Bedjo Untung in Jakarta, September 2012.

Interview with Slamet Effendi Yusuf in Canberra, 16 March 2013.

Interview with Nursyahbani Katjasungkana in Hague, 19 September 2013.

Interview with Nurlaela Lamasitudju in Jakarta, 8 May and in Palu, 26 September 2014.

Interview with Ifdhal Kasim in Jakarta, 22 September 2014.

Interview with Aminuddin Kasim in Palu, 25 September 2014.

Interview with Haliadi in Palu, 25 September 2014.

Interview with Muliati in Palu, 26 September 2014.

Interview with Rusdy Mastura in Jakarta, 26 September 2014.

Interview with Netty in Palu, 28 September 2014.

Interview with Sidarto Danubroto in Jakarta, 10 October 2014.

Interview with Haryo Wibowo in Jakarta, 9 May 2016.

Interview with Firman Jaya Daely in Jakarta, 9 May 2017.

Index

Note: Page numbers followed by "n" denote footnotes.

For Product Safety Concerns and Information please contact our EU representative GPSR@taylorandfrancis.com
Taylor & Francis Verlag GmbH, Kaufingerstraße 24, 80331 München, Germany

www.ingramcontent.com/pod-product-compliance
Lightning Source LLC
LaVergne TN
LVHW011130300926
849160LV00008B/595
9781032084558